PLOWSHARES

PLOWSHARES

Protest, Performance,

and Religious Identity

in the Nuclear Age

KRISTEN TOBEY

The Pennsylvania State University Press
University Park, Pennsylvania

Library of Congress Cataloging-in-
Publication Data

Names: Tobey, Kristen, 1978– , author.
Title: Plowshares : protest, performance, and
    religious identity in the nuclear age /
    Kristen Tobey.
Description: University Park, Pennsylvania
    : The Pennsylvania State University
    Press, [2016] | Includes bibliographical
    references and index.
Identifiers: LCCN 2016012660 | ISBN
    9780271076720 (cloth : alk. paper) |
    ISBN: 978-0-271-07673-7 (pbk. : alk.
    paper)
Summary: "Explores the actions of the radi-
    cal Roman Catholic antinuclear activist
    group Plowshares. Focuses on the
    closely interwoven religious and social
    significance of the group's actions and
    subsequent legal trials, which rely on
    performances of moral distinction to
    achieve the activists' aims"—Provided
    by publisher.
Subjects: LCSH: Plowshares Eight (Group)
    | Antinuclear movement—Religious
    aspects—Catholic Church. | Antinucle-
    ar movement—United States. | Nuclear
    disarmament—Religious aspects—
    Catholic Church. | Nuclear disarma-
    ment—United States.
Classification: LCC BR115.A85 T63 2016 |
    DDC 261.8/73206—dc23

LC record available at https://lccn.loc
    .gov/2016012660

The Pennsylvania State University Press is
a member of the Association of American
University Presses.

It is the policy of The Pennsylvania State
University Press to use acid-free paper. Publications on uncoated stock satisfy the min-
imum requirements of American National
Standard for Information Sciences—Perma-
nence of Paper for Printed Library Material,
ANSI Z39.48–1992.

Dedicated to

Sara Schmitt

and to the memory of

Martin Riesebrodt (1948–2014)

CONTENTS

ACKNOWLEDGMENTS

My first thanks are due to Martin Riesebrodt, Clark Gilpin, and Winnifred Fallers Sullivan, who saw this project through its early years with unfailing intellectual generosity and remarkable patience. It is my great pleasure—though marked by the sadness of Martin's untimely death—to thank them here.

For vital contributions to this book as product and process, I am also grateful to Barbra Barnett, Michael Budde, Spencer Dew, Debra Erickson, Greg Johnson, Paula Kane, Sheila McGinn, Dan McKanan, Kathy Merhar, Linda Penkower, Sara Schmitt, Susan Silver, Charles Strain, Kathryn Yahner with Hannah Hebert and the rest of her team at Penn State University Press, and the many other colleagues, students, friends, and relatives who have asked questions, shared insights, challenged my interpretations, or wished me well during a decade spent thinking about the Plowshares.

For institutional and financial support I am grateful to the Martin Marty Center for the Advanced Study of Religion at the University of Chicago Divinity School; the Dietrich School of Arts and Sciences at the University of Pittsburgh, especially its Department of Religious Studies; and the John Carroll University Department of Theology and Religious Studies. Material from this project has appeared in "Beyond Religious Freedom: Religious Activity in the Civil Disobedience Trials of Plowshares Anti-nuclear Activists," *Journal of Religion* 96, no. 2 (2016), and in "'Have We Made Ourselves Inaccessible?': Plowshares Disarmament Activists' Rhetoric of Marginality," *Journal of Political Theology* 13, no. 1 (2012): 76–92.

Introduction

"September 9, 1980," wrote Jesuit priest, poet, and peace activist Daniel Berrigan. "We rose at dawn after (to speak for myself) a mostly sleepless night."[1] Daniel Berrigan and his brother, Philip Berrigan (formerly a Josephite priest); Oblate priest Carl Kabat; Sister of the Sacred Heart Anne Montgomery; and Catholic laypeople Molly Rush, John Schuchardt, Elmer Maas, and Dean Hammer—the Plowshares Eight—weren't sure what the consequences would be when, early on that September morning, they trespassed into Building Number Nine of the General Electric plant in King of Prussia, Pennsylvania, but they anticipated lengthy prison sentences for what they were about to do. They understood their compulsion to act, regardless of possible outcomes, as a repetition of the calls to prophetic witness found in the Hebrew scriptures. Specifically, they read Isaiah 2:4 as a command: *They shall beat their swords into plowshares, and their spears into pruning hooks. Nation shall not take up sword against nation; they shall never again know war.*[2] Armed with household hammers and plastic baby bottles, the Plowshares Eight intended to enact Isaiah's prophecy.

Once on site two of the eight handed pamphlets to the security guard on duty, which read, in part, "In confronting G.E., we choose to obey God's law of life, rather than a corporate summons to death. Our beating of swords into plowshares today is a way to enflesh this biblical call. In our action, we draw on a deep rooted faith in Christ, who changed the course of history through his willingness to suffer rather than to kill. We are filled with hope for our world and for our children as we join this act of resistance."[3] Declaring to the guard that their intentions were nonviolent, an assurance they repeated throughout the action, two of the eight restrained him—either with a hand on the arm, a grab of the arm, or a bear hug, depending on the account—while the other six proceeded through the building, despite the guard's shouts that they were unauthorized and entering prohibited space. Once the six had crossed the lobby and entered the farther reaches of Building Number Nine, the two who had been restraining the guard left him and followed the others. At that point the guard called his superior, and he and other employees began to hear the "banging of metal," according to his later report.

Going after the eight, the guard found them hammering on what he and other guards, in subsequent write-ups of the events of that day, called "government material": four-foot-tall nose cones, for use with the then-new Mark 12A reentry vehicle system for the Minuteman III nuclear missile, which had been manufactured by the General Electric Space Systems Division beginning in the 1970s. The eight then laid down their hammers and began to pour red liquid, later identified as their own blood, from the baby bottles over the dented cones and documents in the room. Once the bottles had been emptied of their contents, the eight joined hands to pray and sing songs from the peace movement. They then returned through the lobby, either of their own volition or "herded" or "shoved" by astonished, frightened security personnel. They continued to sing and pray as the Upper Merion Township police arrived at the site and while they were taken to the police station, where the FBI shortly arrived. The Commonwealth of Pennsylvania charged the eight with criminal trespass and criminal mischief. Eleven additional charges, including several referring to assault and threatening behavior, were added in the coming days, as part of a legal process that was not resolved until a decade later.[4]

Two years earlier, in a 1978 letter from prison to his brother, Daniel, Philip Berrigan, serving a short sentence for a civil disobedience action at the Pentagon, had written, "We're passing more firmly into middle age. But it seems to me that the fact of deepening age suggests not a run-down of the clock or declining powers, but more renewal—better husbanded energy, more 'effectiveness' in the true sense, more firmness in the long haul." At the time of the letter both brothers had been in the national spotlight for years, rising to fame (or infamy) during the 1960s with their outspoken dissent against the Vietnam War. Their dramatic antiwar demonstrations, which included burning and pouring blood on draft files, galvanized the nascent Catholic Left and the larger peace movement. To many they exemplified the spirit of reform and engagement that accompanied the Second Vatican Council. To many others they exemplified that spirit taken much too far. They were lionized by many in the peace movement and the counterculture, ridiculed and maligned by others. By 1978 both had been arrested dozens of times and served multiple prison sentences; both had been disciplined by their respective religious orders for their antiwar activities and felt the censure deeply, though it fueled their deeds rather than curtailing them. Their actions up to that point had received wide media attention and provoked heated debate in both religious and secular circles on the morality of war, and the punishments they faced for those actions had become increasingly harsh. But in another year they would start planning for what they imagined would be, as Philip's letter predicts, their most "effective" action to date—and their riskiest. "It seems then to me that the better fun is yet to come," the letter continues, "and that we will be called upon by the Lord, summoned if you will, in increasingly serious ways. What this means God alone knows, but perhaps its broader outlines are already somewhat clear."[5]

Philip conceived of his next action, which would eventually take the form of the King of Prussia Plowshares action, as a way to continue the momentum of the heady Vietnam days, during which a religiously infused peace movement grew exponentially before the Berrigans' eyes, and in no small part as a result of their own efforts. The 1980 action he forecasts in his 1978 letter, in which he and Daniel and six others entered the General Electric plant to "symbolically disarm" the nose cones, similarly inspired followers, though on a far smaller scale than their earlier resistance. For the most part Plowshares activists, who continue to carry out their so-called divine obediences (the term they prefer to "civil disobedience"), adhere to the template established by the King of Prussia action. Participants enter facilities, military or private, where equipment to be used in the production or deployment of nuclear weapons is manufactured or stored; pour their own blood over the equipment and beat on it with household hammers; and perform what they often describe as a liturgy at the site. Most Catholics would probably not recognize in the actions what they know as liturgy, and many in the church's hierarchy have decried the Plowshares' actions. Plowshares activists don't mind. Though many are priests or nuns, and virtually all consider themselves to be devout Catholics, they often proclaim their distance from the institutional church. They also proclaim an indissoluble connection to it, and the actions rely on elements—trespass, blood, and hammers—that the participants understand in Christian and specifically Catholic ways. Each of the three elements is imbued with deep theological and sociopolitical resonances that blend with and layer over one another—as they should in the true church, according to the Plowshares.

Typically in a Plowshares action, activists are not immediately apprehended, so they wait to be confronted by private guards or military police. Upon their discovery participants declare that their intentions are nonviolent, kneel, and pray. They are invariably arrested, jailed, and await trial for charges that include criminal trespass, destruction of federal property, terroristic threat, and conspiracy to commit a felony, among others. Plowshares activists have received prison sentences of varying lengths, from twenty days to eighteen years, in past cases. In three cases, charges have been dropped just before the trial (inexplicably, the Plowshares say), and in rare instances their cases have been dismissed after mistrials or hung juries. In the United States, Plowshares defendants have never been acquitted.[6] Despite the harsh consequences that await the activists—or, as I will suggest, because of them—the Plowshares' symbolic disarmaments continue, though they remain unknown to most people, including other Catholics. Since 1980 there have been just over fifty Plowshares actions in the United States. The most recent took place in July 2012 at the Y-12 nuclear facility in Oak Ridge, Tennessee. This action was carried out by three activists, aged fifty-seven, sixty-three, and eighty-two, and nuclear experts called it the highest breach of nuclear security in the United States' history. Plowshares activists say that they will carry on until nuclear weapons have been abolished—not reduced, not limited, but entirely eradicated. Reading the Bible as a mandate to Christians to enact God's kingdom through political resistance, they believe they have no choice.

Courtroom Declarations and the Origins of the Project

In March 2000 I attended the trial in Baltimore County's circuit court of four Plowshares activists facing charges for the action they had performed at a Maryland Air National Guard Base the previous year, called Plowshares Versus Depleted Uranium. (Each group of Plowshares activists gives their action a name, which often refers to a particular site or weapon.) During that trial, an unusually well-attended and emotionally charged one, which I discuss in chapters 4 and 5, my interest in the group began to crystallize around the issues and questions that structure the work at hand. It was immediately apparent that the trial wasn't going well for the four defendants. Their every word and behavior provoked the judge, whose patience for the defendants and their cause, limited to begin with, quickly wore razor-thin. The jury, too, seemed largely baffled and frustrated by the proceedings. Not that the judge made it easy for the defendants: they were not allowed to call expert witnesses to speak about nuclear weapons, nor were they allowed to mention the weapons or their effects or speak about their motivations in performing the action. They responded to the judge's repeated reminders to this effect, which they called a gag order, by turning their backs on him and refusing to participate further in the trial. Did they think, an observer could have asked, that such behavior was going to encourage the judge and jury to be well disposed toward them? And, with all signs indicating from day one that that was not to be the case, why was the trial, to all appearances, a downright celebratory event, regarded as anything but a failure, even when the defendants were found guilty and sentenced far more harshly than anticipated?

Of course, like many civil disobedients, the defendants and their supporters were not primarily concerned with receiving a verdict of not guilty. The trial was important, even successful, no matter the outcome, because (among other reasons that I explore later) it provided an arena for the defendants to declare themselves as obedient to a more binding, truer justice than that of the earthly courts and thus morally distinct from the sinful world in thrall to what Philip Berrigan called "Lord Nuke." This much was evident at the time, when I was an undergraduate religious studies major interested in the intersection of religion and political activism. During my graduate studies in the sociology of religion, by which time I was primarily interested in questions of religious identity formation and community maintenance, the significance of the legal arena for the Plowshares came into clearer view. In the courtroom the Plowshares were trying to demonstrate their own self-understanding, a set of identity claims based in moral distinction. As I argue in the pages to come, that self-understanding lies at the heart of the Plowshares' religious life and resistance, which they understand as successful to the degree that they embody a scripturally based ideal of prophetic witness. It is very much the point of their resistance that doing so sets them apart from a war-making state, a complicit church, and an apathetic society. As such, public disapproval and legal consequences corroborate the Plowshares' self-understanding as persecuted for the sake of witness and as fundamentally different from the social, political, and religious institutions that they consider to be immoral. In finding the four Plowshares Versus Depleted Uranium defendants guilty, the court had confirmed the activists' own characterizations of themselves, which they had attempted to demonstrate throughout the trial, as well as in the action itself. The courtroom had served as a space not only for expressing religious identity claims but for *constituting* those claims. The actions themselves, I argue here, work in this same dual manner.

Unpacking the ways that Plowshares activists communicate a sense of themselves as morally distinct—in the actions, in the courtroom, and in the rhetoric that surrounds both—is the central task of the work at hand. So while this book is not only about the Plowshares' trials, it owes its contours to the questions that began to emerge from thinking about the Plowshares' trials as essential components of their actions and as profoundly important to their understanding of what the actions are meant to accomplish. These questions concern how the Plowshares' sense of moral distinction plays out in the actions and the trials; how it shapes their and their peers' understandings of what they and the actions achieve with tactics that many find baffling or foolish or misguided or even dangerous; and how it stitches together the strands of a religious world produced and performed across multiple settings (very few of them "religious" in the sense usually employed by sociologists, who primarily have observed aspects of religion such as congregational life) through an array of social interactions.[7] And, though I did not anticipate this when I began the project, it ends in the courtroom, where the norms of carefully secularized space become the backdrop for the display and enactment of the Plowshares' religious ideologies and identity claims, even though religion is seldom an explicit focus of the trials.

This book examines the religious logic of the Plowshares and their symbolic disarmaments, but by "religious logic" I do not mean simply a series of beliefs that inspire and legitimate their distinctive practices. Rather, as I will show, the Plowshares' religious logic is as embodied, spatial, and emotive as it is cognitive. The activists' sense of themselves as morally distinct, which lies at the heart of that logic, is correspondingly embodied, spatial, emotive, and cognitive, all at once. The question of how the Plowshares convey their sense of distinction on those several overlapping levels and to various overlapping audiences—sometimes quite intentionally and sometimes less so—is the animating question of this book. I argue that it is the multivalent demonstration of this sense of distinction (and by demonstration, as I discuss later, I mean not only expression but enactment) that anchors the Plowshares' religious world and their resistance and that they and their project become intelligible when viewed from this angle, which I call, going forward, their boundary work. Their case also suggests what scholars of religion in America have to gain from looking more closely and intentionally at the boundary work of religious groups than we have tended to do.

Showing, Doing, and the Performance of Religious Boundaries

Sociologist Thomas Gieryn coined the phrase "boundary work" in 1983, to describe scientists' attempts to assert and defend the credibility and superiority of "science" over and against "non-science" in public discourse.[8] Social scientists, the foundations of whose field include studies of class groups, status groups, ethnic groups, and more, quickly found uses for the concept of boundary work beyond the question of epistemic and disciplinary demarcations, especially for studying social groups and movements and for probing the mechanisms and ramifications of social difference—the ways that a group conceives of itself, and expresses and experiences that conception, as different from and better than groups that it classifies as "other."[9] While Gieryn analyzed scientists' boundary work as a rhetorical style (scientists' way of describing what they do as distinct from what nonscientists do), social scientists have also analyzed boundary work as it is accomplished through a variety of other means, including consumption patterns and cultural tastes, for example.[10]

As I am using the term, boundary work—rhetorical or otherwise, conscious or not—simultaneously reflects and asserts ideas about difference and distinction so that those ideas become apprehensible, both to the group in question and to the others from whom it distinguishes itself. Much of it takes place in the space between what Michèle Lamont and Virag Molnar, in their review of the recent attention to boundaries in the social sciences, identify as "symbolic boundaries" and "social boundaries." Symbolic boundaries, according to Lamont and Molnar, are "conceptual distinctions made by social actors to categorize objects, people, practices, and even time and space"; social boundaries are "objectified forms of social difference manifested in unequal access to and unequal distribution of resources (material and nonmaterial) and social opportunities." Symbolic boundaries "serve as tools by which individuals and groups struggle over and come to agree upon definitions of reality . . . separate people into groups and generate feelings of similarity and group membership . . . [and] are an essential medium through which people acquire status and monopolize resources," and when they are widely agreed on, symbolic boundaries can become social boundaries, as they "take on a constraining character and pattern social interaction in important ways." Social boundaries, at the same time, cannot exist without the conceptual distinctions or symbolic boundaries that underpin them.[11] The relationship between social and symbolic boundaries is complex and variable; there is not always a neat correspondence between the two categories.[12] Rather, symbolic and social boundaries are deeply interwoven, forming an elaborate meshwork of conception and assertion whereby, as social scientists have long noted, group identity is constituted and fortified.[13]

Religious groups are no exception, and the American religious landscape, throughout history and into the present day, teems with small- and large-scale religious communities intent on declaring their distinction from one another, in a variety of ways. Clothing, for example, was an important means by which religious groups in eighteenth-century America distinguished themselves. Evangelical Methodists and Baptists, among others, chose "plain dress" over and against the ornate fripperies of the unsaved as a way to signal their piety and visually define their community.[14] Those same Methodists and Baptists wrangled over the proper method of baptism into the faith—dipping versus sprinkling, adults versus infants. Their heated debates, often polemical, allowed for theological refinement on both sides as the two denominations defined their positions each in contrast to the other, and it allowed for the presentation of distinct denominational identity before an enthusiastic sea of religious consumers. R. Laurence Moore, in his study of religious outsiders in America, argues that claims of difference advanced in the early and mid-nineteenth century by Joseph Smith's young Church of Jesus Christ of Latter-day Saints created a "usable identity," allowing Mormons to "become a people."[15] The link between physical removal and the demonstration of piety, a kind of spatial boundary work, is a recurring theme in American history, evident in countless examples from Joseph Baumler's Zoar Separatists to Mother Ann Lee's Shakers to present-day Amish, who avoid using electricity in the belief that electrical wires would connect their rural communities to the outside world. And Christian Smith argues that the strength of evangelical Christianity in contemporary America comes from its ability to resist the twin lures of assimilation and separation and maintain a fluid but unambiguous distinction from society at large. "In a pluralistic society," Smith posits in what he calls a subcultural identity theory of religious strength, "those religious groups will be relatively stronger which better possess and employ the cultural tools needed to create both clear distinction from and significant engagement and tension with other relevant outgroups, short of becoming genuinely countercultural."[16]

Smith's theory suggests a permeability and elasticity to religious group boundaries, and, indeed, as often as boundaries are asserted on the American religious landscape, they are transversed and refigured.[17] In colonial New England, for example, devout Mary Rowlandson experienced an alarming breakdown of distinctions between her decorous Puritan self and the Native Americans who took her captive during King Philip's War.[18] The breakdown became ever more pronounced as Mary ate the Indians' food, participated in their economy, and, in tandem, began to assign to the Indians moral qualities that previously she had identified only with her own community. In her enormously popular captivity narrative, an early best-seller first published in 1682 and reprinted several times that year and over the next two centuries, Mary seems constantly startled to notice as at least semiporous the spatial, physiological, and moral boundaries that, in her mind prior to the trials of her captivity, sharply demarcated the Christian (herself, namely) from the heathen. And yet she plays a role, if a hesitant one, in the erosion of those boundaries. Mary demonstrates how the overturning of a social boundary, however unwilling, can lead to a reworking of symbolic boundaries, however unexpected. As she tells it, she gradually began to eat the Indians' food (even to enjoy it, thanks to God's grace) and participate in their economy, deliberate social experiences that inadvertently led her to reevaluate her previous thinking about the differences between herself and the Indians. They were, in these social encounters, kind to her, generous—one could almost say, in a whisper, civilized. This was unexpected, to say the least.

Mary's story is a dramatically personal one, but the erosion or elision of boundaries happens at the group level as well. A recent study suggests that the breakdown of boundaries between religious groups has proceeded so far apace that the sole remaining boundary on the American religious landscape is the one separating believers and nonbelievers. Overwhelmingly, the authors of the study find, Americans regard atheists as a threat to the national moral identity, and as a result atheists are excluded in both public and private life, less accepted than other groups that are also perceived as threatening. Survey respondents were less likely to vote for an atheist presidential candidate or to approve of a child marrying an atheist versus a member of several other groups with a history of being viewed as suspicious in American culture. The perceived moral distinction between believers and nonbelievers

Erosion of boundaries

is particularly notable, the authors of the study suggest, because it remains stoutly intact even though divisions between religious groups, such as the denominational disputes of the eighteenth century, are on the wane.[19]

Such a narrative, of the decreasing relevance and strength of religious boundaries, is often applied to American Catholicism, usually told as a story of increasing attention to—and success at—assimilation. At the same time, another narrative strand often applied to American Catholicism, this one by detractors more than historiographers, characterizes that which sets Catholics apart as inherent and permanent, a lasting mark of difference that prevents true assimilation. Hence the urgent push to assimilate, so that these two strands are braided together into a master narrative whereby American Catholics flee from, yet cannot ever quite escape from, their own difference. There is little room in this narrative for Catholics cultivating difference, or insisting on distinction, as a central feature of religious life.

Yet despite the important specifics of Catholic history and historiography, in this regard Catholics share a fate with many other American religious groups, whose boundary work is seldom studied as such. Perhaps a prevailing sentiment that religious distinctions have all but vanished in the present-day United States explains why only a small body of work in American religious studies starts with boundary questions, though a great deal of work ends with boundaries, a few examples of which I have already mentioned: Leigh Eric Schmidt, in his prescient call for scholarly attention to the material and visual culture of early American religion, asks what "what they saw" (such as clothing styles), in addition to what they heard (sermons, prayers), tells us about the religious worlds of colonial Americans. It tells us, he argues (though not in these terms), about boundaries. R. Laurence Moore asks how the Mormons "became a people" and concludes that boundaries played a pivotal role. Christian Smith comes to the same answer, having asked why evangelicals thrive in contemporary America. Works like these leave little doubt that religious groups are exemplars of boundary work, laboring to articulate and demonstrate understandings of themselves as pious contra the wicked, moral contra the immoral or amoral, saved contra the damned, chosen. While work that ends with boundaries shows boundary work as important to religious communities, it also suggests that boundary work is merely attendant to the other work of being religious (professing creeds or practicing devotions, for example). Far less work in American religious studies *begins* with boundary questions, asking after the why and especially the how of boundary work as such and positing it as central to religious worlds.[20]

The case of the Plowshares illustrates this centrality. It also shows what there is to gain from starting with boundaries, from thinking about religious distinctions with the phrase and the frame of "boundary work" squarely in mind. First, as a broad heuristic, the lens of boundary work can bridge aspects of religious studies often treated by scholars as vastly different objects of study, addressing vastly different questions—theological debate and bodily practice, for example. People's religious worlds are not often as compartmentalized as that, nor should be our frames for studying them. Second, the lens of boundary work focuses our attention on the social aspect of practices or propensities in which the social aspect might otherwise be overlooked, a theme I revisit in the pages to come. With its boundary work, a group defines itself *in relation to* groups that are perceived as somehow less worthy or less good, for its own sake but also for the sake of other constituencies in its social world, like the funding organizations to whom scientists make their pitches in Gieryn's example or the revival-goers to whom eighteenth-century itinerant ministers made theirs. Boundary work, with its specifically social nuance, directs our attention to the ways that religious actors are also social actors and to their agency in negotiating social space. It trains our gaze on the fact that negotiating social space is, indeed, work—that asserting identity claims, conveying a particular sense of self, takes strenuous effort across a variety of domains. It reminds us to guard against the opposed yet equally hazardous trends of seeing religious distinctions and boundaries as inherent or as artificially imposed. Thematizing boundaries and boundary work through the lens of a Catholic group is especially important, as the history and historiography of American Catholics have been so much influenced by the effects of both these trends. Also, thematizing boundaries obliges us to probe the identity claims of the groups we study, approaching them not as facts but as processes of which we can (and should) ask not only "why," but "how." Many observers, for example, have repeated the Plowshares' claim that they are outsiders, without looking into the ways that the Plowshares themselves work to make that claim a social reality and the different ways that they do so for different audiences. That overdetermination on outsiderness, I argue in this book, limits our understanding of the Plowshares and other groups who work to construct their own difference.

For the Plowshares it is theologically imperative that their symbolic boundaries—the schema that posits their moral rightness contra those citizens who do not do the work of Christian witness as they conceive it—become instantiated as social boundaries. I do not mean to suggest that the Plowshares are not very much concerned with unity, solidarity, and community. Literature from them and about them leaves no doubt that they are. But they are, at the same time, very much concerned with distinction and boundedness, both symbolic and social. Because of their simultaneous concern with community and distinction, the Plowshares nicely illustrate the dual character of boundaries, as the sites where differences are both shored up and elided, depending on the audience at hand.

I use the term "audience" deliberately, to reflect the performative quality of the Plowshares' boundary work—a performative quality that, I argue, is necessary to the efficacy of the Plowshares' witness as they conceive it. "Performance" has a handily dual sense, suggesting both display and achievement. One performs an aria or performs a surgery—that is, presents something or makes something come to pass or, sometimes, both. Richard Schechner, a founding figure in the field of performance studies, captures this duality when he defines performance as a "showing of a doing."[21] Ritual theorist Ronald Grimes notes that Schechner's definition fails to accommodate all the types of performance generally considered to fall under the heading, specifically Grimes's own métier, ritual. He argues that "very few ritualists would say their primary intention is to show their doings. More characteristically they say they are doing, and that their doings may, incidentally, be seen or overheard."[22] Grimes's critique of Schechner suggests that to consider an audience as anything but incidental to the doing of religious acts detracts from the primary meaning of the actions and the primary intentions of the actors. But for the Plowshares the showings of their doings are not incidental. Showing is certainly not the Plowshares' only motivation, and I am not suggesting that it is a more primary intention than, for example, obeying what they read as scriptural mandates or working to abolish nuclear weapons. But showing is vitally important for the Plowshares—so important, I argue, that their other intentions cannot be realized without the element of display and that the doing of the actions indeed depends on the showing. The Plowshares illustrate the role that performance plays in the process of instantiating conceptual, symbolic boundaries as social boundaries.

I argue in this book that performances of various kinds, including embodied and discursive performances, allow for the actualization of the moral boundaries central to the Plowshares' project—the production of religious identities and meanings, as well as the expression of those identities and meanings. The Plowshares are always conscious of an audience, and that imagined audience—always watching, always judging—is crucial to their multivalent religious logic. The Plowshares thus help us to think more carefully about the ways that audience and performativity can be central to the work of religious groups, in the same way that they help us to think more [handwritten: Then focus on boundaries] carefully about boundaries as the product of strenuous work, a constellation of endeavors central, not incidental, to religiosity. The two lenses of performance and boundary work also help us to understand the Plowshares, and what it is they believe themselves to be doing, better. They enable us to make sense of a group that may initially seem counterintuitive and counterproductive, claiming to work for certain changes in ways that the activists acknowledge are unlikely to bring about those changes directly. But they do not regard their actions as futile—far from it. Efficacy for the Plowshares, as I will show, hinges on the negotiation of physical and sociomoral space; boundaries are the sites where these spaces, and the moral qualities attendant to them, can be girded and sustained or can be rethought and reworked, not only for the Plowshares themselves but also for their various audiences.

Terminology and Methodology

[handwritten: Not really a "movement" b/c it doesn't recruit]

Readers who are familiar with other work on the Plowshares probably will notice, and perhaps wonder, that I do not refer to a Plowshares "movement." This is intentional, and it is not always easy. Literature on the Plowshares, including earlier work of my own, presumes the label almost without exception, and Plowshares activists themselves use it from time to time, though not regularly. In avoiding the term here, I do not mean to suggest that it can never be fruitful to think of the Plowshares as a movement. Sharon Erickson Nepstad's 2008 book on the Plowshares is framed around a movement question—how do participants remain committed to a movement that makes serious demands of its participants, without ever seeming to achieve its desired ends?—and the resulting study yields important insights about the Plowshares and about social movements and high-risk activism in general. A great deal of recent social movement theory can account for a movement that does not achieve instrumental goals or obvious political results, and many of these characterizations, like Barbara Epstein's notion of the politics of moral witness on which Nepstad draws, go a long way toward making sense of the Plowshares.[23] But movements, whatever else they do or do not do, work to recruit, to attract new people to the cause. The Plowshares do not. The larger communities of which they are a part do work to recruit new members to the broader causes of antimilitary and antinuclear activism, but increasing the number of participants in their specific activities is not a concern for the Plowshares. Indeed, that their numbers are small is an important component of their resistance. To emphasize this aspect of their project—that is, to focus on what they *are* doing, even if they are decidedly not growing—I refer simply to "the Plowshares," by which term I mean an elite subset within a larger Catholic resistance community. I have taken a cue from a phrase that appears occasionally in Philip Berrigan's writings, "Plowshares people." When Plowshares activists write about their actions,

the context is often such (or assumed to be such) that they do not need to label themselves at all (though when they do, they do so in telling ways that I explore in chapter 3). But Philip's "Plowshares people," though he does not use it with any great regularity or frequency, nicely evokes precisely what I am arguing in the work at hand: that the efficacy of the actions is bound up with the activists taking on and performing particular identity claims. Simultaneously, embracing the identity to which they feel called happens as the actions are performed.

My concern in this book is to probe how the Plowshares' actions, their legal trials, and the rhetoric that surrounds the actions and the trials work as performances of a self-conception based on moral distinction and how those performances are interpreted and conveyed as efficacious. When I talk about performances, I am interested mainly in the tellings and retellings of the actions. In part this is because those retellings—in texts, in the courtroom—are more accessible than the actions. The visible nature of the Plowshares' actions is essential to their efficacy. But very often, the actions go largely unobserved. They are cloaked in secrecy up to the moment when they are committed, and, even then, most take place at locations decidedly *not* public and usually not heavily peopled. The physical audience for a Plowshares action or its aftermath is usually quite small. But that audience expands as accounts—those of the activists themselves and their supporters, of the military or police, and of various media outlets—circulate. The actions become more fully public in the telling, where they go from being public *in theory* (which is not unimportant) to being *actually* public. The telling of the actions is necessary to make the actions work as performances: they allow for the showing of the doing. Those tellings take place on paper, in the letters and pamphlets and books that Plowshares activists write about their actions; and they take place in the courtroom, as Plowshares activists explain what they have done and why they have done it. Trial transcripts paint a vibrant picture of interruption, reiteration, objection—in short, of discursive battles being waged as the events of a Plowshares action are recounted from significantly different perspectives. As crafted accounts, constructed by constituencies who have a stake in stressing certain aspects of the actions while glossing over others, courtroom accounts, like textual accounts, highlight the activists' intentionality, the choices they make in narrating the actions. What do they want to convey about the actions and themselves as perpetrators of the actions? Why do they describe their actions in the terms that they do? What rhetorical tactics do they use as they address various audiences, to bolster and even complete the aims of the actions themselves? I am interested in the work of dissemination, of communication, but I am interested in them as *more than* retellings. They are echoes, recapitulations, reactualizations of the acts that they describe, and as such they are necessary components of the actions. They are the performances of a performance—performance multiplied for multiplying audiences, all essential for the realization of the Plowshares' goals.

Chapter Overview

Chapter 1, "'We in the Underground Are Trying to Do Something Else': The Plowshares' History and Development," presents the Plowshares' history, locating the group's origins in the Vietnam War–era Catholic Left, and examines the group's demographics, including shifting trends over the past thirty-five years. This chapter explores how Philip and Daniel Berrigan came to equate moral distinction and marginality and how that pairing came to structure Philip's vision for the first Plowshares action. I argue that the affiliations the Plowshares claim and eschew (they do not, for example, think of themselves as part of the larger disarmament movement that was at its apex just as the first Plowshares actions were taking place) give the first insights into the Plowshares' emphasis on symbolic, moral boundaries.

Chapter 2, "'Something Deeper than Reason': The Logic and Tactics of Symbolic Disarmament," analyzes the Plowshares' actions and the religiopolitical worldview that undergirds them, examining what precisely constitutes "symbolic disarmament," the elusive designation that, according to the Plowshares, renders their actions distinct from other disarmament and peacemaking activity. I consider the genres of performance, ritual, and liturgy as constitutive of symbolic disarmament, and I analyze the rudiments of the Plowshares' actions—trespass, blood, and hammers—in light of these genres, to explicate their overlapping levels of theological, political, and social significance. I argue that in a Plowshares action, the elements of trespass, blood, and hammers are re-marked as symbols; at the same time, the activists undergo a similar re-marking by which an exclusive ritual community is created. I also examine innovations that have taken place within the general template of a Plowshares action and argue that these innovations have revealed ambiguities and tensions within the group that most observers overlook. This chapter begins to demonstrate the book's central argument, that their actions are embodied performance of the sociomoral boundaries at the heart of the Plowshares' self-understanding, even for activists who don't explicitly voice that sense of distinction in the same way that the founders did, and that the extent to which the actions are considered efficacious hinges on the extent to which boundary performance is accomplished.

Chapter 3, "'Our Only Real Credential': The Rhetorical Performance of Symbolic Boundaries," looks at the formats and media that the Plowshares use to talk about their actions. Writing about the actions, and about themselves, is crucially important for the Plowshares; how do they construct the narratives of their actions for various audiences, and how, in turn, do those audiences receive these narratives? I examine key tropes that emerge as the Plowshares talk about themselves and their actions, explaining their motivations and intentions both within the group and to various outside audiences. I argue that their rhetoric both displays and helps to instantiate the Plowshares' symbolic boundaries (this is the dual sense of "performance," as both depiction and achievement, that I employ throughout), even as it strives to be inclusive, and that these rhetorical boundary performances are necessary to complete the embodied performances of the actions themselves.

Chapters 4 and 5 analyze the Plowshares' legal trials, where rhetorical and embodied performances come together in striking and complex displays of boundary work. Chapter 4, "'Just to Speak the Truth': The Plowshares' Theory of the Case," lays out the communicative aims of the trials. I analyze two typical opening statements, arguing that they reveal the moral framework that undergirds the Plowshares' legal strategy. The statements contain, in seed form, several of the elements important in the unfolding of the Plowshares' defenses, which I explore in detail in chapter 5. "'Your Honor, I Object. . . . She Is Talking About God': Boundary Negotiations in the Courtroom" examines the Plowshares' choice of defenses and their courtroom behaviors and language, all of which contribute to the defendants' performances of "nonbelonging." The trials reveal with especial clarity the character of boundaries as sites of both the maintenance and merging of difference, as the Plowshares both restrict and expand their symbolic boundaries, demonstrating their ability to work either within or outside the conventions of the legal system and their self-reflexivity with respect to their boundary work. The Plowshares are idiosyncratic in their resistance, but in the courtroom they stand in for a parade of religious actors whose time in the courtroom threads vividly through the tapestry of American religious history. Analyzing the Plowshares' legal activity as religious activity not only illuminates their particular religious world but also expands the model of the relationship between religions and the courts as one of control, regulation, and limitation, to allow for the agency of religious actors within a space particularly suited to the production of religious discourses and identities, even when religion is not an explicit focal point.

As I delved into the kinds of boundary work the Plowshares do to distinguish themselves from a sinful world and lackadaisical church, my thoughts turned often to the trial I observed in 2000, where I found myself in the midst of a throng of the Plowshares' extended Catholic activist community, gathered from across the country to show their support for the four defendants. Sharon Nepstad has pointed out the deep community that sustains Plowshares activists, and that sense of community was strongly evident at the trial. But it was also quite clear that the community was socially stratified. Plowshares activists were accorded a deference that reflected their elite status within the larger Catholic resistance community. Even in a group composed primarily of career high-risk activists, their peers seemed to regard the Plowshares—not only the four defendants, but those who had participated in other Plowshares actions—as somehow different. The Plowshares' elevated status made sense in that context, among nonviolent activists for whom prison sentences are a mark of commitment and integrity. But the awed respect that their peers displayed toward the Plowshares revealed a tension that has surfaced often during my examination of the Plowshares' boundary work. For the most part Plowshares activists are noticeably humble and talk about themselves and their actions as part of a larger network of Catholic activism that they hold in high esteem. Usually, they do not explicitly claim to be exemplars or virtuosi, and yet many of their peers characterize them that way. How does that happen? That is to say, how is it that the distinctions Plowshares activists assert between themselves and the court and its agents, for example, which are crucial to their sense of identity and their notion of efficacy, also come to distinguish them in the midst of their community of supporters, close friends, and allies, such that even their closest kin regard them as morally distinct?

In this book I aim to connect the social dynamics I saw at play during the trial with the Plowshares' larger project, to tease out a link between the ways they posit themselves as outsiders with regard to the state and the church and the social stratifications evident in their activist community. In other words, how do external boundaries (boundaries between the group at hand and the "other" from which it distinguishes itself) shape internal boundaries, the subtle distinctions within a group, such as those between the Plowshares and closely allied activist communities, whom they explicitly include in their milieu? Nepstad concludes in her study of the Plowshares that activists remained committed because community sustains them, supporting them materially and emotionally and also reinforcing their theology and ideology. This is undoubtedly the case. I want to take a step back, to ask how the Plowshares themselves produce and present the tropes and ideals that the community then supports. How do the Plowshares' words and actions encourage the notion that their resistance is Catholic resistance par excellence, even when they would not characterize it as such? How do those words and actions shape the religious world of the community that supports them *so that* it supports them? Again, I do not believe that Plowshares activists intentionally set themselves apart from, or elevate themselves above, their friends and supporters. But the processes by which a group's internal boundaries take shape as a product of, or corollary to, external boundary work, their hierarchies shaped and replicated accordingly, is a theme that deserves more attention in boundary work studies, and I take it up explicitly in the conclusion.

Creating and maintaining boundaries is, for the Plowshares, not simply attendant to the work of being a religious group. It lies at the very heart of what it means to be religious. The Plowshares are idiosyncratic, but in their energetic attunement to what an academic like myself might call boundary work, and they would simply call performing their witness, is not unique. Indeed, I hope with the work at hand to suggest the importance of boundary work to religious worlds. But foremost, this is a story about the Plowshares, generally regarded as little more than a footnote to a more glorious Catholic past, but to my mind a striking case study in their own right, both continuing and departing from a lineage and a mode of religiosity with deep roots in American Catholicism. It is my aim to use the frame of boundary work to tell their story from a new perspective and more fully than has been done before. At the very least—and this is no small thing, I hope the reader will agree— centering my analysis of the Plowshares on their boundary work allows me to tackle a perennial question asked not only of the Plowshares (and of me, during the decade I have spent studying them) but of a host of groups like them, religious activists who trade in the symbolic: *Do they really believe that works?* And, of course, its incredulous follow-up: *How?* The answer to the first question is simple: Yes. The answer to the second question is more complex, involving a sacramental, liturgical worldview that plays out on overlapping levels of political, metaphysical, and social efficacy. The results of a Plowshares action or trial occur not only on a symbolic plane, but in social spaces that they share with detractors and supporters alike, through practices that have discernible effects on the larger community whose religious worlds their actions, words, convictions, and commitments help to generate. The Plowshares' savvy as social actors is as striking as their intensity as religious actors—indeed, the one cannot be separated from the other, as these pages show.

"We in the Underground Are Trying to Do Something Else"

The Plowshares' History and Development

Headlines tinged with surprise trumpeted the news of the King of Prussia Plowshares action, and every twist and turn in the complicated legal trial that followed, across the nation in the early 1980s. The *New York Times*, *Washington Post*, *Christian Science Monitor*, and *Newsweek* were among the high-profile publications that proclaimed the return of sixties activism during their coverage of the dramatic events at General Electric Building Number Nine, the week-long trial that drew crowds of supporters to the courthouse in Norristown, Pennsylvania, and its drawn-out aftermath of appeals and resentencings. Eight people had taken part in the action, all veteran Catholic peace activists who felt that pouring their blood and hammering on the nose cones at General Electric was an appropriate and necessary response to the threat posed by nuclear weapons to the planet and to humanity. They had prayed about their action together over a period of several months, discerning that it was indeed God's will for them and that it did indeed fall within the parameters of nonviolent witness, to which they were entirely committed. They had planned its details together, considering contingencies and devising backup plans in case the map they had of the GE facility, an old one, proved to be inaccurate. And, finally, they had committed the action together. But media attention focused overwhelmingly on two of the Plowshares Eight: Philip and Daniel Berrigan, brothers who had achieved celebrity status years before for their dramatic acts of protest against the war in Vietnam.

In 1970, a decade before the Plowshares Eight undertook their symbolic disarmament at General Electric, writer Francine du Plessix Gray had lauded the Berrigans as "some of the purest, sternest Christians in the country," at the vanguard of a burgeoning movement of "new Catholic radical[s]" that would prove to be the "leaven of reform" in America. She profiled the Berrigans for the *New Yorker* that same year, in an article that, along with a 1971 *Time* magazine cover story, both signaled and reinforced the fame and controversy that surrounded the anti–Vietnam War activities of the "rebel priests" (as *Time* labeled its cover sketch of the two in clerical collars). Those activities were greeted simultaneously with admiration and consternation, depending on whom was asked.[1] During the 1960s and 1970s both devotees and detractors regarded the Berrigans as largely responsible for the development of a sizable movement of religiously motivated antiwar activists. Even observers who were ambivalent about their actions, such as a Jesuit priest who, in 1971, questioned whether the adjective "prophetic" could properly be applied to the Berrigans, were loath to dismiss them outright: "Until the day when we shall know for sure [whether they are true prophets], the wise Christian ought to consider well the issues Fathers Dan and Phil Berrigan have raised."[2] And their most vocal critics, who saw them as dangerously misguided and self-righteous, acknowledged their influence by warning against their undeniable allure.[3] Admirers and critics alike continue to invoke the Berrigans as emblematic of the Catholic Left in its heyday.[4]

For all the lasting renown of its central founding figures, the Plowshares, though still active, are little known in most circles today. The flurry of media interest that greeted the King of Prussia incident slowed with each subsequent action, and today, more than fifty actions later, what little media coverage there is tends to characterize the Plowshares not as the exciting sequel to sixties activism but as the aging relict of a more glorious past. This trend reversed somewhat after the most recent action in July 2012, which received attention from several major media outlets due to the serious nature of the security breach. But the characterization of Plowshares activists as a holdover of an earlier era, clinging to their fight against nuclear weapons when most peace activists have moved on to more relevant campaigns, has shaded most media coverage of their actions for the better part of three decades. It is a characterization that is neither entirely accurate nor entirely false. The Plowshares emerged directly from the Vietnam War–era Catholic Left and frequently acknowledge that lineage, to the exclusion of any connection to the larger nuclear disarmament movement flourishing in the United States as the first Plowshares actions took place. At the same time, Philip Berrigan conceived of the King of Prussia action as a departure from the tactics and the mindset of the earlier peace movement, as well as those of the disarmament movement.

The history that the Plowshares tell, the affiliations and influences that they claim or do not claim, the ways they characterize their actions in contrast to other disarmament activities, and the ways the group has taken shape and developed over three decades provide the first insights into the moral boundaries central to the Plowshares' sense of self, which in turn is central to way they understand the actions' efficacy. In subsequent chapters I turn to the logic and strategies of "symbolic disarmament," the actions themselves and their consequences, and I argue that the actions "work" for the activists because they function as boundary performances. But it is necessary to start the Plowshares' story here, in the decades leading up to the King of Prussia action, from which time emerges the system of moral distinctions that structures the Plowshares' religious worldview and resistance strategy and necessitates the strenuous boundary work that the next chapters examine. Who do the Plowshares say they are and are not? Whom do they perceive themselves to be like and unlike? These questions lie at the heart of the Plowshares' project.

The Rebel Priests

Today characterizations of Philip and Daniel Berrigan as resolute outsiders, fringe figures who remained committed to a particular moral vision despite painful consequences, are ubiquitous and automatic. But the two did not always locate success on the fringes. In coming to espouse a mode of resistance premised on a direct link between success and social opprobrium, the Berrigans demonstrate the combination of biographical and circumstantial factors, or emotions and resources, that James Jasper argues is at the heart of the moral protester's strategy.[5] Resonances of their upbringing and responses to tension within their religious orders and within the larger Catholic Left met the circumstances and resources that they encountered as the Vietnam era came to a close, and the combination gave rise to a new model of activism that placed a heavy emphasis on contingency and marginality as necessary to true Christian witness. From there, Plowshares actions would eventually emerge.

The Berrigans were born in small-town Minnesota, Daniel in 1921 and Philip in 1923, to staunchly Catholic parents. Daniel joined the Jesuits directly out of high school and was ordained in 1952. Philip fought in World War II, where he was struck by the poor treatment black soldiers received. Upon his return from combat he followed Daniel into the priesthood, joining the Josephite order, which is dedicated to ministry among African Americans. He was ordained in 1955. Both became involved in the civil rights movement and ultimately took the position that the United States' participation in the Vietnam War—and, later, in the arms race—was the root cause of a host of social ills, including racism. Placed in a poor African American community in New Orleans, Philip was deeply troubled that the government spent billions on the war while African Americans were segregated into poverty, and that oppressively racist sentiment in the United States did not diminish even as a large percentage (disproportionate, Philip concluded) of African Americans joined combat troops in Vietnam.

Even among the Josephites Philip's exhortations against racial injustice were considered dangerous in the South, and in 1963 his superiors sent him from New Orleans to New York. But he continued to make waves. In 1965 he gave a public talk in which he decried not only racism but the escalating war. Members of the audience, angered by his antiwar message, complained to his superior, who had previously ordered Philip, a known firebrand, not to speak or act against the war in any way. Philip was moved again, this time to Baltimore, where he remained silent on the war for a few months, before realizing that he no longer could. He later wrote, "My love for the Catholic church, and for the Josephite order, had not diminished, but I kept thinking about how Jesus might respond to seeing children trapped in a sea of napalm. . . . I had sworn fidelity to the church, and I had never violated my vows, yet my conscience dictated that I speak openly, clearly, and honestly about the war in Vietnam."[6]

Daniel experienced similar tension with the Jesuits. By 1965, as a professor of New Testament studies at LeMoyne College in New York, he was already far more vocal in the antiwar movement than his superiors felt was appropriate. When Roger LaPorte, twenty-two years old, immolated himself in November of that year to protest the war, Daniel's superiors, including the easily provoked Cardinal Francis Spellman, ordered him not to make a public statement about the young man's death. Spellman's official statement, which was to be the only statement, announced that LaPorte had sinned by committing suicide. When, a few days later, Daniel spoke at LaPorte's funeral and called the self-immolation a potentially hopeful and redemptive act (he later wrote that he did not think he was disobeying the order by doing so), his superiors immediately sent him from New York to Latin America, without specifying a purpose or length of time for the trip. Many of his Jesuit brothers as well as a mass of supporters outside the Jesuits rallied publicly to his defense, and his superiors brought him home after four months. The experience of "exile" was hardly total, but Daniel refers to himself still as an outsider within the Jesuits (though they have never expelled him from the order, and he has never left). He had always dreaded the possibility of separation from his order, feeling a deep and previously unfamiliar sense of belonging there. His feeling of being cast out by his superiors affected him deeply and infused his theology, perhaps also undermining his attachment to the Jesuit ideal of obedience to superiors as a central aspect of piety. He wrote of this experience, "Violent dislocation went beyond the fact: it emerged as a symbol. I was becoming something crudely known as a standoff. I was morally placed at a distance, by forces beyond accounting—from my order, from my church even."[7]

Yet Daniel reports in his autobiography that the ideals of his order and the church became more real than ever before to him during his exile. The Jesuit emphasis on self-abnegation and suffering for Christ became significant to him in a new way in Latin America, where he observed priests and laypeople working to address social concerns in their communities, under circumstances of dire poverty. These priests exemplified for Daniel the ideal of the "worker-priest," a model of clerical life that arose in France in the 1940s as way to put priests in touch with the lives of the impoverished, and which had been deeply influential to him in seminary. Upon his return he resumed his co-chairmanship of Clergy and Laity Concerned About Vietnam, the organization he had founded with Abraham Heschel and Richard Neuhaus before his abrupt departure, and took a job at Cornell University, where he became a central figure on the school's prominent antiwar scene. But he was deeply shaken by feelings of alienation and abandonment. Increasingly, his theological and poetic writings foregrounded themes of suffering and being an outsider for Christ. Philip's thinking developed along the same lines, and he eventually wrote in his autobiography, "It is a Biblical theme that change always begins in the desert, which is a metaphor for slums, the jails, the docks when one is in court, those margins of society where people are speaking truth to power."[8]

By no means were the Berrigans alone as they began to think of the true Christian as a marginal figure and to think of the "margin"—of the church, of society—as a space of radical sociomoral potential. They were tapping into a rich vein of Christian thought stretching back for centuries. Early Christians helped create the script that the Berrigans were beginning to follow (and to which the Plowshares still allude) by characterizing themselves as "others"—aliens, sojourners, foreigners in a land to which they did not belong—to form and strengthen their Christian identity against the sinful world.[9] By the midsixties the Berrigans' close friend Dorothy Day had been embracing the margins of society for years with her Catholic Worker movement, based on the ideal of voluntary poverty. In the 1970s sociologist Guenther Roth noted that marginality made possible the *imitatio Christi*, the imitation of Christ. Roth describes marginality as beginning in privilege, from which the Berrigans, for example, had opted out. Marginality could be embraced by those who did not need to earn an income or were not burdened by financial concerns (a departure from classic sociological definitions in which "marginality" applies to those who are shut out from economic opportunity). As such, Roth argues, the margin functions as a site of great possibility for religious and ethical creativity, for which those who are constrained by ties to the economic system have limited opportunity. The Berrigans did not originate this phenomenon, but, for Roth, they exemplified it.[10]

Neither Catholics specifically nor Christians generally had the market cornered on marginality as a site of potential. Activist bell hooks, not long before Philip penned his autobiography, reflected on the long struggles of oppressed peoples, describing the margin as a "site of resistance" that one might choose to stay in for the creative possibilities it can offer and the ways it can nurture principled opposition to injustice. And historian of religions Jonathan Z. Smith notes that the periphery has long been understood, across cultural and religious traditions, as the realm of the strong, of freedom and transcendence, and of "virtues uncontaminated."[11] In short, the Berrigans during the midsixties were beginning to adopt a familiar mode of thinking and talking about resistance. But it was not the mode that they had anticipated for themselves initially. Both had thought, in their earlier years of advocating for social justice, that influencing people in power would prove the most effective means of change. For Daniel, exile increased his celebrity, and Sargent Shriver courted him for the Kennedy's coterie of priests upon his return in 1966, a position that he was pleased to occupy.[12] Philip, too, had dealt mainly with well-situated political figures, an approach he later came to see as misguided and undemocratic.[13]

In addition to being new for the Berrigans, the mode of peripheral witness did not have many prominent Catholic examples prior to the Berrigans (a point to which I return later), but, more and more, after their experiences of so-called exile, it was a mode the Berrigans felt they could not ignore.[14] In their prolific writings from the late sixties onward they emphasize tropes of exile and shunning and explicitly align true Christian witness with ostracism and punishment. But the impact was not only rhetorical. Their approach to resistance changed as well, as they began to consider the moral potential of the outsider, the symbolic potential of what Daniel called "violent dislocation." If their respective "exiles" were meant to chasten the Berrigans' outspokenness and humble them to ecclesial authority, they failed. The Berrigans came away from those experiences feeling that the church had fallen far short of its duty to critique state power and that they were called to step into that lacuna, no matter the consequences. Their antiwar activities became increasingly radical as they took it upon themselves to fulfill the role that they felt the church had abandoned. In the wake of the Second Vatican Council, their disappointment with the church became even more acute.

The story of American Catholicism often has been told as one of increasing assimilation, of demonstrating belonging in a nation that historically mistrusted and maligned Catholics for their supposed allegiance to their countries of origin and to the Pope and for their assumed opposition to the ideals of freedom and progress. Scholars note the late nineteenth- and early twentieth-century events and processes by which Catholics increasingly demonstrated their participation in the life of the nation and its institutions and mark the mid-twentieth century as the period in which Catholics began to be perceived as Americans on a large scale.[15] In the early decades of the twentieth century—what has been called the era of "public Catholicism"— middle-class, American-born Catholics started to become more politically and socially involved, intent on bringing their religion to bear on society.[16] At a time when Christian values were explicitly shaping the agendas of many Protestant social reformers, advocates of public Catholicism wanted the values of their religion to move beyond the realm of private belief and concern with individual salvation, into the arenas of public policy and action. Labor and other economic issues were the first to be approached by the public Catholics. The new attention to social issues became an important component of a fresh model for being Catholic in America, in which Catholic values would influence not just the individual but society, through welfare programs and policy changes. Historian David O'Brien calls this the "republican" style of public Catholicism, taken up in full force by American Catholic bishops in the 1930s following the papal encyclical *Quadragesimo Anno*, which emphasizes the need to attend to issues of economic disadvantage and disparity.[17] The Berrigans grew up with republican Catholicism, were raised by parents who took Catholic social teaching quite seriously, and joined the priesthood based on its promise. Republican Catholicism culminated in the Second Vatican Council (1962–65), called by Pope John XXIII with the aim of bringing the Catholic church into the modern world and making it more relevant to adherents and their concerns. Vatican II represented a great achievement for proponents of institutional church reform, which, in the early 1960s, still included the Berrigans.[18] Both were tremendously excited at the prospect of the Council.

The Berrigans had been facing their congregations and saying Mass in English for years before the aggiornamento (updating) of Vatican II swept the church, and their civil rights work was well known and highly praised. Their ever-growing concern with social ills, and the role of the priest in addressing them, meshed (briefly) in the early sixties with the spirit of reform that led to Vatican II's extensive changes. The most immediate and best-known changes were liturgical; for example, Mass would now be said in the vernacular rather than Latin, by a priest who faced the congregation. But those liturgical changes reflected a larger reformulation and expansion of the roles of both clergy and laity.[19] Post-Vatican, instead of the priest as a remote cultic figure solely responsible for administering ceremonies and the congregant as the recipient of grace that flowed through those ceremonies, both were to utilize their particular gifts to shape their communities and engage with the world. In the years to come the Berrigans would assert greater and greater distance from the church, but the "rebel priests" made the stir that they did in part because they had been, before their antiwar activities escalated to a level that ecclesial leaders found inappropriate, promising young clergymen who demonstrated, in many peoples' estimations, the best side and greatest potential of the American Catholic Church, finally coming into its own. But the Berrigans increased their antiwar activities and drove their superiors to frustration, in direct proportion to their own frustration with the post-Vatican church. The flare of their optimism burned itself out as the church, in their view, failed to measure up to its promises of reform, progress, and worldly engagement.

Underground

The Berrigans were not the only Catholics to feel let down by the church as the sixties marched onward. A spate of books published in the years immediately following Vatican II on the New Catholic Left, the New Catholic Radicals, and Catholicism and social reform indicate that a sea change was taking place in American public Catholicism, spurred in part by Vatican reforms but also by deep disappointment with the limited extent of those reforms. O'Brien notes that the republican style of public Catholicism, typified by the 1966 founding of the National Conference of Catholic Bishops, left more "evangelical" Catholics, who had hoped for more from the promises of the council, dissatisfied.[20] The Berrigans spoke to that dissatisfaction, providing an example of a more radical, less governmentally acquiescent Catholicism, especially on the part of clergy. Simultaneously, they began to move further away from the mainstream of the church as a result of their involvement in the peace movement and further away from the mainstream of the peace movement as a result of their sense of what it meant to be a priest. Philip made headlines for leading the 1967 Baltimore Four draft board raids, in which he and three other activists poured blood (their own, supplemented with poultry blood from a local butcher) over the Selective Service records at the Baltimore Customs House. The next year he and Daniel spearheaded the Catonsville Nine action, in which they and seven others raided a draft board office in Catonsville, Maryland, removing draft files to the parking lot where they set them on fire with homemade napalm. Now-iconic images of the two priests in clerical collars standing over flaming trash cans in a posture of prayer seared and stunned the nation and sent federal agents chasing after them, suddenly wanted fugitives.

The Catonsville action cemented the Berrigans' fame and notoriety. It also reflected (and, predictably, intensified) their increasing tensions with their respective orders and their growing sense of themselves as righteous outsiders, as did its immediate—and then prolonged—aftermath. Along with the new and shocking use of blood and fire in their demonstrations, the Berrigans had a new plan for what they would do after Catonsville. In keeping with the norms of nonviolent resistance, they would not evade arrest, but instead of reporting for their sentences, they planned to go "underground." It was a plan that they suspected would alienate them from many in their circle, just as they had suspected that even their closest friends and mentors, such as Dorothy Day and Thomas Merton, would not support their use of blood and fire. Indeed, both Day and Merton worried that the presence of those elements would call into question the nonviolence stance of the Catholic Left. But it was precisely that traditional notion of nonviolence with which the Berrigans were starting to break during these years. Both of the means by which they did so—using blood and fire and going underground—were meant not only to serve as a more trenchant critique of the authorities and thus a more solid resistance to the war but also to mark off a new cohort of activists, limiting their numbers to those truly willing to face serious consequences for increasingly dangerous actions.[21]

Both Philip and Daniel planned to go underground rather than submit to authorities after Catonsville (as did two others of the nine). Philip was apprehended after ten days, but Daniel stayed in hiding—surfacing frequently to attend rallies or give sermons, but always a step ahead of authorities—for four months, during which time his successful evasions mobilized the Catholic Left like never before. The media characterized their post-Catonsville exploits largely as a publicity stunt or a way to antagonize J. Edgar Hoover, both of which were indeed outcomes, and probably the Berrigans did not mind either. But, primarily, the decision to go underground was both demonstration and enactment of the ideology and identity claims that the Berrigans were developing during the late sixties. Daniel and Philip eventually ended up in prison together, where they were able to spend their longest stretch of time together since boyhood. It gave them an extended opportunity to think about where the work of resistance was taking them, as their example of prison witness continued to galvanize the peace movement and change American Catholicism.

John Cogley ends his 1973 study of American Catholicism with the lines, "The Berrigans (however one may criticize their practical judgment or style) have pointed out that, while Catholicism can exist very well with separation of church and state, its best representatives will always refuse to separate religion and life. And that makes all the difference."[22] For much of its history, American Catholicism wrestled with the separation that Cogley mentions, as Catholics in America worked to prove that their religion would not impede their ability to be good citizens. But the Berrigans demonstrated another choice. Writing sixteen years after Cogley, R. Scott Appleby, in his essay on the Berrigans in a volume titled *Twentieth-Century Shapers of American Popular Religion*, observes that during their "most significant period of leadership" from the mid-1960s to early 1970s, the Berrigans "made their fellow American Catholics aware of the pluralism of the Catholic tradition on questions of social action. . . . They lent a certain prestige to yet another option in American Catholicism, the role of radical pacifist and social revolutionary. Scores of urban priests and nuns were emboldened by their example and began to refashion ministry in sometimes dramatic, sometimes subtle ways."[23]

To many, the post-Vatican figure of the priest as an active figure in the world was represented in an extreme version, for good or ill, by the Berrigans. A "new priesthood" emerged, composed of socially conscious clergy who felt their role to consist of calling parishioners to service in the world through resistance.[24] Nuns too radicalized, leaving their cloisters and getting involved in activism in large numbers.[25] Lay ministry also thrived, and Jay Dolan reports that, in the new context of socially engaged clergy and laity, Catholic involvement in the movements of the sixties continued and even grew during the 1970s, approved and seconded by the church hierarchy, up to a point.[26] But the Berrigans and others saw the church's support for projects of social reform as recapitulating rather than challenging the church-state pattern that they had hoped Vatican II would transform. The church's attention to anodyne reform left many frustrated, ready to see, if not necessarily to repeat, the new kind of action with which the Berrigans were experimenting. In a 1971 interview Daniel Berrigan characterized the emerging Catholic Left as

> that small and assailed and powerless group of people who are non-violent in principle and who are willing to suffer for our beliefs in the hope of creating something very different for those who will follow us. It is we who feel compelled to ask, along with, let's say, Bonhoeffer or Socrates or Jesus, how man is to live as a human being and how his communities are to form and to exist and to proliferate as instruments of human change and of human justice; and it is we who struggle to do more than pose the questions—but rather, live as though the questions were all-important, even though they cannot be immediately answered. My purpose in life is not to set up an alternative to the United States government. We in the underground are trying to do something else.[27]

His going underground post-Catonsville was meant at least in part as a demonstration of what that "something else" entailed—risk, uncertainty, but also relying on the goodwill and kindness of others, whether friends or strangers, in times of contingency, all for the sake of catalyzing a new society. As I discuss at length in chapter 3, the Berrigans began to conceive of their prison terms in the same way, as a kind of social death with profound regenerative potential, and it was from that sensibility that the idea for the first Plowshares action would emerge nearly a decade later.

While the Berrigans were in prison for the Catonsville action, the Catholic peace movement thrived under the leadership of nun Elizabeth McAlister, of the Sisters of the Sacred Heart of Mary. She had grown close to the Berrigans through her work in the movement, and she and Philip, unbeknownst to everyone, had fallen in love. The two secretly wed in 1969, not announcing their marriage until three years later. But letters they exchanged while Philip was in prison, turned over to J. Edgar Hoover by an FBI informant that Philip and McAlister had trusted to smuggle correspondence, led to the two of them and five other members of the Catholic Left—the "Harrisburg Seven"—being charged in 1972 with plotting to kidnap Henry Kissinger and blow up tunnels under government buildings. Destroying tunnels and making a citizen's arrest of Kissinger had indeed been suggested but discarded as ideas, and the rickety case against them did not uniformly impress the jury, which remained hung on the major charges. A mistrial resulted. Philip and McAlister were, however, convicted of smuggling letters in and out of federal prison, and while those letters did not reveal any secret kidnapping plot, they did disclose the nature of Philip and McAlister's relationship. Many among the Catholic Left were dismayed at that disclosure, even as they were relieved by the larger outcome.[28]

Sharon Nepstad tells the story of the Harrisburg Seven trial with a happy ending, culminating in a "sense of victory and hope that Catholic war resistance would continue." But Berrigan biographers Murray Polner and Jim O'Grady report that the Catholic Left was "exhausted and disillusioned" by the trial and by the end of it had disintegrated grievously. Both assessments are no doubt true in part, but Philip's and McAlister's writings from this time make clear that the Harrisburg episode left them with a pressing need to display more clearly than ever their commitment to nonviolence and to religiously grounded resistance. A need for "deep community" emerged at this time. "I had no intentions of being anyone's leader except my own. Neither had Dan," wrote Philip in 1973. He insisted that his priorities lay elsewhere: "In the last few months we [he and McAlister] have worked with a small group of friends growing toward nonviolent resistance. We are presently seeking a center out of which that work can continue."[29] Gone was the sense of exultation in a growing resistance network composed of differently motivated activists, or the desire for it; the focus had shifted, emphasizing the importance of a small, discrete group of similarly motivated, morally grounded resisters.

Catonsville and Harrisburg stand at either end of a paradigm shift in the Berrigans' thinking and strategy, as they moved progressively further away from the traditional model of civil disobedience and from their previous intent to work for change from within the system, and at the end of which they no longer considered institutional, policy-based reform to be an option.[30] They knew that the Catonsville action might create tension with some of their allies. Indeed, two of their closest, Day and Merton, seriously questioned the use of tactics that they feared could be construed as violent.

They knew with even greater certainty that the decision to go underground would create tension in the Catholic Left, even as it galvanized the movement as a whole, by calling into question a fundamental component of nonviolent civil disobedience: the willingness to submit to consequences. More than a media ploy or a mobilization tactic, going underground was a way to demonstrate and enact a shift in their resistance strategy. The Berrigans' new resistance mode was premised on the notion that evading prison could more effectively communicate disregard for the sinful authority of the state and heightened regard for God's authority. It unambiguously communicated new norms about what the content of true Christian witness ought to be. That witness was not, they knew, for everyone, with its risk of prison sentences far greater than the night or two most antiwar activists spent in jail for participating in a die-in or Pentagon demonstration. But as the tensions surfaced in the antiwar movement that would explode during the Harrisburg trial, embracing a mode of resistance that few people would emulate seemed less like a liability and more like an advantage. As Philip reflected in 1971, between Catonsville and Harrisburg, "one or two or a handful or a small number can do something significant for justice and peace, but it will never begin outside the one or two, who are faithful to Christ, their consciences, and their brothers."[31]

Following the Harrisburg trial and the weakening of the Catholic Left, Philip and McAlister began to consider the value of small communities of faith and resistance as an alternative to large movements. McAlister characterizes this period as a transition "from dissent to resistance" that began with the 1967 Baltimore draft board raid and culminated in the Harrisburg trial. As she explained not long after that pivotal time, and shortly before the first Plowshares action,

> Through [the draft board actions] we became enemies of the State, a threat to its political hegemony. Intimidation, defamation, harassment followed. We were subject to massive persecution. Big guns aimed to cut off our credibility, if not our future. Harrisburg was a time of evaluation, reflection, redirection. The war continued

unabated, being met more and more by public silence, acceptance, weariness. For resistance to flourish we faced the need to begin again, to rebuild, re-form, over and over and over. . . . We needed to work so that community would become strong, real, Christian. After Harrisburg we began again with a position paper and a small group.[32]

What mattered more than anything, now, was how people perceived them— that their Christian nonviolence never be called into question again. The small group that McAlister describes as essential to restoring their credibility took the form of Jonah House, an intentional community that Philip and McAlister founded in Baltimore in 1973, which borrowed its name from the unlikely, initially unwilling prophet of the Hebrew scriptures. They explain the founding of Jonah House as borne out of several conclusions: "First, our country's addiction to war was long-term, maybe terminal; second, resistance would become needed more desperately than even during the most genocidal years of the Indochina War; third, the resistance communities of the Sixties and Seventies were too shallow and ad hoc to serve as models for a lasting community; fourth, some of us would have to accept God's word as a handbook and try to embody it."[33]

In time Jonah House would become the hub of the Plowshares' work and of the Atlantic Life Community, an extensive network of intentional faith-based resistance communities in the eastern United States, which meets regularly for retreats and to collaborate on civil disobedience actions. But the founding (and sustaining) vision of Jonah House was that a small community—"a handful," as Philip envisioned it; "some of us," as Philip and McAlister together wrote—could accomplish what a large network could not. Specifically, a small community could nurture the moral potential of the outsider that had begun to take root for both Berrigans after their respective experiences of "exile" and had solidified as their mode of resistance by the end of Harrisburg. A few years after the founding of Jonah House, that resistance mode would find new and dramatic expression in the Plowshares' actions.

One or Two Faithful

Deeply disappointed at the divisive effect of the Harrisburg episode on the Catholic Left, Philip wanted to continue the momentum of the antiwar movement in a way that would more completely instantiate the commitment to nonviolence that Harrisburg, with its charges of kidnapping and explosives, had called into question. In this new phase of resistance, actions would be undertaken by small groups of similarly "faithful" participants, all of the same spiritual mettle, thus ensuring a more efficacious witness as well as an unassailable example of nonviolence—the "better fun" and "increasingly serious" witness Philip had predicted in his 1978 letter to Daniel. Philip's idea for the first Plowshares action, at the General Electric plant in King of Prussia, was inspired by a regular vigil that members of Pennsylvania's Brandywine Peace Community had held there since the late 1970s, to protest GE's manufacture of first-strike nuclear weapons. Among the participants in the vigil was John Schuchardt, a lawyer and former marine who lived with Philip and McAlister at Jonah House. By this time Philip had come to feel about nuclear weapons the way he had felt about militarism in general for decades—that the nuclear weapons industry was the source of all other social ills, draining billions of dollars away from where it ought to be spent on improving the lives of the disadvantaged and oppressed. In conversation with Schuchardt, who previously had thought of breaking into the GE plant upon observing that security there seemed rather lax, he decided that "symbolic disarmament" of the weapons, to be achieved by hammering and pouring blood on them, would be the most appropriate and effective action.[34]

For the other seven of the Plowshares Eight, seasoned activists steeped in the performative and symbolic aspects of antiwar protest and influenced by the Berrigans' earlier resistance activities, the idea of symbolic disarmament made immediate sense. Each eventual participant needed to discern whether the action was right for him or her, especially in light of the unknown but probably harsh consequences that were anticipated, but they intuitively understood the logic of the action, the compulsion to do something beyond a routine Pentagon demonstration, to take a greater risk against the nuclear threat. Molly Rush, forty-four years old, was a longtime, deeply religious peace activist in Pittsburgh, who initially had found Philip to be strident and judgmental and had considered the mess of symbolic protest—ashes dumped in the secretary of state's outer office, blood or paint spattered across the Pentagon steps—to be "too much." But learning more about nuclear weapons and thinking about the futures of her children, she became "more ready to hear the Berrigan message." She came to feel that the message blood conveyed was of vital importance and that the Berrigans represented an unflinching commitment to religiously grounded, nonviolent witness. Despite the entreaties of her husband, parents, and brothers, who knew that she was planning to take part in an action that might result in a lengthy prison sentence but didn't know what that action entailed, she believed the General Electric action was a way to demonstrate "fidelity to the truth in a Gospel way."[35] Carl Kabat had been sent on missions to Brazil and the Philippines as a young Oblate priest. Those trips opened his eyes to injustice and "radicalized" him. After meeting Philip in the late 1970s, he "hurled himself into the antinuclear weapons fight."[36] The others—Elmer Maas, a former college professor and composer from New York City; Dean Hammer, an activist from New Haven, Connecticut; Anne Montgomery, a Sister of the Sacred Heart from New York City; and Schuchardt—told similar stories of longtime involvement in peace activism and the influence of Philip Berrigan. The last of the eight to be persuaded was Daniel, who signed on at the eleventh hour. His desk calendar for the month of September 1980 is a palimpsest, an intended trip to Ireland visible only in ghostly form, where plans for the day of the action and the weeks following have been erased (and nothing else has been written in the September 9 square, a testament to the secrecy and mystery that surrounded the action), as though to prepare for any eventuality.[37] No one knew what the outcome of the action would be—Schuchardt suspected he might be in jail for life.[38]

Perhaps due to the still-fresh memory of the Harrisburg trial, precipitated by intercepted letters, the mountain of correspondence Philip sent and received during the months preceding the action lacks any direct mention of the action, though it was being planned for almost a year. In a note to sister- and brother-in-law Carol and Jerome Berrigan only a few weeks before the action, McAlister wrote that she would have to put the children in school "if this thing in PA comes off."[39] It did come off, resulting in the arrest of the Plowshares Eight. Charged with burglary, criminal trespass, criminal conspiracy, simple and aggravated assault, terroristic threat, and seven other related charges, the eight were given an offer—all charges would be dropped if they would simply go away, refraining from civil disobedience for six months. Insisting that their action be brought to trial, they turned down the offer. After the original sentencing, their case remained under a series of appeals for the next ten years, and eventually the Eight were sentenced to time served.[40]

Though Philip was, by all accounts, a natural leader, he led with the force of his enthusiasm and energy rather than by organization. He hoped that the action might inspire others, but there was not a plan in place for securing another crop of activists or setting up another action. The second Plowshares action was undertaken singly and spontaneously by Peter DeMott, another member of the Jonah House community, three months after the first. (I treat it at greater length in chapter 2.) Over the next twenty-five years, there were usually two to three Plowshares actions per year. The period of greatest frequency was between 1984 and 1988, when a total of twenty-one actions took place, as many as six in a year. There were actions in every year but one during the eighties and every year during the nineties, but frequency waned after 2000. Since 2000 there have been eight Plowshares actions, as compared to twenty-eight in the movement's first decade and fifteen in its second. Two actions took place in 2009, following a three-year period in which there were none, and one took place following a similar hiatus in July 2012.

More than one hundred individuals have participated in fifty-two Plowshares actions in the United States since 1980. The vast majority of them are white, mirroring the demographics of the peace movement and the nuclear disarmament movement.[41] Slightly more than a third are female, though that third includes several of the most frequent participants. Just under 20 percent of the total participants are members of religious orders, either priests or nuns.[42] About a quarter of the total participants, including six of the original Plowshares Eight, have participated in more than one action. (Philip Berrigan participated in six actions during his lifetime, and Daniel Berrigan and Elizabeth McAlister each have participated in one.) In most cases more than one means two, but some Plowshares have committed as many as seven or eight, seeing the actions as their life's work or, in the case of the vowed religious, as their vocation, often one that supplants or supersedes the religious vocation. Certainly, this was the case for the Berrigans. Though they interpreted resistance as part and parcel of their religious vocations, when forced to choose, they felt more tightly bound by what they understood as the obligations of witness than by ecclesial authority. Some vowed Plowshares activists' religious communities are highly supportive of their Plowshares actions, such as the Dominican Sisters of Grand Rapids, Michigan, which counts among its members three of the most frequent Plowshares activists. Others are less supportive, and at least two ordained Plowshares have gone against the explicit orders of their superiors to commit their actions—eight of them, in one priest's case. Like the Berrigans, they regard their commitment to resistance as the indispensable kernel of what it means to be a Catholic, even when it precludes obedience to ecclesial supervision.

Lay Plowshares also characterize their actions as a way of living out Christian and Catholic values, and several of the most frequent participants come from the laity. Among the repeat participants the percentage of priests and nuns increases only slightly, to just over 20 percent, though in the past decade nearly half of Plowshares activists have been priests or nuns. Far fewer people, vowed or otherwise, have performed Plowshares actions since 2000 than in the first two decades of the Plowshares' existence, and fully half of the participants from the most recent decade are repeat participants, a significant increase from earlier decades. The activists who are still performing Plowshares actions thirty years on have committed themselves to the cause as a focal point of their lives, securing the "biographical availability" that allows them to perform action after action, risking a significant jail sentence each time. Many sociologists have pointed to biographical availability, whereby one is relatively free from lifestyle constraints (such as familial or professional obligations), as an important element of high-risk activism— someone without children is more biographically available to serve a long prison sentence than someone with two toddlers; someone who is a family's sole breadwinner is less biographically available than someone with no dependants. Vowed religious certainly qualify. As Sister Megan Rice, an eighty-two-year-old nun who took part in the most recent Plowshares action, described herself and her fellow older nuns to the *New York Times*, "We're free as larks. . . . We have no responsibilities—no children, no grandchildren, no jobs. . . . We can do [the actions.]"[43] But not only the vowed religious possess the important quality of biographical availability. Laypeople achieve it too by living in intentional community, as Nepstad has shown. That is, living in a like-minded community enables activists to share economic responsibilities and child-rearing duties, for example, thereby freeing them from the constraints that might otherwise deter them from committing a high-risk action, providing emotional support, and fostering a sense of shared worldview.

That shared worldview is explicitly religiously grounded, as are most of the intentional communities in which Plowshares activists live or with which they are affiliated. In contrast to the closely allied Catholic Worker movement, many of whose members are not Catholic or even necessarily Christian, the vast majority of Plowshares activists identify as Catholic and understand their actions in explicitly Catholic terms. Plowshares activists characterize the existence of nuclear weapons as a betrayal of the stewardship of the earth that God demands, as a form of idolatry and thus an affront to God, and as a failure to love universally as the example of Jesus Christ requires. They emphasize the weapons' potential for massive destruction, rather than the imminence of destruction, as itself an evil at these three levels. For that reason they insist on the complete abolishment of nuclear weapons, and partial limitations or bans do not impress them. For the Plowshares, the very existence of nuclear weapons represents people's failure to do their duty as humans toward the planet, one another, and God. While they consider the sense of moral obligation that directs their actions to be universally binding, they conceive of and carry out their response to it as religious acts, which are suffused with elements (the subject of the next chapter) that resonate deeply within their particular Catholic milieu. According to the worldview of the Catholic resistance community of which they are a part, which characterizes Jesus as a political revolutionary undeterred by ridicule, arrest, and eventual martyrdom, the Plowshares represent a pinnacle of faithful witness.

To be sure, not all Catholics or Christians would agree that a life dedicated to civil disobedience is, as the Plowshares suggest, the way to be fully obedient to God. But the Plowshares' larger community holds fast to the example set by the Berrigans and Dorothy Day during the years immediately following Vietnam, reinforcing and valorizing their particular mode of Catholicism and hearkening constantly to their examples. The example of Philip Berrigan is especially close at hand for the Plowshares, many of whom describe their participation in the action as due at least to some extent to his influence and friendship. The importance of a personal connection to a man who died in 2002 in generating enthusiasm for the project in part explains why the average age of Plowshares activists is steadily increasing. In earlier decades many Plowshares activists were twenty- or thirty-somethings who took part in one action (before they became less biographically available). In contrast, most Plowshares activists from the past decade are in their fifties and sixties. Several are in their seventies or eighties. Most have performed several actions, as many as seven or eight. Following in the example of Day and the Berrigans, resistance is their life's work, and they participate in that endeavor with others who share the experiences and influences of a particular moment in American Catholicism—experiences and influences that shape their ideology and their resistance in profound ways.

According to sociologist Karl Mannheim, generations are composed of individuals who share a "common location in the historical dimension of the social process." Those within a particular generation have a "specific range of potential experience, predisposing them for a certain characteristic mode of thought and experience, and a characteristic type of historically relevant action." But Mannheim notes that not all individuals within a generation can be expected to think or take action in precisely the same way. Within each generation, different generational units are made up of those who, based on other social factors and affinities, "work up the material of their common experiences in different specific ways."[44] It is the generational unit, bound by "greater intensity" than the generation as a whole, from which particular responses to common experiences—slogans or art, for example—emerge.

Generation, then, is not merely a chronological signifier; it also reveals the interplay between biological facts and a range of sociohistorical phenomena. In comparing the Plowshares to the larger disarmament movement, the distinction between a generation and a generational unit comes to the fore in their vastly different approaches to the nuclear issue.

As the particular response of a generational unit that has not gone out of its way to make what Mannheim calls "fresh contacts" with younger generations, Plowshares actions are declining in frequency and number.[45] Also, Plowshares actions in the past decade have been performed in smaller groups than in the past—one group of five, three groups of four, two groups of three, one group of two, and one action undertaken by one activist. In the Plowshares' first two decades, though there were actions undertaken by one or two people, larger groups of as many as eight or nine activists were more common. But it is a mistake to regard these shifting demographics as signs of failure or decline. Small numbers and advanced age map directly onto the Plowshares' vision for their actions as high-risk endeavors undertaken by a few deeply committed people of faith. Demographic trends that might signal decline in other contexts reinforce the Plowshares' ideals of faithfulness and commitment, as I discuss in later chapters. They also assure a great deal of cohesion within the group, keeping at bay the differences and divides that can make group identity difficult to constitute and communicate. Cohesion helps to ensure that all the things that could go horribly wrong during their actions don't. It also helps Plowshares activists to hew to a clear sense of self and present it coherently and sincerely to others. That sense of self, protected by their small numbers and similar backgrounds, allows the Plowshares to differentiate themselves from others doing work that might seem similar at first—but, to the Plowshares, is not.

Symbolic Disarmament and the Larger Antinuclear Movement

Plowshares actions began as both a continuation and a reworking of modes of resistance from the Vietnam era and its aftermath, to which the majority of Plowshares participants trace their awakenings as activists. Born out of the Berrigans' turn to a resistance based on the moral potential of the outsider, the actions themselves emphasize the importance of embodying the principles of nonviolent Christian witness as a small group on the margins of society, intentionally distinct—morally and socially—from the larger Catholic church and from groups who do not share their particular religious orientation and commitment. The Plowshares have never been alone, of course, in their concern over nuclear weapons. From the earliest phases of the Manhattan Project, the destructive potential of nuclear weapons prompted anxiety within the scientific community. Following the dropping of atomic bombs on Hiroshima and Nagasaki in 1945, a grassroots popular movement came forward to call for a halt to the development of nuclear weapons, which progressed as quickly as did the worry that other nations would build superior arsenals. The nascent disarmament movement grew during the late 1940s and 1950s, even though the larger peace movement from which it emerged had weakened significantly over the course of World War II. The early disarmament movement included secular and religious groups, scientists, and pacifist groups working together to stage demonstrations, circulate pamphlets, and otherwise influence public opinion on the matter of the bomb and its perils, but despite its sustained efforts the arms race proceeded apace, and it and the disarmament movement grew in tandem.

But by the mid-1960s many in the disarmament movement had shifted their attentions elsewhere, to the anti–Vietnam War campaign. By the end of the 1960s and early 1970s, policy limitations in the form of the Limited Test Ban Treaty (1963), the Nuclear Nonproliferation Treaty (1968), and the SALT treaties (1972 and 1974) assured many citizens that reasonable limits to nuclear proliferation were now in place, contributing further to the waning of the popular disarmament movement. With the end of the Vietnam War in 1975, the attention of the peace movement shifted back to nuclear weapons, out of dismay that those treaties had done little to halt the arms race and that President Ford's policies had moved further away from such limitations on nuclear testing and proliferation. The disarmament campaign again gained strength, motivated anew by concerns about nuclear power plants and their potential environmental hazards.[46] Beginning in 1977 with the Clamshell Alliance's occupation of the construction site of a proposed nuclear energy plant in Seabrook, New Hampshire, during which 1,401 people were arrested, a series of high-profile protests against nuclear energy (including those at Diablo Canyon between 1977 and 1982 and at Lawrence Livermore between 1981 and 1984) forced the nuclear issue back to the nation's attention.[47]

In the early 1980s, with the election of President Reagan, who opposed arms control and instead took decisive steps toward a renewed demonstration of nuclear supremacy, the antinuclear movement reached an apex of concern and involvement. In 1980 the American Friends Service Committee, a Quaker group at the forefront of the peace and disarmament movements, developed the idea of a "nuclear freeze" to mobilize peace groups around the issue of disarmament. Involvement quickly reached unprecedented pro-portions, at the grassroots level and from progressive political and religious groups, including the U.S. Catholic Bishops, who issued a pastoral letter in 1983 decrying nuclear weapons. In 1982 the largest political demonstration in American history took place in New York's Central Park, where 750,000 people gathered to protest the nuclear-arms race.[48] As at Seabrook and the other power plant sit-ins, the Central Park demonstration involved scores of distinct "affinity groups." Each affinity group included activists joined by a common interest, ideology, affiliation, or location. These affinity groups served as smaller organizational units for mass protests in which numerous affinity groups gathered around an issue that concerned them all. The net-work-based demonstrations reflected the coalitional nature of the freeze movement, which, along with the larger disarmament movement, derived its strength from various small groups uniting to address a common cause, across differences such as those of religious creed.[49]

The Plowshares took up their actions during precisely these years, when many groups were railing against the proliferation of nuclear weapons. Though many of those other groups were doing so in demonstrative modes not unlike the one that the Plowshares would develop, the Plowshares came to consider themselves as distinct from the larger disarmament or freeze campaigns, despite shared roots in the peace movement of the 1960s and shared trepidation over the arms race. In some cases the larger antinuclear movement disavowed the Plowshares, shocked and upset by their tactics.[50] But the mistrust was not entirely one-sided. During the Vietnam era, ten-sions had erupted between the religious and secular factions of the peace movement, and the coalition that so many had celebrated became fraught with ill will, which the events of Harrisburg reflected and exacerbated. Along with many others, Philip Berrigan emerged from those disputes with his trust in large-scale coalitions shaken. The strong sense of moral distinction reflected in his emphasis on the "one or two faithful" gave rise to the King of Prussia action, and it is still at play, though for the most part less explicitly, in distinguishing Plowshares actions from other types of resistance activities. Then and now, Plowshares activists frequently take part in other civil disobe-dience actions that are not considered Plowshares actions: the Plowshares designation is reserved for a very particular type of witness, a specific subset of the religious activism that they and their larger community routinely un-dertake. The chapters to come illuminate what, more specifically, makes a Plowshares action a Plowshares action, but it is important to note here that, both tactically and functionally, the Plowshares themselves and their larger peacemaking milieu consider symbolic disarmaments to be distinct from what other disarmament activists do and what other peace activists do.

This distinction has something to do with what happens during a Plowshares action, but, more fundamentally, it has to do with how the activists *interpret* what happens in the actions, what they have done and why they have done it. Plowshares activists understand their actions to have specific motivations and very particular outcomes, and they understand themselves to be enacting certain roles as they perform the actions. Motivated by what they read as biblical mandates, especially from the prophetic books of the Hebrew scriptures, the Plowshares' goal is not to change specific policies or to freeze the production of nuclear equipment or nuclear power but to "symbolically disarm" the equipment itself, piece by piece, and thereby turn the nation away from its idolatrous worship of nuclear weapons. In doing so, they consider themselves to be fulfilling the roles of prophet and martyr that God commands. To participate in disarmament activities out of different motivations, with different goals in mind or with a different sense of one's role, is not as effective by the Plowshares' standards and is not symbolic disarmament. That is to say, the Plowshares conceive of their motivation, their goals, and their role in the work of disarmament in a way that imposes a symbolic, moral boundary between them and many other groups working for disarmament. They believe that they are doing something fundamentally different because they understand their motivations and the outcomes of their actions to be fundamentally distinct from those of other disarmament activists. To them, that makes all the difference.

The Plowshares and the Larger Catholic Resistance Community

Plowshares activists certainly do locate themselves firmly within global and local, historical and contemporary, circles of nonviolent resistance. During their actions and trials they invoke their place in a self-constructed lineage, claiming as close kin not necessarily people working actively on the same issue (the abolishment of nuclear weapons) but rather people who have similar ideas about why one should engage in political resistance, where its true effectiveness resides, and the importance of religious grounding. The "small group" that Philip and McAlister envisioned for their new mode of resistance began with Jonah House, but Jonah House quickly grew into something larger. When Philip and McAlister penned their book *The Time's Discipline* in 1989, a reflection on their nuclear resistance over the previous decade, they referred repeatedly to a "nonviolent movement" of which their antinuclear activism was one component part. That movement included campaigns opposing U.S. military policy in Central America, working for human rights in Latin America, and working to end apartheid in South Africa; all were envisioned as of a piece. The activists involved in these several campaigns—and, importantly, who believed that living in intentional community was an essential part of effective peacemaking—came together under umbrella organizations like the Atlantic Life Community, an affiliation of intentional peacemaking communities in the mid-Atlantic region. The ALC coalesced around Jonah House by way of periodic retreats that its residents began to organize soon after Jonah House was established in 1973. In addition to the retreats that it still holds, the ALC provides infrastructure for the Plowshares, as well as the larger Catholic peace community. Through these events and other support mechanisms, it reinforces the worldview according to which the Plowshares' resistance is an exemplary form of Christian witness.[51]

Chief among the Plowshares' cohort in the ALC are their close kin from the mid-Atlantic Catholic Worker houses. Dorothy Day and Peter Maurin founded the Catholic Worker movement in 1933 as a way to meld Catholicism, to which Day was a convert, with social reform. They started a newspaper to call attention to the plight of the poor and began to establish houses of hospitality, where volunteers and those in need lived and worked together. They began a farm commune in rural Pennsylvania to be a setting for retreats and programs designed to stimulate spiritual and intellectual development. Similar houses of hospitality, rural and urban, sprang up elsewhere as the movement gained popularity. The *Catholic Worker* newspaper was a fixture in the liberal Berrigan household during Philip and Daniel's upbringing, and Day was their close ally from the sixties until her death in 1980.[52] Day stirred up controversy when she stepped into the arena of politics and pacifism, but the church has consistently lauded her emphasis on the works of mercy (her cause for canonization, approved in 2000, remains open). Many Catholic Workers today, however, consider the works of mercy to be only one component of the more radical social vision that Day propounded, and anarchism and civil disobedience are significant parts of the lifestyle for many.[53] She was a profound influence on the Berrigans, and she continues to be a profound influence on the Plowshares. Responding to a questionnaire that Nepstad circulated, Plowshares activists named Dorothy Day as their primary influence, stronger than Gandhi, Martin Luther King Jr., and Thomas Merton, and almost 90 percent stated that Catholic Worker communities had been extremely or very important in sustaining their activism.[54]

At many points of affiliation and overlap, Jonah House and the Catholic Worker movement are deeply intertwined. Indeed, "like a Catholic Worker house" was a description of Jonah House that I heard many times over the course of my research into the Plowshares, though never from a resident of Jonah House. Though it works closely with several Catholic Worker houses, Jonah House does not itself identify as one. Jonah House residents say that because they do not provide hospitality, they don't qualify. But the distinction is hazy. In his recent study of the contemporary Catholic Worker movement, Dan McKanan shows that many Catholic Worker houses don't provide hospitality; he argues that the defining feature of the movement today is its diversity and the autonomy of each house to find its own way of living out Dorothy Day's vision of solidarity. Accordingly, he considers Jonah House, which does give out bags of food to needy neighbors every week, as of a piece with the Catholic Worker movement (while acknowledging that Jonah House has never identified that way).[55] At the same time, many individuals and communities do not see the kind of activism with which Jonah House is primarily concerned, which consists of Plowshares actions as well as a range of other nonviolent civil disobedience actions that are not designated "Plowshares," as the most salient feature—or, indeed, as an appropriate feature at all—of the Catholic Worker. For both the Plowshares themselves and the other activists who make up the ALC, Plowshares actions, while certainly related to the activities of the Catholic Workers, are indeed "something else." Plowshares actions are demarcated by the level of commitment they require and the risks attendant to them. For most, participation in a Plowshares action comes only after a great deal of work on other peace and justice campaigns.[56] A Plowshares action is considered advanced activism, given the risks it entails. That Plowshares actions set a high bar for others in the Catholic Left is noted by Catholic Workers who express regret and disappointment that they don't quite measure up to that level of commitment. One Catholic Worker activist remarked on his time in jail for a non-Plowshares civil disobedience action, "I only did two months. I haven't done that much time since then. I continue to be challenged by the Plowshares people and feel a call to do more but feel, at this point in our history as a Catholic Worker, that it's not possible for me."[57]

It is certainly not the case that the Plowshares think of themselves as unmoored from tradition or independent of all wider resistance communities and networks—they feel and proclaim a close connection with a number of allied groups, like the Atlantic Life Community and the Catholic Worker movement. But even as the Plowshares are network- and community-oriented and allied with peers whose work they consider to be consistent with their own, boundaries appear between them and their closest allies. Even as they hope fervently that others will follow their example to take action for change, they do not go to any lengths to persuade others to take *their* kind of action. Talking to reporters about the Plowshares Eight action, Philip Berrigan referred to the "thirty groups" that supported the action. But Plowshares activists quickly recognized that support was one thing; enlistment was another. The minutes from a 1983 support meeting for the imprisoned participants of the third and fourth Plowshares actions recount a debate among supporters about what character the Plowshares and their actions should take on, vis-à-vis the respective virtues of radicality and accessibility. Some in attendance worried that Plowshares actions were too extreme, and incurred too much punishment, to attract widespread support or participation: "Have we made ourselves inaccessible and do we perpetuate the 'mystique' that surrounds us?" Others countered that an emphasis on large-scale participation would water down radicality such that the actions would lose their meaning and impact.[58] No resolution to the debate emerges in the minutes—for seven bullet points the two sides volley back and forth. But it is clear that three years into the Plowshares' activities, participants had recognized a fundamental incompatibility between the radicality that would ensure efficacy versus the accessibility of a mass mobilization. While the 1983 meeting was inconclusive on the issue, the fact that the actions continued in the same fashion, if anything becoming more and not less radical, indicates an eventual consensus concerning the importance of radicality, even if the result was a moral boundary that most people felt was not theirs to cross.

Consistently since the early eighties the Plowshares' rhetoric has reinforced this boundary by emphasizing tropes of self-sacrifice, martyrdom, and marginality. But those tropes coexist with another, more inclusive rhetoric. Few Plowshares activists are as severe about the moral distinction separating the Plowshares from everyone else as Philip Berrigan was when he wrote, "Let's begin by saying that jail is the bottom line. Most American peace people never come to grips with that. As we know, this attitude arises from idolatry, an ignorance of demonic activity in superpowers and major institutions, a superficial grasp of nonviolence; from willingness to offer excuses for the system; from ignorance of its lying and murderous character; from lack of vision as to the new society that needs building."[59] Much of the Plowshares' rhetoric is expansive, embracing a wide range of resistance campaigns and activities. But subtle distinctions remain, voiced by the Catholic Workers who want to "do more," but feel they can't. That "more" refers to the longer prison sentences that Plowshares activists have often received, but it also refers to other aspects of the Plowshares' project that communicate distinction even when their words say the opposite. In the next chapter I turn to an analysis of the Plowshares' symbolic disarmaments, the logic behind the blood they pour and the hammers they wield, and I examine how the subtle distinctions that demarcate the Plowshares' witness are communicated performatively during their actions. What makes a Plowshares action a Plowshares action? And what happens in a Plowshares action so that it speaks so much louder than words, distinguishing the Plowshares from the tradition in which they follow and the wider community with which they affiliate?

2 "Something Deeper than Reason"

The Logic and Tactics of Symbolic Disarmament

Just before dawn on a Saturday morning in late July 2012, three Plowshares activists—Mike Walli, sixty-three, and Greg Boertje-Obed, fifty-seven, Catholic laymen who had each taken part in previous Plowshares actions, and Megan Rice, an eighty-two-year-old nun who had been involved in antinuclear activism since the 1980s—trespassed onto the Y-12 nuclear reservation in Oak Ridge, Tennessee. The majority of the nation's weapons-grade uranium is processed and stored at the Oak Ridge site, and they wanted to get to it. They didn't know their way around the site but later reported that they were steered by God to exactly the right spot: the highest-security area of the plant, the newly constructed Highly Enriched Uranium Manufacturing Facility (HEUMF). "We feel it was a miracle; we were led directly to where we wanted to go," Boertje-Obed explained.[1] The three, who called their action "Transform Now Plowshares," used bolt cutters to sever the fences around the HEUMF. Once on the other side, they hammered on the building with household hammers, poured their own blood over it, and spray-painted messages on its outer walls, including "Woe to the empire of blood" and "Work for peace, not for war." Finally they hung banners reading "Swords into Plowshares, Spears into Pruning Hooks" and draped police tape between its pillars. When guards eventually confronted them, the three presented them with various items that they explained in a statement they read aloud: bread to signify the strength that all people will need to build a new world free of nuclear weapons; white roses, the flower of forgiveness and reconciliation; candles, "for light transforms fear and secrecy into authentic security"; and a Bible, "to remind ourselves to become sources of wisdom and to inspire our acts of conscience as we carry on." Their statement further explained,

> We come to the Y-12 facility because our very humanity rejects the designs of nuclearism, empire and war. Our faith in love and nonviolence encourages us to believe that our activity here is necessary; that we come to invite transformation, undo the past and present work of Y-12, disarm and end any further efforts to increase the Y-12 capacity for an economy and social structure based upon war-making and empire-building.
> A loving and compassionate Creator invites us to take the urgent and decisive steps to transform the U.S. empire, and this facility, into life-giving alternatives which resolve real problems of poverty and environmental degradation for all.[2]

The government contractor that operates the facility temporarily shut down all operations in response to what several nuclear experts labeled an unprecedented breach of nuclear security, and the activists were indicted in Knoxville's federal court on three counts: depredation of federal property, damage to personal property, and trespass. The charges (two felonies and a misdemeanor) carried a combined maximum prison sentence of thirty years and more than five hundred thousand dollars in fines. Their sentencing judge opted for leniency, and in 2014 they were sentenced to prison terms ranging from three to five years and fines of several thousand dollars.

The Transform Now Plowshares participants, among the most recent to follow in the footsteps of the Plowshares Eight and beat swords into Plowshares, were not the first activists to set their sights on Oak Ridge. Two years earlier, in 2010, a group of thirty-six protesters—including residents of Jonah House and other intentional communities in the ALC and several Plowshares activists—had staged a demonstration there, blocking the road leading into the facility, holding banners, and singing. A dozen of those protesters proceeded onto the grounds of the facility itself. While the rest of the protesters were arrested on state charges for blocking a roadway, the dozen who had stepped onto the facility proper were arrested on federal trespass charges and eventually received sentences ranging from time served to eight months. Both Y-12 actions had certain elements in common: the site, of course; the aim of drawing attention to its operations; and the activists' religious grounding and nonviolent stance. Some of the earlier Y-12 activists' signs even read, "Swords into Plowshares." But the 2010 Y-12 action was not designated as a Plowshares action or as "symbolic disarmament." The later Plowshares action, structured by a specific logic and an exacting set of tactics, incorporated a number of elements that the earlier action did not share. In acting on that logic with those tactics, the Plowshares activists understood their action to accomplish a distinct function and to be efficacious in very particular ways.

Three elements take center stage in the majority of Plowshares actions: trespass into spaces where the activists are not authorized to be, the pouring of their own blood, and the use of household hammers to strike the equipment or the land and facilities around it. Any quick gloss of the Plowshares' actions would include these three essentials, two of which (blood and hammers) were not present during the earlier Y-12 action. But the question of what designates a Plowshares action as such becomes more complicated with closer inspection, which reveals that the three elements are not unique to the Plowshares' actions nor are they deployed consistently by the Plowshares. Though there is, for the most part, close adherence to the template established by the first action at King of Prussia, there are also innovations and departures from tradition, both small and quite significant, when it comes time to put those elements to work. The Transform Now Plowshares, for example, brought bread, white roses, and candles to the site along with blood and hammers. Three years earlier a group of Plowshares activists had scattered sunflower seeds along with blood. In a 1987 action two Plowshares activists buried a miniature coffin on the grounds of the Naval Air Development Center in Warminster, Pennsylvania. Longtime Plowshares activist Carl Kabat (one of the Plowshares Eight who is still among the most frequent participants) routinely dresses in a clown suit for his actions, to represent that he is a "fool for Christ." Innovations like these fit seamlessly within the Plowshares' tradition and symbol system and do not undermine a cohesive sense of self for the activists as a cohort. But years before the Transform Now action, another group of Plowshares activists decided to use a jackhammer in their action instead of household hammers—a rather more dramatic and potentially problematic innovation.

Despite ambiguities raised by some of their innovations, Plowshares activists see their actions as consistent and, as a mode of resistance, as distinct from other peacemaking and disarmament activities, including those in which Plowshares activists themselves participate. Plowshares actions, for those who perform them and for those in the Plowshares' communities of support, are set apart both by their tactics and by their aims. Like the Plowshares Eight and the hundreds of Plowshares activists who have performed similar actions since 1980, the Transform Now activists intended their action to symbolically disarm the equipment they targeted and to call attention to and atone for the nation's idolatrous worship of nuclear weapons. To do so they carried out a highly symbolic action, replete with elements meant to resonate with a Catholic audience but also far beyond. To many outside the Plowshares' milieu, their actions seem wildly ineffectual against the threat they purport to address. For the activists themselves, however, the semiotic work that each element of a Plowshares action does, both on its own and in combination with the others, ensures what the activists understand as the particular efficacy of their actions. The actions "work" as symbolic disarmament because trespass, blood, and hammers operate in very particular ways, but also because they are complex, multivalent, and occasionally even contradictory symbols.

Trespass

Several of the 2010 Y-12 protesters were arrested on federal trespass charges, but they hadn't actually made it very far onto the Y-12 grounds. Moreover, they had trespassed in the context of a sizable demonstration, in broad daylight. Trespass of this sort is a common element of nonviolent protest, in which demonstrators risk arrest by "crossing a line" into spaces they are not allowed to enter, to call attention to a particular location or situation. The Transform Now Plowshares' action entailed trespass of a different order, carried out under the cover of near-darkness by an elite few who were prepared to walk for hours through a highly secured area, where deadly force was authorized against anyone entering the site without permission. Plowshares activists typically attempt this more extreme type of trespass; the Transform Now Plowshares action received quite a bit more media than a Plowshares action has received for some time, and more than the earlier action at Y-12, because of the extent of their trespass and the pressing questions it raised about nuclear security. While it is not their only aim, spatial transgression is chief among the Plowshares' intentions and a defining feature of their actions, even though the activists don't usually get as far as the Transform Now Plowshares activists did. In trespassing onto sites purported to be highly secure, Plowshares activists hope to demonstrate that relying on nuclear protection for national security is false and idolatrous, since only God can offer true security. As Philip and McAlister wrote in *The Time's Discipline*, "Experience has taught us that the weapons factories, military bases, and storage facilities are not as securely 'protected' as their guardians believe. Nor are they are secure as we've been led to believe. Time and again, the illusion was shattered as the hammers fell." And the 2009 Disarm Now Plowshares activists wrote in their action statement,

> Nuclear weapons can never be guardians, defenders, or upholders of peace. . . . They are sheathed in stainless steel and metal coverings that conceal the evil incarnate lying within. They are filled with death-dealing agents that tear apart humans and leave survivors scarred for life. They leave no place for human care for the thousands who suffer and die in agony. Nuclear weapons are a lie. Their protection is an illusion.[3]

The element of spatial transgression is central to a Plowshares action, as a way to show that sites of nuclear production and storage are not invulnerable. Spatial transgression is important for a number of other reasons as well. It puts the activists in closer contact with the materials they wish to disarm; ensures a level of risk that signals the extent of their commitment; and delineates a stage on which the two primary symbols of their actions, blood and hammers, can achieve their fullest redemptive potential.

By 1980 nuclear proliferation had become a central issue for peace activists in general and for the Catholic Left, which had been motivated by Pope John XXIII's 1963 encyclical *Pacem in Terris*. In it, the pope warned against the testing of nuclear weapons as a danger to life on earth, but many in the Catholic Left had been disappointed with what they saw as the episcopacy's hesitation to become more actively engaged in the push to halt the arms race.[4] Accordingly, Pennsylvania's Brandywine Peace Community, a hub of peace activism founded in 1977, had held a weekly vigil in front of the General Electric plant in King of Prussia since 1978. The first security guard to notice a car full of unfamiliar people, one in a priest's collar, driving toward the

General Electric facility for the first Plowshares action, later recalled thinking that though it seemed rather early in the morning, this was just another group of demonstrators—nothing out of the ordinary, nothing worrisome. He planned to let other guards know of their presence, but with no particular urgency.[5]

Blockades and vigils at nuclear sites—like Brandywine's and, on a larger scale, the Clamshell and Diablo Canyon occupations—were popular forms of protest at the height of the antinuclear movement. For the Plowshares and other disarmament activists, such demonstrations continued a trend from the Vietnam era, when vigils were held in front of government buildings, especially the Pentagon, to refute the secrecy of the policy decisions made within—"witness" in the literal sense. Philip and McAlister saw great value in such activities: "By our presence, we name [the Pentagon] as a temple of death that indeed it is; without such a presence, the place would remain nameless, secure in the darkness where its evil deeds can be perpetrated."[6] To facilitate the goals of naming and exposure, staging such demonstrations in public, licit space ensured that demonstrators would be visible to employees entering the site in question as well as passersby and that they would be able to remain as long as they wished, for maximum impact. This was precisely the logic of the 2010 Y-12 action, where protesters and their signs blocked employees from entering the facility for hours.

The decision of the Plowshares Eight to trespass onto the General Electric grounds and into Building Number Nine rather than join the vigil outside the facility, like the Transform Now Plowshares' decision thirty years later to walk as far as they could onto the Y-12 site, signaled a distinct goal at the heart of the Plowshares' actions. If the aim of witnessing outside a facility is to expose it as sinful, the Plowshares Eight meant going inside to extend the reach of witness and exposure. But they also went farther to come into closer contact with the materials they wished to disarm, to purify the site that they characterized as an altar of idolatrous sacrifice to the god of war. Plowshares activists have performed their symbolic disarmaments at nuclear-equipped submarines docked at sites from Washington to Rhode Island, sometimes swimming to get to them; at air force bases from North Carolina to New York; at production and assembly facilities from Texas to Massachusetts; and atop the missile silos that dot the Midwest. They have walked for hours and cut fences of every design to reach their action sites. In 1984 two activists broke into the office of an electronics company to hammer on two computers that provided navigation information for nuclear-equipped submarines and aircraft. For all these activists, the purpose of their often-strenuous efforts in reaching their action sites is to confront more directly and take purifying action against what Philip Berrigan called the "National Security State's idols."[7]

In doing so, activists intend to call into question the right of the sites themselves to exist, especially as protected spaces, temples to Lord Nuke. Through the act of trespass, Plowshares activists challenge the normative designations and ideological underpinnings attached to sites of nuclear production and storage, at the same time spatially proclaiming their own ideology of self-sacrifice.[8] Trespassing is an embodied performance of transgressive ideology, intended to reveal and instantiate an ideological difference that, to the Plowshares, mirrors a fundamental moral distinction between those who would worship and even protect Lord Nuke and those who would resist. That transgression can happen in other ways. Two Plowshares actions, the 1998 Gods of Metal action and the 2003 Riverside action, took place during public events (a Department of Defense open house in Maryland and New York City's annual Fleet Week events, respectively) so that the bomber and submarine the two sets of activist boarded were, at the time of their actions, licit space. Their actions at the site, however, left little doubt about their transgressive ideology. But trespass maps that ideology onto space, rendering a moral boundary visible through the breach of a spatial boundary.

That moral boundary is closely tied to the risk that Plowshares activists take during their actions, which hinges the personal and legal consequences that the act of trespass entails for participants. Because of how they are directly connected to risk and punishment, issues of space and boundary are important in civil disobedience circles. At vigil and demonstration sites, the boundaries between legal and illegal space are usually clearly demarcated, as during the 2010 Y-12 demonstration. Decisions about where one places oneself in physical space are undertaken quite consciously in such situations, and placement can signify a great deal about level of commitment and status within the group. Thus, it is not only in the eyes of those who "belong" in the spaces into which they trespass (military, security, and governmental personnel) that a significant crossing-over occurs during a Plowshares action. Their larger resistance community also recognizes the act of trespass as an extraordinary transgression of boundaries—perhaps boundaries that *should* be transgressed, but that most commonly are not. Plowshares activists make a choice that others do not. On an April morning in 1992, Good Friday, about fifty people caravanned with Fr. Carl Kabat and Carol Carson to a missile silo site at Whiteman Air Force Base near Kansas City, Missouri, where several Plowshares actions have taken place. They stood in a circle, watching as Kabat and Carson cut through a fence to access Silo Number

Five. They watched as Carson beat on the silo cover with a sledgehammer and Kabat, an Oblate priest, performed a rite of exorcism. When air force guards arrived half an hour later, their fifty supporters linked arms around Carson and Kabat, physically creating a tight circle of song and prayer and support around them. When the police arrived, only Carson and Kabat were arrested, on trespass and property destruction charges.[9] Only Carson and Kabat were designated as Plowshares activists; only they had committed the spatial transgression attendant to that designation.

That action wasn't typical—more often, a high degree of secrecy surrounds Plowshares actions so that no more than one or two supporters know the details of the action beforehand, and supporters do not join Plowshares activists at their action sites. Plowshares activists often commit their actions in deadly force areas (media coverage of the Transform Now Action stressed the lethal risk to the participants more than it has in other actions, but the risk undertaken is often tantamount), which is not a risk they expect others to shoulder. Neither grave bodily harm nor death has come to pass in a Plowshares action, though both are theoretically possible; just as significant to the Plowshares and their milieu are the legal risks the actions entail. "We have invaded one of the government's atomic temples, offended the high priests of megadeath, poured blood over the National Security State's idols. Lord Nuke will exact revenge," Philip wrote of the Plowshares Eight action.[10] Trespass is what irrevocably renders the actions illegal—often, trespass charges stand even when others are dropped, and activists are convicted on trespass charges when not on others. Because it is the fulcrum on which legal consequences hinge, trespass is the mechanism that allows Plowshares activists to enact an ideology and an identity grounded in the value of self-sacrifice. In her trial notes for her 1983 Plowshares action, McAlister wrote,

> When Jesus said: "You will be my witnesses" (Acts 1:8) he wasn't giving advice to his disciples or recommending a course of action. He was telling them what had happened to them and what would continue to happen to them. Witnessing isn't so much something you do—it is something that happens to you. . . . To witness is to risk yourself. How I'd like to know an easier way. But I sense that any other way would involve turning my back on all the clues I've had about a decent, meaningful life.[11]

Within the Plowshares' symbol system, trespass signals the great commitment that is key to the efficacy of their actions. The larger Catholic resistance community notices, regarding Plowshares actions as very serious and deeply admirable. The element of trespass, with its promise of consequences, thus shapes the social world that Plowshares activists inhabit. In transgressing physical boundaries the Plowshares enact symbolic boundaries between themselves and all those who would not and will not so transgress—the protectors of Lord Nuke but also the people of faith and conscience who have not made the same choice as the Plowshares.

"Real symbolic action," wrote Philip and McAlister, "draws on symbols to break real laws. Jesus broke the temple laws and the laws of the land; his criminality is not to be doubted. We are called to create new events, open new possibilities, in the spirit of the traditional symbols. We are called to break into this world, as Christ broke into the temple, in nonviolent rampage against those who rattle the missile keys and level the megaton guns."[12] The image of Christ breaking into the temple is an important one for the Plowshares, inviting and even commanding them to violate good order. It is their legitimation for the crime of trespass, in which "breaking into" and "breaking the law" come together. Trespass into illicit spaces brings with it the considerable personal and legal risks essential to the designation of symbolic disarmament. For the Plowshares, the spaces that they enter are God's spaces, made unholy through the manufacture or storage of nuclear equipment, from computer programs to missile components, from submarines and aircraft to enriched uranium. Trespass is a way to take those spaces back, to reclaim them for God's kingdom through the deployment of the biblical symbols of blood and hammers. It is the context of trespass, figured as entry into the profane kingdom of death and also the means of self-sacrifice, which delineates a stage on which the primary symbols of the action, blood and hammers, can function at their fullest purifying, redemptive potential.

Blood

The most immediate rationale for the Plowshares' spatial transgression is that trespassing brings the activists into closer contact with the materials they intend to symbolically disarm with hammers and, conspicuously, their own blood. Plowshares activists draw their blood before the actions and usually carry it to their action sites in baby bottles. The bottles are convenient, and they are also a visual reminder of a prominent trope in the Plowshares' rhetoric, which I discuss at length in the next chapter, of performing the actions for the sake of their own children and all the children of the world.

Once they are as close as they can get to the nuclear material (which might be a submarine or a bomber, a component part of a missile, a blueprint, or a computer), they pour the blood with abandon over the equipment and the facilities that house it and the ground on which it sits, sometimes in the shape of crosses, sometimes stamped into bloody handprints. Plowshares activists rely on blood to ensure the metaphysical efficacy of their actions.

The Plowshares Eight activists were not the first to pour their own blood in the context of a civil disobedience action. The Baltimore Four draft board raiders had done so a dozen years earlier at the suggestion of their lawyer, who was horrified by their initial plan to blow up the customs house where the draft files were kept (when no one was inside or near the building) and hoped they would like his idea better. At first unconvinced, Philip Berrigan and his co-raiders eventually agreed that blood was an appropriately biblical symbol and that by drawing their own they could identify with the soldiers and civilians whom the war put at risk on a daily basis. They supplemented their own blood with poultry blood from a local butcher, of necessity, so they would have enough to douse the files.[13] Many nonviolent resisters, including the Berrigans and their cohort, had already been using and would continue to use "blood-like substances" in their demonstrations, spattering red paint over sidewalks, government buildings, and the prone bodies of corpse-simulating protesters, especially at the Pentagon, where "die-ins" occupied a primary place in the repertoire of nonviolent civil disobedience during the Vietnam era. Following the Baltimore Four raid some protesters began to use human blood in these demonstrations, especially in Catholic circles, and while paint was also considered effective as a way to make bloodshed visible, as Philip and McAlister note in *The Time's Discipline*, human blood had an extra resonance, implying the willingness to sacrifice oneself for the sake of peace. Following on the heels of the Baltimore Four action, however, the Catonsville Nine decided not to pour blood. Philip felt that the presence of blood in the Baltimore Four action had only confused people and that it hadn't been clear enough as a symbol.[14] Dorothy Day and Thomas Merton, towering figures in the Catholic Left and close friends to the Berrigans, had indeed been disturbed by the use of blood, though they were just as disturbed by the use of homemade napalm that the Catonsville Nine opted to use instead. Both, they felt, undermined or at the very least destabilized the coherent presentation of a commitment to nonviolence, and such ambiguity ran the risk of reflecting back on the nonviolent movement as a whole.

Day and Merton's discomfort and the Catonsville activists' decision not to use blood speaks to its ambiguity as a symbol and the ease with which it can be taken to represent precisely the opposite of what the Plowshares intend, for which red paint will not suffice. Though media accounts often speak only of the "red substance" that Plowshares activists pour at their actions sites, for the Plowshares it is of the utmost importance that they pour their own blood. Plowshares activists continue to use blood substitutes in other actions in which they take part. Since the escalation of anxiety about AIDS in the 1980s, they and their cohort have been much more judicious about using human blood, making sure that it comes into contact only with inanimate objects and that it is used only in situations where its meaning is "clear" and its presence "essential," as Philip and McAlister have explained. Plowshares activists regard the presence of their own blood as essential because it makes bloodshed visible, but their reasoning goes further. "We pour our blood on this ship to reveal the blood of the innocent already shed by the use of this weaponry. We also pour our blood to repent for our complicity in the pervasive violence of our world," wrote the four activists who performed the 2003 Riverside Plowshares action during New York's annual Fleet Week events, as surprised onlookers watched.[15] Visibility and repentance are only two of the several overlapping resonances that Plowshares activists intend blood to invoke, and these several layers of meaning map onto various populations to whom the blood is ascribed. That is, the blood that Plowshares activists pour is purposefully their own, but it is also identified with the victims of foreign policy and with Jesus Christ.

Though blood has not been poured in every Plowshares action, Plowshares activists commonly characterize it as the most theologically laden and most significant element of the actions and talk about it *as though* it is always used. Often, they talk about it as though its meaning is self-evident. "We agreed on blood," wrote Philip Berrigan in his autobiography, "because of its Biblical symbolism."[16] He didn't elaborate further. He didn't need to, at least not for the sake of his immediate audience. Like almost all Plowshares writings, Philip's autobiography is addressed to supporters, readers who share his interpretation of the Bible and of blood's special role in the Christian story: a sign of Christ's sacrifice for all of humanity and the concomitant ideal of redemptive self-sacrifice, but also a sign of violence and injustice. He and McAlister wrote, "For Christians, blood signifies the new Covenant of justice and peace. The pact of sisterhood and brotherhood is sealed by Christ's blood. . . . When resisters use blood as a symbol, poured on the Pentagon, White House, arms factory, or weapon . . . blood as a resistance symbol means 'Stop the bloodshed. The blood is yours!'"[17]

Even in its "Biblical" meaning, blood signifies at a number of overlapping levels; for the Plowshares, blood's multiplicity renders it an essential component of the actions. Perhaps most immediately, the blood Plowshares activists pour represents the blood spilled by the foreign policy decisions they oppose, especially those concerning the use and proliferation of nuclear weapons. They intend to expose the deaths of those who are killed as a result of those decisions, whose blood, according to the "pact of sisterhood and brotherhood," is the blood of all. Plowshares activists liken the deaths that nuclear weapons perpetrated in Hiroshima and Nagasaki, as well as the deaths that contemporary foreign policy decisions bring about in countries such as Iraq and Afghanistan, to misguided offerings to a false god or to Cain's slaying of Abel. As Philip and McAlister explained in *The Time's Discipline*, "Much discernment has gone into our efforts to offer symbols and symbolic actions that are, if not adequate to the horror humanity faces, at least evocative of such horror. . . . If only the horror with which people respond to the blood as symbol can be transferred to the reality of shedding blood!" And Anne Montgomery, one of the Plowshares Eight and one of the most active Plowshares participants until her death in 2012, wrote, "Much of our creativity focuses on the choice of those symbols that will become our action or accompany it. Some have aroused emotions and raised serious questions of propriety, such as the pouring of blood on doors or weapons. The very 'offensiveness' of bloodiness is part of the message. War is not polite; dismembered bodies are messy and nauseating. But symbols can point in many directions."[18]

Plowshares activists use blood for its shock value and its ability to evoke a visceral response as a visual reminder of death, but that is only one of the directions in which blood points for the Plowshares. In pouring blood they are also invoking the healing power of Christ's blood spilled for humanity and the message of Christian redemption. This message lies at the heart of the Roman Catholic liturgy, during which, for believers, Communion wine turns to the blood of Christ and bread to his body, in a renewal of the covenant between Christ and the church and a memorialization of the sacrifice that brought it about. The technical term for the memorializing function of the Mass is "anamnesis," from the Greek words for remembrance. Traditionally and most specifically, anamnesis refers to the portion of the Mass, following the consecration of the host during the Eucharistic Prayer, which commemorates Jesus's passion, resurrection, and ascension. It may also refer to any part of the liturgy in which memorialization takes place or to the liturgy as a whole. Theologians and liturgists often define anamnesis as a "reactualization" of Christ's sacrifice, highlighting the active character of the memorialization.[19]

For the Berrigans and many in their cohort, the church's silence on the Vietnam War and social issues since that time demonstrated that the church had fallen short of its potential to reactualize Christ's sacrifice, failing at the task of anamnesis. They hoped Vatican II would reinvigorate the anamnetic function of the Mass and the church as a whole with the significant changes it introduced to the liturgy, long considered to be an absolutely fixed form. Specific changes, such as Mass in the vernacular and a different format for receiving Communion, reflected a broader understanding of key liturgical concepts. In the postconciliar church the Mass was to be adaptable (within parameters), based on the needs of congregants who were to have a more active role in the liturgy, and liturgical components were to be more broadly applied, beyond the specific rubrics of the Mass. Explicitly, anamnesis was to take place beyond the walls of the church on Sunday morning, enacted by the community of the faithful in their daily lives. To those who believed, with the Berrigans, that Jesus's example was best reactualized through political activism, this new interpretation of the Mass was a justification for the work of resistance. But the church itself did not follow suit to the degree that many in the Catholic Left would have liked. Summarizing the opinion of the church that he and his brother shared from the late sixties onward, Daniel Berrigan wrote, "The prophetic voice of the church . . . cannot be found because the church is married to the state instead of to God. Beholden to the state for assets and property, our religious institutions have become imprisoned in their own temples."[20] The Berrigans and their cohort, however, took the expanded notion of anamnesis and the broadened sense of liturgy in general very much to heart.

Daniel Berrigan explained his participation in the first Plowshares as an attempt to reclaim potent liturgical symbols that had been "borne away" and "lost in a secular vortex." Especially, he lamented that blood had been debased and desacralized. "To undo the blasphemy," he wrote, "what a labor!" Echoing his assessment, many Plowshares activists describe their time at the action sites as liturgical, referring to the prayers they recite and the songs they sing while waiting to be apprehended. Some activists have shared Eucharist at the sites. Liturgical elements during the actions are meant to demonstrate the activists' identity as religious, specifically as Catholic. They also signal the continuity the Plowshares see between their actions and the anamnetic task of the liturgy. For at least some Plowshares activists, the actions do not simply contain liturgical elements or continue the message of the liturgy; more than this, the actions themselves function as liturgies, intended to reactualize Jesus's passion. Blood, as a symbol and a substance, is the element on which this liturgical, anamnetic function hinges. As Montgomery wrote, blood "speaks of human unity and of the offering of oneself, in however small a way, in a new liturgy of life and hope."[21]

Montgomery's statement describes a profound substitution that the activists believe is taking place in a Plowshares action. To reinvigorate the liturgy as a healing, redemptive, atoning rite, Plowshares activists pour their own blood as a stand-in for Christ's. The Plowshares characterize themselves as countering the state's bloodshed with a bloodshed of their own that is not merely suggestive of the liturgy and its message of redemption but is *itself* liturgical and redemptive, a memorialization and repetition of Christ's sacrifice, an improvement on the liturgy that is meant to refresh the power of anamnesis. Plowshares actions are an attempt to do what the activists see as the necessary work of a church that has fallen short in its task. The *Baltimore Catechism*, which was the standard text by which schoolchildren were taught the rudiments of Catholic doctrine from the late nineteenth century through the middle of the twentieth century (meaning that many Plowshares activists would have learned the church's teachings between its covers), describes the Mass as an unbloody sacrifice, but the Plowshares insist it is not the case that "Christ can die no more," as the *Catechism* states.[22] Christ dies, according to the Plowshares, when children in Iraq die from the effects of depleted uranium; a blood sacrifice is still necessary to right such wrongs.

"So what did we accomplish and what will we be accomplishing by our life in prison?" asked Paul Kabat (whose brother, Carl Kabat, is also a Plowshares activist) in a reflection written for supporters following the 1984 action that resulted in eighteen-year prison sentences. "Because we are religious people we hope we have had some redemptive and salvific value for eternal life as well as intercessory power before the throne of God."[23] That redemptive, intercessory power is contained physically in the blood that Plowshares activists pour, which serves a liturgical purpose—ensuring that the actions redeem the idolatrous sites, purifying them and reclaiming them as part of God's kingdom—in two distinct ways. As a repetition of Christ's sacrifice, the blood the activists pour is meant to remind humanity of the covenant, the pact of sisterhood and brotherhood, that Christ's blood sealed, according to which nuclear weapons are a grave social sin. As the activists' own blood, it is meant to atone, to make amends for Americans' collective sin of nuclear idolatry, and to reactualize Christ's sacrifice rather than simply recall it. Theirs is the intercessory offering; theirs is the countersacrifice.

The Plowshares understand their actions to be liturgical because the blood they pour echoes the presence during Mass of Christ's blood, wine's miraculous substitute; at the same time, it is crucial that the blood also retain its character as the activists' own, as their willingly undertaken, bloody sacrifice. Following her 1982 action, Marcia Timmel wrote, "As I poured my blood in the crude form of a cross on the hatch in front of me, and watched it drip down to the silo, I realized that before me was the nuclear cross that might soon crucify all of humanity, Christ's Mystical Body. I prayed that like Christ's offering of his life's blood for the lives of all, our own blood would be found a worthy offering to God, in atonement for the sin of [nuclear submarine] Trident."[24] Timmel's description articulates the sentiment evident in many Plowshares activists' accounts of their actions. They mean the blood they pour to represent, in addition to Christ's and foreign policy victims' willing or unwilling sacrifices, their own sacrifice. But blood is not merely representational. Blood is the visual accompaniment to the Plowshares' theological claims about the necessity of self-sacrifice, and it is also the way they bring about the sacrifice. The spilled blood, resolutely their own, makes visible the risks they embrace in undertaking the actions, simultaneously representing and demonstrating their own willingness to make extreme sacrifices for the sake of peace and for the sake of reactualizing Christ's redemptive death.

Blood also makes visible their solidarity with the victims whose deaths they intend to expose. Here again, blood is enactive as well as representational: the Plowshares wish to call attention to victims' deaths but also to connect with the victims through bloodshed. Paul Kabat made this link explicit when he identified his action with child victims who also go unnoticed on the world stage.[25] And the Disarm Now Plowshares wrote in their statement, "On this day of remembrance, All Souls Day, we bring our own blood in solidarity with the victims of war, who are invisible to those who target them." Blood signifies that, for the Plowshares, solidarity is not merely a supportive stance. Rather, it necessarily involves sacrifice on the part of the activists themselves. The spilling of their own blood makes solidarity active by serving as a countersacrifice, an enfleshing of their resistance to idols through worthy offerings to God. The countersacrifice is meant to metaphysically tip the scales or right the wrongs committed by policy makers and complacent Americans who do not actively resist the government.

These overlapping layers of meaning raise questions about the extent to which blood's meaning in the Plowshares' actions is as obvious as Philip and McAlister suggested, when they wrote that in addition to using blood

61

only when it was essential to the character and functionality of the action, they would be more "careful" about using blood by using it only where its meaning was clear. Given the complex semiotics of blood as it is used in a Plowshares action, its several deep valences that might easily be interpreted as being at odds with one another, how is it that the Plowshares consider the meaning of the blood they pour to be clearly apprehensible? Plowshares activists themselves acknowledge the ambiguity of blood and indeed rely on that ambiguity for the symbol to be fully effective. Because blood is open to a range of interpretations, it can convey a message that reflects what Jason Bivins calls the actions' "doubleness," referring to the overlap between the theological and political. Blood also signifies multiply as it refers simultaneously to the blood of victims, the blood of all humanity (according to the pact of sisterhood and brotherhood), the blood of Christ (who dies anew when a victim dies), and the blood of the activists themselves. Blood stands simultaneously for violence and nonviolence, for sin and redemption, and for willing and unwilling sacrifice. Its multivalence as a symbol ensures a successful symbolic disarmament, but that same multivalence means that it is often misconstrued to mean the opposite of what the activists intend.

Even when blood is not actively misconstrued, its "real" meanings do not always come through clearly to observers. Descriptions of the actions from anyone but the activists themselves and their close supporters often fail to mention blood at all or fail to confirm that the "red substance" at an action site is blood. In official accounts of the 1984 Silo Pruning Hooks action, a military spokesperson explained, "There is a red substance at the site. . . . However, it has not been confirmed as to it being blood."[26] In the trial of the Plowshares Eight the prosecution and judge insisted that the blood they poured be discussed only in terms of its type—A and O—and not its theological or political significance. Though blood signifies greatly for the activists, outsiders often disregard the activists' own interpretations of its semiotic power. To mitigate against the public's failure or refusal to apprehend the symbolic logic behind the pouring of blood, some Plowshares activists spell out in detail their reasons for using blood in their action statements. For example, the Transform Now Plowshares activists wrote, "We bring our life-symbols: blood, for healing and pouring out our lives in service and love. Our very humanity depends on lives given, not taken. But blood also reminds us of the horrific spilling of blood by nuclear weapons."[27] Many, however, do not. For the Plowshares, the solution to blood's ambiguity and ambivalence is inherent in the nature of symbolic action. McAlister explained that symbols are effective because they don't require intellectual comprehension to be effective, nor do they require explanation to be understood. Rather, they "get beyond the assumed rationality of it all" and function as "something deeper than reason."[28] In *The Time's Discipline*, she and Philip wrote,

> the purpose of symbolic action is not to convey information but to touch and disclose previously unknown depths of awareness lying unplumbed at the center of being. Merton wrote:
>
> *Traditionally the value of symbol is precisely in its apparent useless-ness as a means of simple communication. Because it is not efficient as a mode of communicating information, the symbol can achieve a higher purpose of going beyond practicality and purpose, beyond cause and effect. Instead of establishing a new contact by a meeting of minds in the sharing of news, the symbol tells us nothing new; it revives an awareness of what we already know and deepens that awareness. . . . The symbol awakens awareness and restores it.[29]*

And Anne Montgomery echoed, "Symbols have a condensed, almost physical power and are especially important in an age when the inundation of words makes us nonlisteners. Symbols touch us on a deep, subconscious level and release memories and fears, aspirations and energies."[30] For the Plowshares, blood functions as a symbol because it evokes truths that all of humanity already knows, awarenesses that all of humanity already possesses. Thus, there is nothing to be lost from elaborating blood's meaning in action statements, but more often, activists take its overlapping levels of meaning to be self-evident because they are meanings that are "true" in a profound sense, needing only to be reawakened or revived. The concern with proper intellectual apprehension by outsiders that kept the Catonsville Nine from pouring blood is not a concern for Plowshares activists, because, according to their post-Harrisburg logic of symbols and symbolic action, people understand blood deeply, even if at first it doesn't make sense at the level of reason. This apprehension at a level deeper than reason ensures that blood works properly in the actions. It also allows for the efficacy of household hammers, which, where blood seems complicated and ambiguous, often strike observers as simply foolish.

Hammers

Hammers

Cultural references to Isaiah's image of beating swords into plowshares, which appears also in the books of Micah and Joel, span a wide range—from a 1987 Ronald Reagan speech ("Cannot swords be turned to plowshares? Can we and all nations not live in peace?") to the 1991 Michael Jackson song "Heal the World" ("See the nations turn their swords into plowshares") to the stirring finale of the musical Les Miserables ("They will walk behind the plowshare, they will put away the sword"), to give only a few examples.[31] Evgeniy Vuchetich's statue Let Us Beat Swords into Plowshares, which stands in front of the United Nations building in New York, casts Isaiah's words in bronze, depicting a well-muscled man with a sledgehammer doing just that; and several philanthropic organizations take their names from Isaiah's verse, hearing his directive to turn the weapons of war into farm implements as an apt metaphor for the work of conflict resolution. Plowshares activists intend to do more than invoke Isaiah's words, however. They intend to enact them, following and "enfleshing" his short instruction with their household hammers. A prophecy, after all, ought to be fulfilled, and Plowshares activists believe that they are doing just that with their actions. They describe the actions as powerful and effective at a symbolic level, but also as "productive," "direct," and "actual" disarmament. In part this is because, for the Plowshares, the symbolic is productive and actual, but it is also because they attach great significance to the tangible aspects of their actions, even if the physical effects are usually negligible. As Montgomery described, hammering during a Plowshares action renders the action "both symbolic and direct, since [hammering] carries out in a carefully defined scenario a small but real disarmament that thousands of treaties and conferences have yet to accomplish."[32]

After the overtly transgressive quality of trespass and the visceral impact of blood, hammers may seem almost like an afterthought, innocuous and not nearly as conspicuous or dramatic as the other two fundamental elements of a Plowshares action. But hammers are crucial to the Plowshares' symbol system. As Plowshares chronicler Arthur Laffin notes, "When someone has done an action using the symbols—basically a hammer—we put it in the chronological list."[33] At an immediate level, hammering moors the Plowshares' actions to the biblical inspiration that motivates and legitimates them, by summoning Isaiah's image of beating swords into Plowshares more directly than either trespass or blood. Often activists write Isaiah's words, along with other messages such as "the war stops here" and "love your enemies" on the hammers' handles themselves or on the illustrations of hammers that frequently appear on their banners and fliers. Like blood, hammers convey a message both theological and political, connecting the Plowshares to Jesus and to those whose deaths they wish to bring to light. Activist Mark Colville linked the act of hammering with Jesus's rampage against the moneylenders in the temple: "Hammering swords into plowshares is the kind of action that builds a solid foundation for a life of true discipleship by following Jesus into his civil resistance and action on behalf of God's word." And the activists who performed the Plowshares Number Four action wrote in their statement, "We come with hope and hammers. Hope, that God's good creation might not be destroyed. Hammers, that the cries of the victims might be given form by our deeds."[34]

The image of hammers giving form to the intangible features of the Plowshares' resistance echoes Montgomery's (and many other Plowshares activists') characterization of hammers as the element that links the actions' symbolic and direct aspects. The bridging of the demonstrative and the enactive is a defining characteristic of the Plowshares' actions, and hammers have a special role to play in building that bridge. As Marcia Timmel described, "I stand on the deck of a nearly finished Trident submarine, a household hammer in my hand. I tremble, my knees weaken. What am I doing here? This is the most deadly weapon in the world; more than 2000 Hiroshimas are under my feet. I feel weak, powerless. What can I do? With my sisters and brothers I, an ordinary woman, can hammer this nuclear sword into a Biblical plowshare. In faith I hammer."[35] In Timmel's description, hammers give form to the abstract and tangibility to the symbolic; hammering is not only demonstrative and symbolic—though it is both those things—but an actual, embodied response, an act of power.

For all its significance, hammering is not prescribed or regulated any more than blood or trespass within the Plowshares' actions. No rules, either formal or informal, govern or even suggest how hammering is to be carried out, and the image of "beating swords into Plowshares" has been interpreted in a variety of ways over the group's thirty years. Ordinary household hammers, the sort that most people keep in a rudimentary toolbox, remain the most common implement, precisely because they are, in terms of instrumentality, so blatantly ineffectual against the equipment that the Plowshares wish to disarm. As Philip Berrigan wrote of one of his actions, "We kept our action symbolic by refusing to do the maximum damage possible."[36] Symbolic action thus links directly to the principle of nonviolence, which entails an eschewal of earthly power in favor of spiritual commitment. But Plowshares activists have also interpreted the directive to beat swords into Plowshares with notable creativity. In doing so they have brought to the fore certain tensions bound up with the Plowshares' project, especially pertaining to the ideal of nonviolence, and the presence of threatening elements in the actions of a group that places great importance on that ideal as a hallmark of its identity and the very trait the activists most hope to instantiate.

Innovative thinking about the symbol of the hammer was evident as early as the second Plowshares action, undertaken spontaneously a few months after the Plowshares Eight's deed at General Electric. Peter DeMott, a resident of Jonah House, was taking part in a sizable protest at a shipyard in Groton, Connecticut, during the launch ceremony for a fast-attack submarine. He noticed an empty security van. Then he saw, upon closer inspection, that the keys were in the van. He proceeded to get into the van and drive it repeatedly into the side of a Trident submarine at the site—a creative interpretation of "beating swords into Plowshares," indeed.[37] There is no record of anyone in his circle taking issue with what most media, as well as the prosecution in his trial, labeled a theft (the vehicle is, in court records and newspaper accounts, a "stolen van") or with the undeniably more destructive nature of the action.

A second case prompted more discussion about the interplay between symbolic and direct action. In the 1984 Silo Pruning Hooks action, which stands out among Plowshares actions both for the tactics the activists used and for the lengthy prison sentences that resulted, Fr. Carl Kabat, Fr. Paul Kabat, Larry Cloud-Morgan, and Helen Woodson chose not to use household hammers, as the activists in most of the ten previous Plowshares actions had done (the notable exception being DeMott and the security van). Instead, they took a rented jackhammer to the Minuteman missile silo covers at Whiteman Air Force Base. The jackhammer malfunctioned a few minutes into the action, but the activists remained at the site praying and were apprehended by military guards about an hour later. Not surprisingly, the judge in their federal trial saw their action as a much more serious threat than previous Plowshares actions. For the first time in the Plowshares' history, the charges against the four included sabotage, which led to shocking prison sentences—as high as eighteen years. (At that point in the Plowshares' history, sentences of several months or a year were typical.)

In explanations of their decision to use jackhammers instead of household hammers, the Silo Pruning Hooks activists made it clear that they didn't think that the jackhammers would actually cause more damage or destruction of property. Paul Kabat observed that even if the four had had days, they wouldn't have made a dent in the silo covers. But even so, he and the others had felt compelled to try what he characterized as a more direct, more productive approach to disarmament: "Even though we knew there were six feet of concrete between us and the missile, and that our efforts would be more symbolic than effective, we felt that somebody had to make a first move to productive disarmament. We knew we would never get near the warhead even if we could have been on the site for a week, much less the few minutes we were actually there. We still had to make some kind of effort to disarm that nuclear bomb."[38] Even though the activists did not consider this act to have any more destructive potential than using household hammers would have had (especially because of its unexpected malfunction a few minutes into the action), it *appeared* more destructive, and that appearance of greater destructive capability, Kabat suggests, related directly to the actions' symbolic import and metaphysical impact. The Silo Pruning Hooks activists' approach was productive because it *seemed* like a threat against the silo covers and was meant to be perceived as such. The extent to which it actually *was* more of a threat than earlier Plowshares actions, at least until the equipment malfunction, did not seem to be a primary concern for the activists (though it was very much on the mind of the judge who heard their case).

The linkage of efficacy with the appearance of a more significant threat is unexpected from activists who go to great lengths to present a coherent, unmistakable commitment to nonviolence and for whom earthly powerlessness goes hand in hand with spiritual authenticity; it highlights an ambivalence surrounding the extent to which the actions are meant to be perceived as threatening. In the Transform Now action at Oak Ridge, the threat to national security and the concerns that it raised dominated media coverage of the action, overriding the other elements that the activists themselves thought were important—the blood they poured, the white roses they presented. But prior to the Oak Ridge action, media coverage largely downplayed the threatening aspects of the Plowshares' actions. A *Kitsap Sun* story on the 2009 Disarm Now Plowshares action, for example, reports that according to the navy's press release, consistent with many official treatments of the Plowshares' actions, "At no time was the safety of Navy personnel, property, or the public threatened in any way."[39]

A retrospective assurance that no threat was posed during the action, however, does not mitigate the real risk that is both present and perceived during the actions. The activists risk their lives when they enter the deadly force areas where many of their actions are committed, and personnel at the sites report feeling some degree of menace from the combination of spilled blood and outstretched hammers and from the simple presence of unauthorized persons on sites that are supposed to be well secured. A security guard who apprehended the Plowshares Eight, for example, reported that "I thought he was going to swing at me [with the hammer], I really did."[40]

And in a letter to the court included in the presentencing report for the 1989 Thames River Plowshares action, which took place aboard the Trident submarine USS *Pennsylvania* (to which the activists had swum and canoed), Rear Adm. W. P. Houley noted that

> The real danger involved with this type of protest activity is that young armed sailors standing topside watch on a submarine cannot distinguish between armed terrorists and unarmed nuclear protests at the precise moment when those attempting to board are first detected. . . . The dilemma faced by the sailor who encounters such intruders is that he cannot determine whether deadly force is required. Even if the intruders identify themselves as peaceful protesters, security training has taught the sailor that true terrorists intent on securing an explosive device to the ship would likely give the same response. Subsequent investigation in this case distinguished these Plowshares protesters from terrorists. However, until such a time as the protesters were apprehended and prevented from further damaging the ship, the possibility of someone getting shot was very real.[41]

The sense of menace present during the actions, even if it is later downplayed, regularly gives rise to charges of terroristic threat and even, on rare occasions, assault. The tension between what personnel at the sites attest to feeling during the actions, the reports they later give that minimize any sense of menace, and charges that suggests a high degree of danger to the actions mirror the tension in the Plowshares' own characterizations of the actions, as nonviolent but doing *something* that deserves to be taken seriously as an actual threat to the security of the sites and the inviolability of the materials stored there. It is the same tension that insists on the value of purely symbolic action while hoping to achieve a measurable physical effect—to not be trivialized as merely symbolic but to have their symbols recognized as efficacious at an enactive as well as a demonstrative level.

The Silo Pruning Hooks activists' attempt to harness greater destructive capability while still considering their action "more symbolic than effective" raises complex questions about how much tangible impact the Plowshares hope to have and about where the lines are drawn between the symbolic and the direct—and, in turn, between violence and nonviolence. What exactly did Philip Berrigan mean when he noted that refusing to do the maximum amount of damage possible was the key to keeping the actions symbolic?

What would constitute "maximum" damage, and is everything that falls short of that unformulated designation acceptable within the repertoire of symbolic disarmament and of nonviolent resistance?

Within the Catholic activist community, nonviolent symbolic action takes a variety of forms—mock funerals processions, the scattering of ashes, and, of course, the pouring of blood, to name only a few prominent examples. But there are actions that the category strains to accommodate, as the case of Plowshares activist Helen Woodson illustrates. Woodson was one of the four participants in the Silo Pruning Hooks action and was sentenced to eighteen years in prison. She was released after ten years, though she tried strenuously to avoid early release. While still in prison, to continue her witness and as part of her campaign to forestall early release, Woodson had acted "in solidarity" with two Plowshares actions that took place during her sentence. It is unclear what her participation entailed aside from adding her name to the two groups' action statements, but the group's chronologies list her as a "remote participant" in these actions. In addition, she performed what was termed the Resistance in Captivity Plowshares action, in which she used nail polish to set a fire in the prison yard. According to Laffin and Montgomery (presumably by way of Woodson herself), prison officials destroyed the evidence of this action so that it could not stand in the way of her 1993 parole.[42]

Her efforts to prevent early release were not only vigorous but atypical; most Plowshares activists welcome early release. But Woodson wrote letter after letter to prison officials, pleading with them to keep her for the full eighteen years, maintaining that the only acceptable shortening of her sentence would have to include the acknowledgement that her action had been appropriate. That acknowledgement, she informed prison officials, could be demonstrated by her sentencing judge joining her in another disarmament action. Her letters failed to sway anyone. Immediately upon her release, and without the participation of the sentencing judge, Woodson undertook a series of further actions that ultimately distanced her from the Catholic resistance community, though previously, through her strenuous and atypical campaign to prevent early release from her long sentence, Woodson had instantiated the movement's deepest ideals about the need for a select few to sacrifice themselves to the consequences in order to catalyze a new society. She also instantiated that ideal by immediately getting herself back into prison after the release that she resisted in every way, but she did so by extremely controversial means: three days after her early release from her Silo Pruning Hooks sentence, Woodson mailed letters, each with a .38 caliber bullet attached, to several corporate CEOs with the message, "Your actions

[margin handwritten note: Woodson tried to help from prison officials destroyed evidence so they could release her.]

are like a bullet through life." She considered this action to be of a piece with the missile silo action, similarly symbolic and nonviolent. Others disagreed.

In Laffin and Montgomery's chronology of Plowshares actions, the authors, Plowshares activists themselves, record that after her participation in the Silo Pruning Hooks and Resistance in Captivity actions, Helen Woodson was "involved in several controversial protests (which went outside the bounds of traditional nonviolent protest)."[43] Though Woodson explained this and subsequent resistance activities theologically, characterizing the letters and the Plowshares actions as all part of one biblically inspired campaign for justice, today she is embraced most enthusiastically by radical secular groups such as the Earth Liberation Front, while many in the Catholic Left, as Laffin and Montgomery indicate, consider her to have overstepped a crucial boundary between violence and nonviolence. But that line is both ill-defined and malleable. Some nonviolent activists, for example, feel that putting others in a position to do violence, which the Plowshares do when they enter deadly force areas, is itself violent. Some feel that destroying property or causing fear is violent. Many observers at the time, from among their supporters and outside that circle, regarded the Berrigans' draft board actions as too evocative of violence to fall under the heading of nonviolent resistance, while now it is generally held up as a paragon of nonviolent witness.

Woodson's characterization of certain financial establishments as life-destroying idols and her use of a violent symbol to evoke that characterization operate at least in an initial sense on the same plane as the Vietnam War–era draft board actions, and, as she apparently intended, as the Plowshares' evocative use of symbols and their characterizations of the victims of warfare as sacrifices to idols. Moreover, the idea of breaking with the tactics and attitudes of traditional nonviolence to shock and startle audiences, even frighten them out of complacency, was central to the development of the Plowshares' resistance; and Woodson's iconoclasm within that tradition was already evident, certainly, when she set a chemical fire for her Resistance in Captivity action, which the Plowshares do include in their chronologies. Woodson certainly made a creative and controversial choice when she decided to enact nonviolence with bullets. But every Plowshares action relies on creativity, from the start attaching a particular interpretation to the image of beating swords into Plowshares. The use of a stolen van or a jackhammer to perform the same symbolic task as a household hammer shows that there is a good deal of leeway in interpreting even those biblical passages that the Plowshares hold to be most fundamental to their sense of who they are and what they do and that a certain amount of innovation is welcomed. So where, exactly, was Woodson's breach located?

In at least one important way, Woodson's mail campaign fails to qualify as a Plowshares action: her target was not nuclear weapons. (Plowshares activists often emphasize the economic ramifications of nuclear production and policy, but only as one in a litany of evils for which Lord Nuke is responsible.) Nonetheless, her example highlights a striking paradox: the distinction between nonviolent and violent resistance, even in a community that adamantly proclaims its allegiance to the former, is at the same time ambiguous and, to those in the Catholic resistance circle, obvious and immediate. That is, even though to Woodson herself the later actions had much in common with the symbolic disarmament actions in which she had participated as a Plowshares activist, others felt—as though by some common instinct—that her later actions, which she continued to characterize as symbolic and nonviolent, failed egregiously on both counts. That ascription of failure illuminates a further key aspect of the Plowshares' symbolic actions: the way the three primary elements, potent in themselves, work together to maintain a delicate balance between the threatening and redemptive capabilities of potentially violent symbols so that they function instead as both signs and vehicles of nonviolence.

[Handwritten margin note: 71 It is hard to make a line between violent / nonviolent protest.]

[Handwritten note: The symbols themselves (hammers) can actually harm, may not be seen as nonviolent.]

Re-marking Symbols, Re-marking Selves

According to most every formulation of what nonviolent resistance does and does not entail, Woodson's bullet letters failed conclusively as nonviolence when they substituted what could have been read as threats to human life (though Woodson reportedly did not intend them that way) for destruction of property. But, as I have related earlier, some personnel at the Plowshares' actions sites have reported feeling threatened by the activists' hammers (hammers are, after all, more immediately threatening than bullets without a gun) as well as the fact of their trespass, and it is likely that spilled blood hasn't always set the minds of site personnel at ease either, despite the activists' repeated declarations that they are nonviolent and intend no harm to anyone. But the Plowshares believe that their actions function as acts of nonviolence—that is, they actively instantiate the ideal of nonviolence—despite possible misapprehensions at the surface level. The actions are able to do so, according to the logic of symbolic disarmament, because the combination of elements within them ensures the highly ritualized context necessary to guarantee each element's proper semiotic function.

Jason Bivins describes the early Plowshares actions as exemplary of "ritual protest," typifying a mode of resistance, increasingly prevalent and visible since the civil rights movement, in which activists use symbolic protest instead of organized political logic to critique "our very understandings of what it means to be religious and political," relying on the demonstrative ability of symbols to "create alternative worlds of meaning to the liberal state." Bivins's characterization of the Plowshares' resistance accords with the activists' own descriptions of the demonstrative power of symbolic disarmament, but the term "ritual" applies in a broader sense as well, of which the demonstrative power of the actions is only one aspect (just as it is only one aspect, for the Plowshares themselves, of symbolic disarmament). Catherine Bell argues that when we think about ritual, we should start with "how human activities establish and manipulate their own differentiation and purpose" and how "certain social actions strategically distinguish themselves in relation to other actions." That is, rather than thinking of ritual as indicated by a set of universal characteristics, we should think of "ritualization" as a social process and examine, within a given context, what it is about certain activities that distinguishes and privileges them over and against other activities. As ritual theorist Ronald Grimes has pointed out, ritualized actions may rely on strict rules to ensure that they stand out as rituals. But in the absence of overprescription, several other features can signal an action's high degree of ritualization.[44] Thus, while neither trespass nor hammers nor blood are highly prescribed in the context of the Plowshares' actions, with no formal rules governing their deployment and a great deal of interpretive leeway accommodated, the actions possess other qualities that imbue them with a distinctly ritualized character, to which the activists allude when they speak of the actions as liturgical and as simultaneously symbolic and direct. For Grimes, these qualities of ritualization include traditionalizing the action in question or associating it with the past; elevating the action or connecting it with sacred values and norms; carrying out the action in a stylized manner or with some special pomp or flair; invoking the power of gods or spirits; situating the action in a particular place or time; and performing the action with specially qualified agents.

The Plowshares' actions demonstrate these qualities in the ways that I have elaborated on earlier. Their action statements indicate the high degree to which the Plowshares associate their actions with sacred values and norms (the ideals of Christian nonviolence and redemptive self-sacrifice in the mold of Jesus Christ and Isaiah's directive to beat swords into plowshares) and with a past both sacred (related in the Hebrew and Christian scriptures) and earthly (demonstrated in the examples of their mentors and exemplars, such as Dorothy Day, Gandhi, and the Berrigans). The secrecy and mystery that surrounds the actions, as well as the many accessories the activists bring with them to their sites (not only blood and hammers, but bread and roses, sunflower seeds, and miniature coffins, for example), indicate the actions' stylized character. Not only their rhetoric but the blood they pour invokes Christ's power. The spatial element is, as I have argued, vitally important to the actions' particular efficacy. And while often the Plowshares deny that they are specially qualified to perform the actions, they do make frequent references to the special preparation that the actions require. As Anne Montgomery explains, "An act of divine obedience such as entering an arms factory or military base and hammering on a missile cone or launcher is not taken lightly but requires that the process followed for other resistance actions be more intense and prolonged."[45]

These qualities of ritualization are determined not by any one of the elements alone, which are neither unique to the Plowshares' actions nor deployed consistently in every action, but rather by the combination of elements, an interaction between space and symbol on which the actions depend. Trespass sets the stage on which the Plowshares' symbols can operate in their intended capacities, while their symbols, in turn, render the act of trespass not merely illegal but transformative. Blood spilled anywhere may signify atonement; for the Plowshares, blood spilled at the altar of Lord Nuke effects purification. Hammers in another context may, in fact, be enormously destructive; hammers used in spaces where they stand little chance of being enormously destructive communicate the message of nonviolence but also the direct nature of symbolic action. Space and symbol combine to ritualize the actions to a high degree, even without a high level of prescription. Symbols interact with one another as well: trespass and hammers may well signify an intent to do harm in another context, but that violent potential is neutralized by the blood the Plowshares pour, which conveys their attachment to sacred norms, according to which they would give life rather than take it. These symbols and ritual qualities are by no means self-evident to everyone, though the Plowshares think of them as operating at a level "deeper than reason." But they resonate immediately for many in the larger Catholic resistance community.

When Woodson sent her bullet letters, she may well have had several of these qualities of ritualization in mind. But the response of the Catholic resistance community indicates that her action did not convey those qualities properly. Where the Plowshares' actions mark them as virtuosi within their larger community, Woodson's estranged her from it. This difference highlights the fact that in addition to the metaphysical and symbolic outcomes for which the Plowshares themselves hope, their actions and the particular combination of familiar elements within them have profound social effects as well. These social effects are also crucial to the efficacy of the actions, which function as intended not only because they are highly ritualized but because they innovate on preexisting rituals. Historian of religions Bruce Lincoln describes ritual change or innovation as a process of re-marking symbols that have become, through repetition, deprived of their original potency. Ritual objects and practices start out "marked," designated as special beyond the characteristics that the object or practice might possess outside the ritual context. The objects are themselves strongly marked and work to mark the rituals of which they are a part. But repeated use of the same marked object in a given ritual lessens its special status. With repetition, symbols lose their marking, meaning, and vibrancy, and so do the rituals of which they are a part. To escape the trap of overfamiliarity and standardization, innovation must take place and symbols must be re-marked or new marked symbols introduced.[46]

For the Plowshares the once-potent symbols and practices in traditional liturgies and traditional civil disobedience have, in the way that Lincoln describes, lost their marking and their meaning. In that process, the Plowshares believe, the church and many political resisters have become complicitous with the state rather than a check against its power. They mean their actions to re-mark those symbols and reclaim the power of religion as a force for countering the state, by using the symbols and practices in new spaces or new ways—pouring blood as part of a "new liturgy of life and hope," hammering as an act at once intentionally ineffective and a show of physical force, trespassing in such a way that they risk bodily harm or even death. But re-marking a symbol and thereby innovating a ritual also serves to "distinguish [the innovators'] performances from those of others, with consequent gains in an economy of prestige." Lincoln notes that when ritual innovation is generated by someone who was a practitioner of the original ritual (as with Plowshares activists, who were once practitioners of the traditional Catholic liturgy and of traditional civil disobedience), the innovation reveals ingenuity, creativity, and boldness so that the innovator can gain in both power and stature.[47] Re-marking symbols, then, also re-marks the ritual agents who undertake such innovation, as in the case of the Plowshares, whose innovations distinguish them within the larger Catholic Left.

To effect such gains (or, as in Woodson's case, losses) in an economy of prestige, a ritual innovation needs to be apprehended by others who can confer or deny prestige. Woodson's bullet letters marked her as deviant, and the Plowshares' actions mark them as virtuosic, because others in their milieu know about those actions. A ritual innovation can reshape the social world, in other words, because it is a performance—not a mere doing, but, in Richard Schechner's apt phrasing, the "showing of a doing." While the Plowshares are ostensibly unconcerned with prestige, they do care deeply about their actions as apprehensible and apprehended by their immediate community as well as a larger audience. Schechner's characterization of performance as a showing of a doing conveys the dual sense of performance as both displaying or conveying something before an audience (performing an aria) and bringing something to pass (performing a surgery), which corresponds precisely to the Plowshares' dual intentions for their symbolic disarmaments—to present or convey their values but also to bring to pass the sacred norms that engender those values, instantiating the roles on which the realization of those sacred norms depend. The actions allow for both. They provide a context in which the Plowshares can display their values: trespass represents the value of "divine obedience" and therefore civil disobedience; blood represents the values of self-sacrifice, atonement, and solidarity; hammers represent the value of nonviolence; and all three represent the value of symbolic action. But that display is valuable for the Plowshares only as a simultaneous enactment of those values. Pouring their blood is, actually, a kind of self-sacrifice; trespass and hammers are, actually, ways to break the law, by which the Plowshares secure a space within the social category to which they feel called—the one or two faithful, criminalized and cast out from a sinful society for their commitment to true justice.

In performing their actions the Plowshares both present and enact moral boundaries between themselves and the sinful world in thrall to Lord Nuke. The actions hinge on distinctions between licit and illicit space, between those who are willing to shed their own blood and those who are not, between those who understand the value of symbolic action and those who do not, so that the actions both visually signify and instantiate their moral distinction from all those who do not so resist—especially the church, on whom the Plowshares believe that the duty to resist state power is especially incumbent (hence their "new liturgy of life and hope" attempts to complete the moral task at which they feel the church has failed, by re-marking its symbols). In performing these moral boundaries between the faithful and the sinful, they intend to bring to life the biblical ideal of the prophet cast out as a punishment for divine obedience and of a small community of the faithful that endures risk and persecution for the sake of redeeming the world. But for these effects to come to pass, their actions have to be apprehended; to function as performance, the actions require an audience. And, practically, the activists have to be caught and punished to face the persecution apposite to prophets and martyrs. For this reason Plowshares activists remain at their action sites if they are not immediately detained, sometimes for hours, to be apprehended (in its own dual sense of being seen and being caught). Further, knowing that not many people will see the actions or their aftermath because of the highly secured nature of the sites where they are usually performed, the Plowshares continue the performance of their actions in writing, disseminating accounts of what they did and why they did it; and during their trials, where they can speak about the actions to audiences beyond the immediate circle of supporters that primarily reads their writings.

Because they have multiple, overlapping audiences, the Plowshares' actions have multiple, overlapping levels of social significance and remake the social world in ways that the activists do not necessarily intend. That is to say, the Plowshares' actions do not only distinguish the activists from the wicked world. The potent combination of elements and the ritualization and re-marking that take place in the actions also place the participants into a category of high-risk activism regarded as unmatched by their wider resistance circle—and that circle pays a great deal more attention to the Plowshares than the wicked world does. The actions thus reveal and instantiate sociomoral boundaries not just between the Plowshares and the protectors and worshippers of nuclear idols but also between the Plowshares and their closest peacemaking allies. As I discuss in the next chapter, most Plowshares participants themselves would probably not characterize their actions this way, at least not immediately. Typically, their rhetoric is expansive, inclusive, based on solidarity rather than virtuosity. But as I have shown here, they also characterize the actions as rituals, liturgies, and performances—all categories based on social distinctions, even hierarchies. Rituals have innovators; liturgies have celebrants; performances have actors and audiences. And, true to those categories, the Plowshares' actions, carefully choreographed to effect metaphysical and political change through a mechanism of self-sacrifice both represented and actualized, show forth the Plowshares as an elite group set apart by a commitment—and consequently a piety—that those in the Plowshares' milieu regard as exemplary. Though not the activists' explicit intention, their rhetoric, to which I now turn, does the same.

3

"Our Only Real Credential"

The Rhetorical Performance of Symbolic Boundaries

"I'm writing to tell you, that if all goes well, on the fourth Sunday of Advent (Dec. 18) several of us will go to the Maryland Air National Guard in Baltimore. Following the words of Isaiah to beat swords into plowshares, using hammers and our own blood, we hope to begin to convert an A-10 Thunderbolt II Warthog fighter jet. Most likely we will all be held in the local jail. . . . Right about now, maybe you are asking: 'Can't you think of something better to do? Are you being effective?'"[1] So wrote Plowshares activist Susan Crane in the days leading up to a 1999 action, in a letter to friends posted after the action on the Jonah House website. For as immediately apprehensible and deeply resonant as they consider their symbols and actions to be, Plowshares activists spend a great deal of time and effort explaining what they did and why they did it, working to allay the misperception and bafflement that often greet the actions and to respond to the perennial "why" questions that Crane anticipated.

Explanation is built into the action itself, as Plowshares activists travel to their actions armed not only with hammers and baby bottles of blood but with action statements written beforehand and signed by the activists. Each action statement, which is handed to personnel at the site and also distributed to the Plowshares' communities of support, presents a summary of the action and its rationale. Generally the action statements fit onto a single sheet of paper; sometimes they are only a few sentences long. While they vary greatly in tone and content, they all present information about the particular equipment or site that the action is meant to target, and they all frame the action in explicitly religious terms, emphasizing the activists' biblical motivations and nonviolent intentions. In 1984, for example, the eight Pershing Plowshares activists, whose action was directed against missile components and a missile launcher at Martin Marietta in Orlando, Florida, wrote,

[handwritten margin note: They hand out statements w/ Biblical reference]

We act in faith in a time when the "doomsday clock" stands at 3 minutes to midnight, in a time of fear, desperation, violence; a violence concretized in the Pershing nuclear sword that is pointed at the heart of the Russian people, intensifies the cycle of threat, deployment, counter-threat on both sides. This nuclear threat holds all people hostage: the people of Germany, the first to die in a "limited" nuclear war; the people of the third world, oppressed under the East-West nuclear umbrella; the poor everywhere, victims now of the $256 billion we spent this year on the arms race. Of the $4.6 million spent on just one Pershing.... We act in love, in this Easter, this "dawn" of new life: responsible love: recognizing our relationship to these weapons which we must transform, to their creators—all of us in our shared violence and apathy, to their victims who cannot act; communal love: conspiring—breathing together—that we may be one: East and West, North and South in a more human and faithful world; obedient love, enfleshing the prophets' command: "They shall beat their swords into plowshares and their spears into pruning hooks; one nation shall not raise the sword against another, nor shall they train for war again."[2]

Just over a decade later the six Jubilee Plowshares activists, four at a shipyard in Virginia and two at Lockheed-Martin in California, handed out statements that read in part,

Our faith commands us to disarm and transform the swords of our time into plowshares. Today, August 7, 1995, we expose with our blood the genocidal nature of the nuclear-capable fast-attack submarine and the Trident II D5 missile built at Newport News Shipbuilding in Virginia and Lockheed-Martin Corporation of Sunnyvale, California, respectively. . . . With blind insanity we have amassed enough weaponry to eliminate all life on the planet many times over. . . . Disarmament is the necessary first step to Christ's jubilee. We refuse to see violence as inevitable, injustice as the order of the day, and death-dealing as the only way of life.[3]

And in 2003 the Riverside Plowshares activists, who performed their action aboard an Aegis cruiser during New York's annual Fleet Week activities, wrote,

> We come here today to enflesh the prophecy from Isaiah, "They shall beat their swords into ploughshares and their spears into pruning hooks" (2:4). With hammers we have initiated the process of disarming this battle ship, of transforming this carrier of mass destruction into a vessel for peace. The USS Philippine Sea uses Tomahawk cruise missiles, depleted uranium munitions and the Aegis radar system to enforce the US empire's will on other nations and regions. We pour our blood on this ship to reveal the blood of the innocent already shed by the use of this weaponry. We also pour our blood to repent for our complicity in the pervasive violence of our world. We are trying to follow Jesus Christ's commandments to love our enemies and neighbours, to forgive those who do us harm and to repent. We seek to stop the injury of war on the human family and heal our communities by living nonviolently and seeking justice for all. The peace and security that comes from an empire wielding weapons of war and intimidation are false and illusory. With hammers we disarm this weapon of mass destruction and with blood we reveal its purpose.[4]

The action statements offer poetic summations of the actions' aims and content, but they are only the first step in the Plowshares' long campaign to render the actions apprehensible through the written word. The work of explaining continues long after the actions, for the benefit of audiences beyond the personnel they encounter at the action sites. Those later writings (or, as in Crane's case, written prior to the action but not distributed until later) describe the actions for friends, family members, and supporters, and they are far more personal. Here too the activists talk about nuclear weapons, about war and violence, about God's commandments and expectations, and about Jesus's example. But they also talk a great deal about themselves.

"This is the tale of a journey, symbolic and actual," wrote Martin Holladay in 1985 from a prison cell. "It is a journey from Lebanon to Vermont to Missouri, where I now find myself in jail awaiting trial for hammering on the concrete lid of a nuclear missile silo." On February 19 of that year, as a show of support for the four Silo Pruning Hooks activists whose trial began that day, Holladay entered another Minuteman II missile silo on Whiteman Air Force Base, where they had committed their action the year before. Confronting what he called the "violence here in the farmland of Missouri," Holladay poured blood over the silo and beat on it with a household hammer and chisel. Writing from prison as he awaited trial, he explained, "The small sound of my hammer was a farmer's anguished 'No.'" Holladay grew up in Lebanon, he relayed in that same letter, and was deeply impacted by the beauty and fertility of the land. At the time of his action he had been a carpenter and gardener in Vermont for ten years, living an idyllic "post-Eden existence." But, he wrote, "My increasing awareness that the nuclear threat reaches everywhere, even to the backwoods of Vermont, brought me to a most difficult fork in the road. Eventually—not without heartache—I gave away my chickens and took leave of the land. I traveled to Missouri, to the missile fields." At the end of the road he chose was a conviction on the charge of destruction of federal property and an eight-year prison sentence, ultimately reduced to nineteen months of time served. Why make such a sacrifice? He explained, "Our love for God requires us to love justice and therefore to implement it, to love all creation and therefore to defend it. . . . In our love for our neighbor, violence has no place. We are called to disarmament, a disarmament of the heart. But our love for our neighbors also calls us to protect them, to prevent harm, to intervene to save them."[5]

Holladay's letter tells a story common among Plowshares activists, of a journey from complacency to action, a progression to a new way of thinking and, consequently, a new compulsion to act. Agnes Bauerlein wrote after her 1983 action, "Slowly, over many previous months of serious thoughts and prayers, I had decided to protest the proliferation and continuation of the nuclear arms buildup in a stronger way than I had previously done. I had decided that civil disobedience would be my way of saying 'no' to an insane arms race that threatens all life on our planet." And after the 2012 Transform Now Plowshares action, Greg Boertje-Obed wrote from jail, awaiting trial, of the action itself as a journey directed by God: "We believe God clearly guided us through the fences to the uranium building where we put up banners, poured blood, spray painted, put up crime scene tape, and began to hammer on a lower corner of the wall beneath an imposing guard tower. . . . We give thanks for the miraculous leading of the Spirit, which is how we understand the action occurred. If God can raise people from the dead, then God can lead people past forces of death to continue the process of transforming structures of death to become structures for life-enhancing purposes."[6]

Part theological treatise, part political manifesto, and part memoir, writings like these seek to convey the activists' sincerity and forethought and reasonableness, their commitment and their conviction. More than mere descriptions of the actions, they are also proclamations of the "truth" about nuclear weapons and humans' responsibility to disarm them and thus a continuation of the Plowshares' prophetic task as they understand it. As such, they are rhetorical performances of the Plowshares' identity claims—a distributable version of the embodied performances of the actions. Central to the Plowshares' explanations of their actions are the ways they talk about themselves. To tell who they are, for the Plowshares, is to become who they are meant to be, which is crucial to the success of symbolic disarmament.

Persuasions and Performances

The Plowshares' rhetoric is primarily inclusive and expansive. Often it explicitly addresses peers in the Catholic Left or posits an imagined audience that shares its religiopolitical sensibilities, as when, in their introduction to *Swords into Plowshares*, editors Arthur Laffin and Anne Montgomery wrote that they hoped the book would help conscientious people choose which form of nonviolent resistance to pursue.[7] Identification of an audience precedes persuasion as rhetoric's first task, and the Plowshares indeed identify an audience of like-minded activists who are similarly motivated by a particular interpretation of Christianity and who understand the type of symbolic logic on which the Plowshares' actions rely. The Plowshares' inclusivity is also reflected in their published chronologies, which include writings not only from Plowshares activists about the nuclear issue but from activists working on other campaigns, such as U.S. involvement in Iraq, violence in Bosnia, or the School of the Americas. But at the same time that they suggest continuity between their work and other religious campaigns for peace, their rhetoric, like their actions, demarcates the Plowshares as occupying a special sociomoral space. Their rhetorical performances work by employing discursive domains that they share with their audiences and at the same time utilizing specific tropes and metaphors in the context of those domains, negotiating the interplay between inclusivity and exclusivity.

James Fernandez defines metaphor as a "strategic predication upon an inchoate pronoun (an I, a you, a we, a they) which makes a movement and leads to performance." The metaphors one assigns to oneself or others, for the sake of either adornment or disparagement, "provide images in relation to which the organization of behavior can take place." A would-be disparager (or adorner, though predications of disparagement are both more prominent in Fernandez's work and more relevant to the Plowshares' story) orients, through metaphor, a group or individual at the lowly end of whatever continuum is imaged for the domain employed ("jellyfish" is at the humble end of the continuum of purposiveness in the domain of sea creatures, to cite one of Fernandez's favorite examples). The group or individual may respond by pointing out what is still lower on that continuum (I may be a jellyfish, but at least I'm not an octopus), by asserting a supposedly higher place on the continuum (You say jellyfish; I say stingray), or by insisting that the supposedly negative predication is in fact not undesirable when compared to the other end of the continuum (Better a jellyfish than a shark!). The disparaged group or individual may also invoke another domain altogether and claim a less modest position within it.[8] These metaphoric strategies allow both the predicator and the predicated-upon—the would-be disparager and the disparaged—to position themselves and each other in social space, both rhetorically and performatively: pronouns often find ways to act out the predications attached to them by others or by themselves (as the Plowshares do).

In what follows I draw from books written by Plowshares activists, as well as action statements and letters and other writings from Plowshares activists in prison. Most of these writings (I note the exceptions) were intended for wide circulation within the Plowshares' circle of supporters; some were intended for outside audiences as well. The importance of different kinds of rhetoric for different constituencies—supporters versus detractors, for example—figures prominently in the strategy of many social movements and campaigns.[9] But the remarkable continuity evident between writings intended for family members or close friends, those intended for a wider audience of supporters, and those intended for outside readers (even detractors) speaks to the degree to which orientation toward a particular sense of identity shapes the meaning of success for the Plowshares. At the heart of that identity, and their project, is the theme of self-sacrifice, to which all these metaphors pertain. Because it is a theme that they share with their posited audience, at the center of the rhetorical domains they share with the wider Catholic resistance community, it sets the stage for the Plowshares' metaphorically driven movements in sociomoral space.

Martyrdom

Martyrs

In his 1987 autobiography Daniel Berrigan notes in a tone both casual and matter-of-fact, "It is common to serious Christians that they exist in the world as in a conscientious limbo, out of their element, walking uneasily."[10] Perhaps more than any other, this sentiment infuses his writing from the late sixties onward. The image of the serious Christian as uneasy in the world, an outsider, became essential for Philip at roughly the same time and later formed the core of his vision for the Plowshares. The trope of serious Christians as facing difficulty and disparagement continues to imbue the Plowshares' rhetoric, but what, precisely, are serious Christians? What does it mean to be uneasy in the world, and how do the Plowshares qualify as such? The Plowshares answer these questions in a myriad of ways, many of which tie back to Daniel Berrigan's theology.

When Philip and Daniel Berrigan began their resistance to the war in Vietnam, each was clear about his intent to marshal people to the cause and assemble a critical mass. Philip by all accounts was a natural leader; Daniel, more retiring by nature, still felt called to serve as a figure around which the student mobilization at Cornell could rally. Voicing dissent and working for reform had been part of the Berrigans' upbringing, but the model of "republican" public Catholicism to which their father adhered would come to be disavowed by both, not only as ineffectual but as a corroboration of the war-making state. Instead of large movements, intentional communities were to be the units of resistance. The support of a community was necessary for resisters, they deemed, because after Harrisburg they had come to accept as axiomatic that true Christian witness would always be subject to persecution and marginalization. Taking on the mantle of marginalization as a way to demonstrate the authenticity of one's witness had emerged strongly as a theme in the writings of both Berrigans by the end of the 1960s.[11]

Self-sacrifice + suffering

They shared that vocabulary of self-sacrifice and suffering with the larger Catholic Left. As Robert Orsi has argued, the "strange cosmos" of American Catholicism in general has always emphasized suffering, pain, and martyrdom, a language and worldview that shaped the urge toward civic engagement and ardent citizenship. The narrative of redemptive suffering has undergirded a different impulse as well, serving as the justification for a life of resistance to the civic order and the norms of citizenship. James Fisher notes the centrality of this language and imagery for the Catholic counterculture in America. He gives the birthdate of that counterculture as 1933, the year that Dorothy Day started the Catholic Worker movement with the publication of the first *Catholic Worker* newspaper. For Fisher, this event also marked the start of the period of "Catholic romanticism" in America. He calls Day the progenitor of this period, marked by a "gloomy" aspect deriving from its focus on self-abnegation. It was Day, argues Fisher, who brought to American Catholicism an intense zeal for mortification stemming from her interest in European literature, emblematic of her convert's "sophistication" that most Catholics born in America, largely working-class immigrants, did not share.[12]

Day's romanticism was an alternative to the triumphalism that characterized American Catholicism during those same years, as immigrants attempted to prove their Americanness (in many ways succeeding, as demonstrated by the election of John F. Kennedy to the presidency in 1960). In an explicit refusal of triumphalism, Day's romanticism emphasized the language of sacrifice and the idea of completing the martyrdom of Christ in one's own life. The language and ethos of self-abnegation became most explicit during the Catholic Worker retreats of the early 1940s that Fisher placed at the high tide of the movement, at the same time a period of controversy and steep attrition, when Day's absolute pacifism was rejected by many erstwhile supporters, as World War II loomed. But even as Catholic Worker houses closed or distanced themselves from the movement—or were distanced by Day herself—the retreats allowed for the concretization and dissemination of Day's theology, one that emphasized the need to assent to suffering and to become a victim alongside Christ.[13] Those associated with the Catholic Worker movement sought after these theological goals by embracing poverty and the social stigma that accompanied it.

The emphasis on a theology of self-abnegation created polarization within the Catholic Worker movement, but the Berrigans later would come to admire Day deeply for this theology, which she and they both understood as the foundation for her unflinching pacifist position even in the face of "public and ecclesiastical scrutiny . . . objection and obloquy even," as Daniel Berrigan characterized it. In an essay on Day written shortly after her 1980 death, Daniel wrote, "She read the words of Jesus, austere and uncompromising, concerning a faith that sunders families, breaks blood ties, violates nature at its marrow. All for the sake of a higher calling, the call of Christ, arranger and wrecker of lives . . . the gospel harrower." Day "resolved to taste the violence of American life, dreadfully apparent in marginal and expendable people," and exemplified solidarity with the outcast and downtrodden.[14] The Berrigan household subscribed to the *Catholic Worker* when Daniel and Philip were children, and Daniel described Day as an omnipresent though unnoticed influence "waiting" to introduce the Berrigans to a "sane and perennial Catholicism" when they became close associates during the Vietnam era.[15]

By that time Daniel's rhetoric was already being shaped by what he understood as banishment by his Jesuit superiors, and through the late sixties and seventies the theme of "social death" became prominent in his writings, as both symbol and prescription. In 1971 Daniel published *The Dark Night of Resistance*, written while he was evading arrest for burning draft cards at Catonsville in 1968. Based on mystic Saint John of the Cross's *Dark Night of the Soul*, a sixteenth-century poem that emphasizes self-abnegation—the *via purgativa*—as the necessary path to union with God, the text is an extended meditation on a new paradigm of moral protest, in which resistance to the state and the church is total, and one undergoes social death to become a "new man" through whom a regenerated society will be catalyzed. As an evocative statement of the theology at the heart of the Plowshares' actions, it bears quoting at some length:

> To save the earth and those who dwell upon the earth . . . it might be necessary to go under the earth. To go underground . . . to resign from America, in order to join the heart of man . . .
>
> I am no more sure than others of what may be the physiognomy of the "new man." But . . . what is to be done, in accord with the truth of things, has something to do with the unmentionable fact of death.
>
> And its analogies. Which are so to speak the political facts of life today: imprisonment, jeopardy, legal pressure, refusal of tax payments, refusal of war-related emoluments and jobs, etc., economic insecurity for one's self and family. . . .
>
> What will he be like? A man of integrity, which is to say, a man with two sides, inner and outer. A contemplative, intellectual, artist; a man of skills and worthwhile intention; a public man, whose life is on the line; whose moral sense includes the mysterious sense of when and how to die. When best, how best, with all the implications of that, for public weal, for the victims.[16]

The "dead man" is the person underground, the prisoner for justice; both are emblems of the truth of resigning America. For Daniel and later for the Plowshares, metaphors of social death locate true Christian witness at the margins of society and church, where only a few will venture; but those few, by virtue of their commitment and sacrifice, hold the keys to a new world order.

The tropes of social death and marginality turn martyrdom into metaphor—self-sacrifice, for the Plowshares, is indeed a sacrifice, but it is enacted socially rather than physically. Following his time in Latin America, Daniel wrote copiously on martyrdom, expressing solidarity with the Jesuits struggling for an end to injustices, and often for their lives, in the countries he visited. Many of these became literal martyrs, of course, but Daniel expanded the category of martyrdom into the realm of metaphor. The church must embrace its responsibility to remember the martyrs, he wrote, and that task falls to the small faithful contingent among the larger church, who, in serving as the "martyrs' living witness" become martyrs themselves: "When the highest authorities of the church refuse to vindicate our martyrs, and thus refuse to confront the powers clearly and unequivocally, only the local community of faith can supply for the moral deficit." There is continuity "between the witness of those who die and those who survive. Both speak up, both pay dearly, some in blood, some in the bearing of infamy and danger."[17] Thus, solidarity is not theoretical; rather, the community of faith is called to be a community of martyrs in its own way: socially dead in relation to a culture of death. "A man is of no use to the future unless the full force of the present world has turned him inside out, like a pocket before a mugger and his knife, stripped clean!"[18] Daniel's language renders unmistakable an oppositional stance with respect to the "present world."

That theological vision, based on an orientation toward self-sacrifice and uneasiness in the world, served as a framework for Philip's resistance in general, and specifically for the Plowshares, within which Daniel is celebrated as a central figure though he participated only in the first action.[19] Thus, unlike some of the accusations I discuss later (prisoner, bad parent), the designation of "martyr" is not imposed externally but insisted on by the Plowshares themselves. Self-sacrifice is the way to be a true Christian for the Plowshares and for their larger Catholic resistance community, following the model of a particularly characterized Jesus, as opposed to the church that, again in Daniel's words, "has forgotten. She literally does not know what [Jesus] is talking about."[20]

Describing themselves in terms of self-sacrifice, the Plowshares place themselves at the positive end of the spectrum of self-sacrifice in the domain of Christian, and especially Catholic, witness. It is worth nothing that their direct linkage between literal martyrs and themselves bypasses the category of the "confessor," who is persecuted but not killed for the faith. "Confessor" would be a literal designation for the Plowshares; "martyr" is a metaphoric one that suggests a claim to moral stature. As such it is seized on by detractors who use "martyr" as a pejorative term, signifying ineffectiveness and self-righteousness.[21] Because of its central place in the rhetoric of the Plowshares and of their detractors, the Plowshares must work to protect their own, internal characterization of "martyrdom" from external characterizations that would undermine it. Notably, the Plowshares respond to disparaging applications of the term with metaphors from a new domain. Philip and McAlister use the metaphors of the sentry and the shepherd, taken from Hebrew and Christian scriptures, to turn "martyr" into an appellation that signifies action and courage rather than passivity:

> From a Judaic view, the prophetic vocation is essentially to become a sentry who communicated God's warning of "sword" to the people. The overall metaphor [in Ezekiel 33:1–6] is that of war . . . but the context discloses that "wickedness" inspires war. The sentry's warning to the people is therefore against wickedness and its lethal companion, the sword. The warning is against war—its roots, its paraphernalia, its consequences. Christ's view of the Good Shepherd clarifies the divine charge laid upon the Jewish sentry. The shepherds are those who lay down their lives for the sheep. . . . Many prefer silence, selling themselves, running away. Most refuse to leave the majority, the rank and file, the flock or herd, to become a sentry or shepherd. . . . The texts from Ezechiel and John lay solemn emphasis on a loving, gentle resistance against wickedness and violence. But if the sentry sees war coming and fails to sound a warning, so that the people are killed, God will hold the sentry responsible for their deaths. . . . Those summoned to God's revelation are sentries and shepherds. We see war or wolf and cry out against the peril, even with our lives. . . . The good shepherd *lays down his life for the sheep.*

The idea of laying down one's life also functions metaphorically for the Plowshares, referring as it does not to literal death but to a life of marginalization—Daniel's social death, which "most refuse" when it entails leaving the majority. Yet it is crucial to the Plowshares' theology that they not remain embedded within larger society. After all, wrote Philip and McAlister in their description of the Plowshares Eight action, those activists "did the truth with a generosity of spirit on behalf of us all." They had knowledge of "Light" and the "truth" that allowed them to see what was good and just and to sacrifice themselves as surrogates for the rest of humanity.[22]

Dean Hammer wrote after his action, "We could have gone in there, did [*sic*] our deed, and left. . . . We went out to Hangar Road to take responsibility for our actions. From a Biblical perspective, we have laid down our lives."[23] Plowshares activists depict self-sacrifice as an active endeavor rather than a passive one, turning it into an orienting value with which they legitimate their actions and through which other forms of marginalization take on value.[24] They did not originate the language of self-sacrifice, nor a theology and lifestyle based on it, but they have placed the trope of "martyr" firmly at the center of their discursive world, from which their other ways of talking about themselves develop.

Prisoners and Criminals

"What sort of society would call these women criminals?" The question is posed on the Jonah House website, next to a picture of grandmotherly Ardeth Platte and Carol Gilbert, gray-haired and smiling beatifically at the camera.[25] Even as the labels are questioned, "criminal" and "prisoner" are central to the Plowshares' identity. Though the accusations themselves are literal—the activists have indeed committed crimes and don't deny it, and they have gone to prison—the Plowshares respond to them and use them in ways that rely upon theologically grounded metaphor. Most often, prison is coded as the "social death" by which the activists align themselves with the persecuted and crucified Jesus. Prison is where the Plowshares understand their ideas about the necessity of self-sacrifice to be actualized, making jail an authentication of their witness, associated not with failure or ineffectiveness but with sincerity and commitment. In a notable switch back from the Berrigans' move away from this aspect of traditional civil disobedience during the Vietnam years, Philip wrote of the biblical precedent for arrest and prison as consequences of Christian living: "The Acts of the Apostles: In nearly every chapter we have a record of harassment, ostracism, torture, flogging, imprisonment, and execution. Like Christ, the disciples preached and lived a new way of justice, peace, love, freedom. The status quo, the Powers, the pharaohs found this intolerable and threatening. . . . Many of the N[ew]

T[estament] letters were written in prison. John, the author of Revelation, wrote it as a prisoner at Patmos. Thus goes our tradition."[26]

During their prison sentences Plowshares understand themselves to be embodying their theological and political commitments, specifically their orientation toward self-sacrifice. As much as the action itself, the prison term serves as a deeply authenticating moment for the Plowshares, wherein a number of their goals are realized. Elizabeth McAlister wrote that upon learning as a young nun, before her activist days, of Bernard of Clairvaux's prison conversion to Christ, "I thought then, that for me to become 'holy' I would need such a jail experience. But it seemed utter fantasy then that such would be my lot. Reality being stranger than fantasy, I have seen the insides of a goodly number of jails but without the experience of becoming holy."[27] Prison time may not cultivate holiness, but it is theologically crucial nonetheless. A Plowshares action is potent in itself for resacralizing unholy materials and landscapes and for providing the means of self-sacrifice, but prison is the necessary culmination of the action because it is the embodied, corporeal analog to the theological statements made during the action. The category of "social death" functions theologically, as an apt and effective metaphor for martyrdom, only insomuch as it has social authenticity, achieved in prison.

The role of prison in the Plowshares' theology and identity has led to the critique that the activists want to go to prison, which Philip and McAlister have attempted to counter: "Contrary to the assumptions of some, we do not seek prison or persecution. But we do try to accept unpleasant consequences when they occur—and to learn from them." They add, "We believe it is inaccurate to equate prison with persecution, especially in this country. North American prisons are not like the Gulag the Soviet dissidents experience."[28] But only a few pages later in the same text, they explicitly link prison with Jesus's crucifixion and write, "The crucifixion articulates God's odd freedom, his strange justice, his peculiar power. It lets us know that without the Cross, without suffering and persecution, our peacemaking is apt to become as strident and destructive as the war making it criticizes. The Cross, suffering, and persecution become the insurance policy, *our only real credential, a guarantee even, of discipleship*."[29] In the latter passage prison clearly is understood as persecution and suffering, and persecution and suffering are understood as useful, even necessary, even if not "sought." The discrepancy reflects an awareness that their marginalization is, while not sought, also not wholly imposed (though prison is surely an imposition, they specifically undertake actions where prison will be the result); the comparison to the Soviet gulag acknowledges that there is some choice and agency involved, and marginality is, at least to some degree, cultivated. Yet to fully acknowledge that prison comes about because of their own agency undermines the claim of persecution. Thus, it is necessary for the Plowshares to emphasize what a difficult choice they make when they decide to undertake actions assumed to lead to prison. They do so when countering the accusation that they are bad parents for leaving their children to go to jail.

Parents

The choice to commit actions that will most likely lead to prison sentences is a difficult one, according to the Plowshares' rhetoric, in large part because it entails separation from loved ones. Leaving their children is especially painful, and it also garners society's disapproval. The predication of "bad parents" who leave their children to go to prison is among the most frequent accusations leveled against Plowshares activists. Plowshares activists turn this disapproval into a positive identity marker, countering the accusation that the activists are bad parents for leaving their children when they go to jail with a strongly developed rhetoric that explains the actions as part and parcel of good parenting. Plowshares activists with children perform their actions, they say, precisely for the sake of those children.

Perhaps no one has faced the accusation of bad parenting more than Helen Woodson, a single mother of eleven children, ten of them adopted or foster children who are mentally or physically handicapped. She was a participant in the 1984 Silo Pruning Hooks action that, due to its tactics, generated unheard-of sentences. Woodson, whose sentencing judge called her irresponsible and a freeloader as he castigated her for abandoning her children, faced eighteen years in prison and refused every opportunity to have the sentence reduced. Her usual response to accusations of bad parenting linked the development of her activist conscience to the birth of her son, as in a newspaper profile written six years into her sentence: "Every single generation of parents had said to their children, 'We will bring peace into the world.' . . . And every generation—we sent them out to die on the battlefields. Now I had a son. Was he going to die 18 years from then? And what about his son?"[30] For the reasons detailed in the previous chapter, Woodson is not an altogether typical Plowshares activist. In many ways she is a problematic Plowshares activist. As a single parent, her approach to parenting differs from those high-risk activists, including Plowshares, who undertake their actions only when a co-parent is not in jail so that one parent is always available to the children.[31] Yet the sentiments she expresses about performing her action for her children, and her children's children, are entirely typical.

Virtually without exception, the Plowshares' press releases, pamphlets, communications from prison, and trial testimonies include the explicit statement that the action was performed not only for the sake of the activists' children but also for the children of the world, as when Susan Crane, in the letter with which this chapter begins, stated that she acted after she "read about the children who have mirasmas [marasmus] because of the sanctions, and cancer because of the depleted uranium and other poisons that result from the war." Crane attached to this letter, intended for wide circulation, a message specifically addressed to Wailifa, an Iraqi woman whose photograph Crane kept on her wall in prison:

> I have a picture of you that I see every day . . . of you and your child, Makarum, in the Saddam Pediatric Hospital in Baghdad. . . . Like you, I am a mother, and I feel tremendously grieved that the country I live in is waging war against you and your children.
>
> I don't know if anything I could say to you would convey how sorry I am. The best I can imagine is to go up to one of the war planes—like the ones used against you and your family—and begin to hammer on it so that it can no longer be used for war. The plane—the A-10 Warthog—is the one that spread much of the 350 tons of radioactive depleted uranium in Iraq, and it has been used to enforce the sanctions. We know that depleted uranium causes sickness and cancer, particularly to children like Makarum.[32]

Crane's account of her action as tied foremost to her identity as a mother and her desire to help all children typifies the Plowshares' counters to the frequent accusation that they are irresponsible parents, with the self-characterization of caretakers to the world's children.

Many Plowshares activists are in fact parents and frame their actions as ways to be good parents to their own children, as did Woodson and Crane and as did Agnes Bauerlein when she wrote, after her 1983 action, "I now can foresee a world for my children and grandchildren. . . . I simply decided that raising and nurturing eleven children was too much of an investment to leave unguarded. In opting for a life without nuclear weapons, I decided to take action myself and not let the future of my family be decided by someone else. I also wanted my children to know that questioning authority is right and that actions of conscience should be the norm." And Kathy Boylan wrote from prison following her 1993 action, "I am a mother of five sons. Many years ago, I saw a poster of a mother pushing a baby carriage through a beautiful park, but just beneath the lush grass, thousands of nuclear missiles pointed skyward. It had a powerful impact on me because I identified with the poster. All I was doing for my children would be meaningless if I didn't act to dismantle the weapons threatening all humanity." Metaphor comes into play when activists describe themselves not only as being good parents to their own children, but caretakers to all the children of the world. Crane suggested this metaphoric move when she described her action in terms of tending to Wailifa's child Makarum; McAlister stated it explicitly when she wrote that her own children are "symbols for us of all the little people for whom we are responsible."[33] Detaching from control and possession of her own children (to leave them in the care of the community, where they would forge other special bonds while their mother was in prison) became its own lesson and value for McAlister, at once a test of commitment and an opportunity for growth. The metaphor of being a caretaker to the world's children is so central to the group's rhetoric that even those who are not literally parents at all—priests and nuns, for example, against whom accusations of bad parenting could not be made—invoke it to a degree. Sister Ardeth Platte, for example, declared in her opening statement during her trial for a 2002 action, "All we could think about were the babies, the children, who had no defense."[34]

For the Plowshares being a good parent is explicitly linked to self-sacrifice and hardship, for it is only truly possible when one has faced marginality and social death. As Woodson wrote, "When I left my beloved children, friends and home to do these actions, I knew I would never return. Many old friends have dropped out of contact, I have a daughter-in-law and grandchildren whom I've never met. . . . Serious resistance is serious business."[35]

Changing Metaphors

As the Plowshares near the end of their fourth decade—as the participants age and dwindle in number, and the urgencies of the nuclear issue shift—accusations of foolishness and ineffectiveness often replace those of criminalization. In turn, the Plowshares assert that their authenticity and efficacy depend on precisely this appearance of ineffectiveness, for it is symbolic witness, undertaken by a small group of true Christians, which will bring about the Kingdom of God. The Plowshares' ideology emphasizes that their actions must seem ineffective as a necessary condition for their actually being effective. Correspondingly, in their rhetoric they emphasize that the actions are performed by groups whose small size seems, at first glance, to render them useless. That sentiment echoes throughout their action statements, which frequently reiterate the (small) number of activists taking part in the action: "the three of us," "we five," "the nine of us," and so on. Action statements also emphasize a distinct "we," in the repeated use of phrases such as "We act in obedience to the prophets. . . . We act in obedience to the law of love," "We who are faithful," and "Governments have proved themselves incapable of respecting the sacredness of human life. We declare our independence from this suicidal course of history," to give only a few representative examples. These phrasings place agency and efficacy in the hands of a select few, denying that failure is indicated by having only five or nine (or fewer) participants in an action and countering the charge that small groups are ineffective. Instead, small numbers become a mark of valor and distinction from the sinful masses. The Plowshares do not use the language of being chosen, but rather of having made a very difficult choice that they do not expect others to emulate.

Another way of countering accusations of inefficacy has been through "fools for Christ" language, by which the specific disparagement of foolishness is refashioned. As the activists in the 2006 Weapons of Mass Destruction Here Plowshares action, who dressed as clowns, wrote in their statement, "We dress as clowns to show that humor and laughter are key elements in the struggle to transform the structures of destruction and death. Saint Paul said that we are 'fools for God's sake,' and we say that we are 'fools for God and humanity.' Clowns as court jesters were sometimes the only ones able to survive after speaking truth to authorities in power."[36] Thus, being foolish comes with its own special efficacy. And Paul Kabat countered the accusation of inefficacy by linking his action's lack of impact with dying children who go unnoticed: "In spite of my fantasies I do not expect my act or my resulting years in prison will have any cosmic effect on history, just as I am aware that the quiet deaths of many children in fourth world situations around the world make any real difference to us Americans and especially to the political and economic leaders of our nation. Millions of children phase out silently and are buried in obscurity. So also we will not be much noted as time and events go by."[37] Success is measured instead by necessarily small groups taking actions that they expect will require self-sacrifice. It is that self-sacrifice that is equated with success—to sacrifice oneself is to do the proper work of God—such that any punishment or response that marginalizes the activists, whether by criminalizing or trivializing, is incorporated into their idea of what it means to be effective. In an excerpt from a Christmas newsletter sent from prison, Plowshares activists wrote,

> There is a tiny bush directly in front of our prison camp which on December 2nd was covered with swelling buds and was bravely waving two fuscia [*sic*] blossoms in the cold 30 degree breeze. This struck us as an especially apt kind of symbol for the Plowshares movement. In the midst of our world's rampant violence and the out-of-control nuclear arms race, we seek—against all odds, against all pundits of popular common sense—to spread our faith and hope that peace and disarmament are possible now. Two thousand years ago there was little hope for world peace and justice. And the night was cold when God laid all our hopes on the birth of a helpless child in a manger—against all odds, out of season.[38]

The "against the odds" nature of the actions, often ridiculed by detractors, is at the core of the Plowshares' vision and their rhetoric. "Success in not measured by passing notoriety or some kind of public acceptance," wrote Paul Kabat.[39] It is measured, rather, by commitment to a biblical vision in which Jesus was martyred for political resistance, prophets are cast out for speaking the truth, and a righteous remnant of true Christians will bring about a new world order. Like their embodied performances, which situate them at the virtuosic end of the spectrum of high-risk activism, the Plowshares' rhetorical performances serve to locate them within the discursive domain that they share with the larger Catholic resistance community, at the virtuosic end of a continuum of roles by which one participates in that biblical vision.

The Plowshares' rhetoric undertakes what sociologists David Snow and Leon Anderson have called identity work, or "the range of activities individuals engage in to create, present, and sustain personal identities that are congruent with and supportive of the self-concept." Personal identity refers to meanings attributed to the self by an actor, whereas a self-concept also reflects social identities or the meanings assigned by others. Identity work tries to resolve discrepancies between the two, not least through "identity talk," or the verbal construction and assertion of identity claims.[40] As an example of identity talk, the Plowshares' rhetoric works to take control of public perceptions, imputing them with meanings consistent with the activists' own sense of self. But the Plowshares' theology, based on the necessity of worldly actualization of spiritual ideals, calls for more than rhetorical constructions of identity claims and metaphoric placement in social space. In addition to crafting a rhetoric that communicates their vision of themselves, the Plowshares feel a pressing need to instantiate a social identity congruent with the personal identity expressed in their rhetoric.

The Plowshares label and the designation of symbolic disarmament depend on the combination of potent elements, reclaimed from the rituals of the Catholic Church and traditional civil disobedience and re-marked through spatial and symbolic innovation. They depend on the motivations behind the use of those particular elements and on a particular understanding of what the outcomes will be and what they will mean. But they also depend on how the activists understand their own roles in performing the actions, the personal characteristics that the actions require and the ones they cultivate and bestow, and the dissemination of those identity claims through retellings of the actions. These retellings complete the actions, and they continue, dramatically, in the courtroom, where behavior joins rhetoric for some of the Plowshares' most complex boundary performances.

They need to act out how they view themselves.

4 "Just to Speak the Truth"

The Plowshares' Theory of the Case

At seven thirty in the morning on October 6, 2002, Dominican nuns Ardeth Platte, Carol Gilbert, and Jackie Hudson, dressed in white jumpsuits they had stenciled with the words "Disarmament Specialists and Citizens Weapons Inspection Team," cut the fence surrounding a missile silo in Greeley, Colorado, a site where several Plowshares actions before and since theirs have taken place. Platte, Gilbert, and Hudson kept to traditional Plowshares tactics. They used household hammers to beat on the silos and poured their blood over the area in the shape of crosses, to "unmask the false religion and worship of national security," as they wrote in their action statement.[1] With time to spare, they cut the fence in several more places. Guards apprehended them praying at the site about an hour later.

In their various accounts of what the three sisters called the Sacred Earth and Space II action, Platte, Gilbert, and Hudson emphasized, as do many Plowshares activists, the time that elapsed before they were apprehended. This discursive tactic is one way that Plowshares activists emphasize their commitment, countering the indeterminacy of the action's denouement with their own determination to wait actively for the consequences, whatever they may be. Consequences matter deeply for the integrity and efficacy of the actions; waiting for them matters deeply for the integrity and efficacy of the activists themselves. In this chapter and the next I unpack the significance of consequences, specifically legal consequences, within the Plowshares' project. Plowshares activists do not always have the chance to "get away with" their actions, but on the frequent occasions that they do, why don't they choose to do so? Why didn't Platte, Gilbert, and Hudson, after successfully enacting the three key elements of a symbolic disarmament, simply let themselves out the same careful way they had entered? If, after all, part of the Plowshares' intent is to point out that nuclear weapons do not deserve our worship because, rather than offering protection, they constitute an enormous risk to humankind, wouldn't getting away with it—gaining access to the sites of nuclear manufacture and storage and then disappearing without being caught—nicely demonstrate this point?

97

The military's use of the opposite discursive tactic, stressing that activists were quickly apprehended after the actions, suggests that, at the very least, longer wait times cause official embarrassment. In the past, during Philip and Daniel Berrigan's famous Vietnam War–era disappearing acts, that kind of embarrassment had proven an effective rallying point for the Catholic Left, in addition to increasing the brothers' notoriety. But the Catonsville and Harrisburg trials gave Philip a different idea about what could be accomplished not by getting away with civil disobedience but in facing legal consequences. By the time of the Plowshares Eight action, the defendants insisted on going to trial despite their suspicion that they would be imprisoned for life, refusing an offer to have all thirteen charges dropped if they would promise not to get arrested for the next six months. The terms of the bargain were unthinkable for such committed activists, but they also recognized that the trial could serve important purposes. As I argue in the next two chapters, the Plowshares' trials are distinct yet continuous components of their actions, functioning as public arenas for communicating about ideology and identity. In the courtroom Plowshares activists can disseminate their ideas about nuclear weapons more widely than the reach of their pamphlets and newsletters allows, and even though it very often looks as though the Plowshares are being silenced in the courtroom, prevented from talking about the events under examination in the moral and political terms that they would prefer, their rhetorical choices combine with a repertoire of behaviors and gestures that allow them not only to communicate but also to enact their identity claims.

THE PLOWSHARES' THEORY OF THE CASE

The courtroom serves as an important locus for the constitution as well as the expression of the Plowshares' religious identity claims for several reasons. The Plowshares' trials almost always end in guilty verdicts and prison sentences, which allow the activists to identify with Jesus. Serving those prison sentences allows for the realization of social forms that the Plowshares and their wider resistance community consider to be crucial in bringing about a better world order. For the most part Plowshares activists do not believe that serving a prison sentence—or several—will result in the overturning of nuclear policy, at least not any time soon, but the rhetoric surrounding their prison sentences reveals that they *do* regard those sentences as powerfully effective, and not only by providing an avenue for living out a particular theology. Prison sentences also have measurable, positive effects on the social networks to which the activists belong, as the exigencies of prison force the activists' communities to put into practice certain principles central to their resistance lifestyle, such as shared child rearing. McAlister related that days before the action for which she would spend time in prison (the sixth Plowshares action, in 1983), she and Philip watched a movie about nuclear destruction with their three young children—ages nine, eight, and two at the time—and talked about their mother's upcoming action.

> I would probably be in jail for some time and apart from them. . . . Both of the older children said that they understood, in a new way, why this resistance was so necessary. They were willing to accept the personal sacrifice of my absence as their part in trying to stop a nuclear war from happening; as their part in trying to avoid the suffering that the movie displayed. . . . They committed themselves to assume more responsibility around the house and be especially helpful in dealing with the questions and fears of their little sister who was not able to understand as they were. It was a moment of extreme closeness for the four of us; a moment of accepting together whatever might come down; and we concluded our conversation with prayer and big, big hugs.

Like other Plowshares parents, McAlister regarded her prison sentence as an opportunity to teach her children by example, but also to widen the circle of resistance by characterizing her children's hardship as a sacrifice of the sort that true resistance entails. McAlister continued, "While they fear prolonged separation, they are proud of their mom and of themselves, for sharing something of the suffering of children in less privileged environments."[2] Prison sentences require the enactment of solidarity, not only on the part of the prisoners themselves, but on the part of their loved ones: their children who are brave and strong along with their parents and the community members who, in a parents' stead, do the work of parenting. Through tangible effects on the community as an entity, imprisoned community members help to bring communal ideals to fruition, such as the new family model that is key to the better world the Plowshares envision. The legal sphere serves as the engine behind those important consequences.

Beyond assigning consequences, the legal sphere is crucial as an arena for public communication about ideology and identity—the threat of nuclear weapons, the responsibility to confront them, the intention with which the defendants did so, and their commitment to meeting consequences actively rather than hiding from them. For the defendants, these themes amalgamate into a unified truth to the events in question during the trial. It is that truth they are attempting to disseminate during their trials, as in the actions themselves, and it has little to do with facts or verdicts. It has to do, rather, with sincerity, responsibility, and obedience to a more binding justice than that of the courts, and it has to do with occupying the roles to which they feel called: sentries, witnesses, good parents, martyrs, and more. In the courtroom, defendants actively and inventively take on those roles.

Communicating the Truth

During a Plowshares trial held over two days in December 2009, jury members were allowed a rare opportunity: to question sole defendant Carl Kabat directly about his decision to cut the fence surrounding a missile silo in Greeley, Colorado (the same one that Platte, Gilbert, and Hudson had targeted in their Sacred Earth and Space II action) and trespass onto the site, wearing his trademark clown costume, to beat on the silo with a household hammer. It was Kabat's second time trespassing at that particular silo. The octogenarian priest had also performed a similar action at another nearby silo in 2000, in addition to several other Plowshares actions, including the first in 1980.[3] For the 2009 action he was charged with criminal mischief and trespassing and faced three to twelve months in prison if convicted. (He was convicted and sentenced to time served.) Kabat began the trial with defense attorneys, friends to the Plowshares who had been involved in several other trials, but he dismissed them during the trial in the hopes that he would be freer to speak about nuclear weapons on his own. As legal professionals, even

[handwritten margin note: Carl Kabat, age 80, tried for hammering silo in a clown suit.]

supportive defense attorneys often feel bound to norms of the court that the defendants themselves, as the next chapter shows, typically reject. The prosecution, however, continually objected to his attempts to do so. Kabat, in turn, refused to continue his testimony, at which point the judge invited the jury to ask questions individually. In responding to many of these questions (for example, why didn't he protest outside the fence rather than cutting through it and trespassing?), Kabat was able to speak more fully about motives and morals and about the destructive potential of nuclear weapons than he had been allowed in his testimony.[4] Kabat had a much freer chance to "witness"—to enact the role of a sentry crying out against the danger of nuclear annihilation and the evil of a government that places idolatrous faith in nuclear weapons—than Plowshares defendants usually do.

They want to tell their story.

As in the actions themselves, at the foundation of the Plowshares' trials there lies a deep desire to communicate—about nuclear weapons and about their decision to symbolically disarm them, even at the risk of significant consequences. Plowshares activists see their trials not only as the inevitable result of civil disobedience but as welcome opportunities to bring their actions and their theological and political messages to a wider audience. The trials, which typically receive more media attention than the actions and include the participation of outside constituencies (legal personnel, juries, reporters), render the actions themselves visible, bringing some measure of public attention to events that would otherwise go largely unnoticed. They provide an opportunity for the activists to explain actions that are often misconstrued, even by those who observe them firsthand. Even while questioning the authority of the court system, Plowshares activists grant and even rely on the courtroom's utility as a space for communicating about their religiopolitical goals.

The Plowshares' aim in the courtroom is not to dispute the facts of the events for which they are being prosecuted. Rather, to the continual frustration of their prosecutors and judges, they attempt to use their trials as opportunities to decry the nation's reliance on nuclear weapons (which they characterize as idolatry) and to educate the public about the danger posed by the weapons themselves. The aftermath of Platte, Gilbert, and Hudson's Sacred Earth and Space II trial illustrates the Plowshares' pedagogical intent. At the trial's conclusion the three defendants were found guilty on two charges, destruction of property and interfering with national defense. But they sought acquittal for only the second of these charges.[5] Their grievance was not with a guilty verdict (all three sisters consider spending time in prison to be part of their vocation) but rather with the particular charge itself, troubling to the defendants because it rested on an explicit characterization of nuclear weapons as "national defense"—exactly the characterization that the activists are attempting to resist in the actions and their trials and against which they aim to educate anyone who will listen.

Thus, while the Plowshares do not expect that their trials will receive wide media coverage or public attention (though some, in fact, do), they do characterize them as the arena in which at least a judge and jury will learn about their actions, their intentions, and their ideologies. During their trials they can explain actions that may seem baffling or silly or frightening or pointless to outsiders, ideally raising questions about nuclear arms along the way. Plowshares activists rely on the actions themselves to communicate on a level deeper than reason rather than to convey information. Conversely, it becomes immediately apparent from an examination of Plowshares trial transcripts that information is, here, precisely what they want to convey— information about international law as they understand it, about nuclear weapons, about what they believe God requires of humans and what they believe their own role to be in confronting nuclear idolatry.

"Truth," however, refers also to what the activists consider to be the truth about themselves: their motivation, their character, what they hope to represent and become during the actions. In March 2000 four Plowshares activists stood trial in Baltimore County Circuit Court for their 1999 Plowshares Versus Depleted Uranium action, which targeted Maryland's Warfield Air National Guard Base and its A-10 Thunderbird aircraft, intended to deploy weapons tipped with radioactive depleted uranium, probably to Iraq. Of the four activists, three were recidivists. The trial was familiar territory for them, except for one considerable surprise: a criminal assault charge leveled at one of the defendants, Susan Crane, who previously had stood trial for Plowshares as well as numerous other civil disobedience actions. As a resident of Jonah House she had provided support for several other Plowshares actions and was well versed in the ordinary contours of a Plowshares trial. But the charge of assault was unexpected (assault charges had been brought against the Plowshares Eight, but not against defendants since), and it deeply rattled Crane, who was charged with threatening or actually attacking one of the officers at the base. The four were convicted of the other, more standard destruction of property charge, but the assault charge was eventually dropped. Even the officer who had claimed to have been assaulted seemed visibly uncomfortable with the incongruity between the assault charge and Crane's quiet, gentle demeanor (and, perhaps, her advanced age). But until it was dropped, Crane, ordinarily composed on the stand, broke down every time the assault charge was brought up, so appalling to her was the idea of it and so counter to the group's nonviolent ideals.

Because the trial was held in Baltimore, the epicenter of the Atlantic Life Community, the trial was especially well attended by members of the Catholic resistance network. And because Philip Berrigan was one of the defendants, it received a good deal of media coverage, beyond the local sources to which coverage of Plowshares trials is most often limited. Probably this latter feature of the trial heightened Crane's chagrin at the assault charge, as she would have been upset at the possibility of casting any doubt on the Plowshares' commitment to nonviolence that would be picked up by the media presence. (The Plowshares have little faith that the media will portray them accurately or fairly anyway, but no doubt they would hate to give the media a reason to portray them in a light so counter to their goals.) Any doubt cast on the Plowshares' absolute commitment to nonviolence would undermine the activists and their actions, rendering the courtroom less effective as a pedagogical arena.

Crane's dismayed response to the assault charge indicates the degree to which the Plowshares wish their motives and ideologies to be apprehended correctly before the court, in response to God's mandate to make themselves heard as sentries and prophets. In a letter written to friends while she awaited sentencing, Helen Woodson plainly conveyed her concern with proper apprehension:

> I got my pre-sentence report. . . . I know you'll be pleased by how they describe "Plowshares." "They enact the biblical prophecies of Isaiah 2:4 and Micah 4:3 to 'beat swords into plowshares . . . ' The main symbols used in plowshares actions are hammers and blood. Hammers are used to literally begin the process of disarmament that thousands of talks and numerous treaties have failed to accomplish. The hammer is used to take apart as well as create and to point to the urgency for conversion of war production to products that enhance life. The blood symbolizes the mass killing that weapons of mass destruction can inflict, as well as the murderous cost they now impose on the poor. Blood speaks too of humanity and the willingness to give one's life rather than to take life." *This beautiful description is now part of the official documents of the courts of the U.S.* (The PSI report, or Pre-Sentencing Report, is written by the federal probation officer and given to both the defendant, US attorney and judge before sentencing . . . *What is written in the PSI is supposed to be true.*)[6]

Woodson's obvious pleasure at the court's official recognition of her deepest commitments indicates the degree to which she wishes to be apprehended properly—"truthfully" with regard to what she did and why she did it. Woodson wrote this letter while awaiting trial for the later actions that distanced her from the Plowshares, as discussed in chapter 2, but the fact that the Jonah House website includes this portion of her letter as an important Plowshares document demonstrates that her concern with proper apprehension of the truth of a Plowshares action is widely shared by other Plowshares activists.

The Sacred Earth and Space II Opening Statement

Ardeth Platte expressed the same concern with proper apprehension in her opening statement for the Sacred Earth and Space II trial. Platte, Gilbert, and Hudson went to trial in April 2003, charged with interfering with the national defense and causing property damage in excess of one thousand dollars. Likely because of their action's proximity to the September 11 attacks, they faced sentences of up to thirty years and $500,000 in fines if convicted on both counts—an unheard-of sentence that many supporters and neutral observers saw as deeply incongruous with the character and motives of the three defendants. Plowshares activists, while cleaving to the ideal of Christian nonviolence, have at times manifested that ideal with confrontational tactics; often they say they are recalling the example of Jesus's angry rampage in the temple. Later in this chapter and the next I examine episodes of noncompliance that regularly take place during the Plowshares' trials, by which the activists demonstrate their lack of attachment to the court's norms and decisions. Platte, Gilbert, and Hudson, however, were anything but confrontational during the Sacred Earth and Space II trial.

At the time of their 2002 action, Platte was sixty-six, Gilbert was fifty-four, and Hudson was sixty-seven. All three had been Dominican nuns for most of their lives. All three had participated in Plowshares actions prior to the Sacred Earth and Space II action, and Platte and Gilbert have committed more actions since. The three nuns have spoken of their repeated participation in Plowshares actions as their ministry and vocation, bound up with the work of ministering to the poor and performing the works of mercy. Following their action all three described themselves as "missioned" to peace and justice work that included their Plowshares action as well as other peace activism. Of the Plowshares action in particular, Hudson explained that she hoped to "enflesh the spirit of TRUTH, which is the hallmark of Dominican spirituality." Similarly, Gilbert hoped to "enflesh the spirit of Dominican life."[7] With these statements they articulated what many vowed Plowshares have expressed over the years, though not always with the support of their orders. At times Plowshares activists have faced direct rebuke from their orders as a result of their actions, but Platte, Hudson, and Gilbert's Dominican community has come out strongly in support of the Plowshares nuns. An atypically wide swath of the public also heard about the action and voiced support for the three nuns when the stringent sentences they faced generated a good deal of local and national publicity. So when Sister Ardeth delivered her opening statement in Denver's federal court (she chose to represent herself, like many Plowshares activists), she did so before judge and jury as well as throngs of supporters and media drawn by the prospect of such lengthy sentences for what was widely characterized in the press as a peaceful protest, carried out by three admirably devout and eminently nonthreatening women.

The trial's many spectators were to observe a prototypical example of a jury trial as described by legal scholar Robert Burns: ongoing discursive struggles between prosecution and defense over their competing moral interpretations of the events at hand rather than the facts of those events. In Burns's model the components of a jury trial interact to convey a particular "theory of the case," a "simple, plausible, coherent, legally sufficient narrative that can easily be integrated with a moral theme."[8] The jury, in the course of a trial, chooses between two opposing moral, not evidentiary, explanations of the act being tried, and the jury's eventual decision reveals that choice. To establish and sustain a particular theory of the case, the argumentative elements of the trial, from opening statements to closing arguments and everything in between, must support a narrative structure that constructs and displays the meaning and moral significance of the evidence to be offered. Burns discusses the subtle but important ways that attorneys present a particular morally imbued characterization of an event or series of events, which is far more important than facts in leading the jury to a shared sense of the "right decision."

Plowshares trials demonstrate Burns's model very well, because facts are seldom in question and because, like other civil disobedients on trial, Plowshares activists are usually not at all shy about presenting their cases in moral terms. The defendants dispute characterizations of events that they see as at odds with their own motives and meanings and fight to have their stories heard in what they consider to be the "right" way. More than anything else, the Plowshares want to convey what they intended with the actions (it is there, in intention, where they locate truth). More often than not, however, they are told that intentions have no bearing on the facts at hand and no place in their testimonies. They continue to reach toward this elusive goal with words and behaviors, which I analyze in the next chapter. Most of these rhetorical and embodied courtroom tactics bring repeated objections from the prosecution, because statements of intention or motivation—the key means by which the Plowshares attempt to show that their actions were necessary—are not generally allowed during testimony. But descriptions of states of mind are permitted during opening statements, which Burns calls the preeminent "constructive" moment of the trial, during which attorneys lay the foundation for the theory of the case, to be supported by everything that follows. Unrestrained by the rules that limit testimony to showing what the evidence *is*, an opening statement can creatively convey what the evidence *will show*, and unlike testimony it can emphasize obviously subjective aspects that that testimony must leave aside. "As such," Burns notes, the opening statement offers a "complete 'God's-eye' narrative of the events that have led to the trial," presenting intentions and beliefs as indeed related to the facts of the trial.[9]

For Burns, opening statements establish an either-or paradigm, at either side of which reside the defense's and the prosecution's respective theories of the case. From those first moments the jury has already begun to choose which theory is a more appealing interpretation of the facts in question—which is right. Opening statements are striking examples of boundary work, in which competing sides are established, and the delineations between them cast in moral terms. In a typical Plowshares case the prosecution's theory of the case is presented in an opening statement that relies on narratives about lawbreaking and criminality and invokes the morality of obeying specific laws and upholding the law in general. Conversely, the defendants establish their theory of the case in opening statements that rely on narratives about conscience and duty and personal responsibility and invoke the morality of a more urgent, more compelling obligation than the laws the court upholds. Platte's opening statement for the Sacred Earth and Space II trial exemplifies the Plowshares' presentation of their theory of the case and introduces several features that recur during the Plowshares' courtroom performances.

Platte began her statement by identifying herself as a nun and blessing the jury and their commission:

> I am Sister Ardeth Platte, and to begin with, I want to give gratitude to God for our being able to be present here with you. I give

gratitude to you who are seated in this jury. The task before you, I know, is very difficult, and I know the grace of God will be with you, that whatever decision you make as it relates to us, that we will continue to bless you, so do not be afraid to speak the truth of what you believe. I also give thanks today to the prosecutor and judge. I want to forgive the prosecutor for some things, one is when he talks about us as "allegedly" being sisters—[10]

She was cut off in midsentence by the prosecutor, but not before she was able to begin rebutting an earlier accusation from the prosecutor that had cast doubt on the defendants' identity as religious. The argument that civil disobedience is not something that real priests and nuns do, or that it is not really a religious action, has been a common one since the Berrigans began to frame their anti–Vietnam War activities in explicitly religious terms. Platte would do so as well, but first she attempted to present her religious character more subtly, displaying her easy familiarity in communicating directly with God, not only on her own behalf but on behalf of the jury as well.

The prosecutor immediately interrupted Platte's introduction: "I don't think this is a proper opening statement. She is not talking about the evidence. She is talking about God." But the unusually sympathetic judge overruled the objection, calling Platte's words so far a "poetic transition to talking about the evidence in the form of its description." His characterization of the religious language as a "poetic transition" cleared the way for Platte to talk about religion—a freedom that most Plowshares activists do not have—and to return repeatedly throughout her statement to the trope of the defendants as deeply religious. In doing so Platte suggested that being religious is about more than being a nun, though she continued to emphasize the defendants' vocations: "I just want you to know that Sister Jacqueline Hudson and I, in our combination of years, have about a hundred years now in religious life in the Grand Rapids Dominican sisters, and Sister Carol has about thirty-seven, going on thirty-eight years, so just to speak the truth, we are Sisters." Platte noted that in addition to being nuns, however, "We are students of the gospel. . . . We are trying to be open to the leading of the holy spirit, the spirit of God." Both of these identities together—nuns and students of the gospel who are open to the spirit of God—make up the sisters' "faith and background," on the basis of which, Platte explained, "We will try to uphold the laws that are also God's laws." Religious identity is multivalent for Platte, having to do with a vocation and a demonstrable Catholic "background," but also with a less tangible "openness" to the spirit of God and the message of the gospel.

The paramount importance of that latter aspect of religious identity is evident in Platte's suggestion of a discrepancy between earthly and divine justice, in the face of which one must acknowledge and actively respond to an obligation to uphold divine laws at the expense of the nation's laws: "We will try to uphold the laws that are also God's laws." The laws that are not also God's laws, Platte none too obliquely hinted, are not worth upholding. Here Platte subtly brought into play the idea of natural law, according to which humans can discover the principles of eternal, universally binding laws. As humans discover and act on eternal laws, they participate in bringing about the realization of natural law. For proponents, the law generated by human, civil institutions—positive law—ought to reiterate natural law and is valid only inasmuch as it does (though civil disobedience does not usually or automatically follow from natural law thinking).[11] Though members of a jury might not have recognized that, in invoking a conception of natural law at odds with positive law, Platte was placing herself within a history of legal thought closely associated with Catholic scholasticism, the mention of God's laws served other, more immediately apprehensible purposes as well, establishing the religious character of the defendants and supporting Platte's broader appeals to conscience and morality. "What we have done," she continued,

> sounds like an extremely dangerous thing, and yet all over the world there are people saying the same thing. There are people who ac-tually believe in what we did. And you are seeing them now by the millions as you turn on your television sets. . . . We are students of the gospel. We are believers in non-violence. We are believers in truth force. We are believers in love force, and we are believers in soul force. . . . We have formed consciences. We are working every day on understanding what is moral and what is immoral.

In Platte's characterization, the three women are not alone—millions across the world are taking a similar stand for conscience—and they are not experts. "Understanding what is moral and what is immoral" is a process, on which they are "working every day." Yet throughout the statement Platte suggested that in one area the women are indeed experts: when it comes to telling the truth, Platte, Gilbert, and Hudson excel, and the urgency of conveying that particular trait to the jury pervades Platte's opening statement.

Throughout, Platte emphasized truth, honesty, and sincerity as the spe-cial purview of the defendants. "I just want to say that even though you are commanded to understand that maybe what we speak is not evidence, I want to assure you that what I tell you is truth. . . . So, even though it may not be considered as evidence, I want to make sure that you understand that everything I tell you will be truthful." "Truth," here, means more than veracity, and Platte's insistence on it functioned as more than an insistence on her own credibility. Platte used truth as a foil for evidence, positing a distinction between that which is true and that which is permissible in the courtroom, a distinction that anchored the Plowshares' theory of the case and the defenses that they employed. Already at the very onset of the trial, Platte understood that her attempts at communicating truth would likely be constrained. The frank acknowledgement that what she was about to say might fall outside the bounds of what the court considered permissible foreshadowed discursive battles to come, which for Platte and the other defendants signified the court's disregard for true justice.

The image of the court's failings in the face of a justice that is more true, presented from the earliest moments of the trial, was the linchpin in the Plowshares' theory of the case, and Platte summoned it repeatedly, both explicitly and more subtly. For example, after an objection from the prosecution regarding the defendant's mention of a book that may or may not be allowed into evidence, Platte responded, "I'm sorry, I don't understand all the laws here." Such a statement—which, as I discuss in the next chapter, is likely more strategic than accurate—served to reinforce the image of a dichotomy between the justice of the courts (a sham, as far as the Plowshares are concerned) and the higher, truer justice to which the defendants adhered, which the courts would stifle. That higher justice is, for the Plowshares, an amalgam of God's natural law and international law. In the vast majority of cases, pretrial motions ban the Plowshares from speaking about either. Often they try anyway, as the next chapter shows; and often, as for Platte, the ban itself serves as an important talking point, to communicate the fact that their speech has been limited by the court: "I think I can say this, because I think it's public knowledge, you know, we had studied every law possible surrounding [the action]. And even though we cannot mention them, evidently, in this courtroom, there were thirty categories that the judge has ruled that we cannot talk about. I still want you to know that's what we studied. And I can't—I can't tell you about it, but it's sincere." "Truth" was presented as being stifled by the court; that which is sincere and that which can be mentioned in the courtroom were presented as direct opposites.

Platte repeatedly spoke of the defendants studying current events and the international laws pertaining to nuclear weapons. She asserted that as a result of intense study coupled with religious conviction, "We had to do something. So this is what we did." With that, Platte began to describe the action in detail. As Burns suggests, the import of her description lies not in the events she related but in the moral qualities that she assigned to those events and to the defendants in performing them. Platte emphasized the careful planning the defendants undertook, to avoid damaging the private property of the farmer whose field they traversed to reach the silo. In doing so, she made a statement not only about the defendants—they are thoughtful, considerate people—but about the nature of the material they eventually did damage as unworthy of such consideration. She described pouring blood over the site and thinking of German concentration camps and noted the defendants' intent "to inspect, to expose and to do a symbolic disarmament." Platte peppered her retelling of the events with appeals to urgent duty and the responsibility to take action, even in the face of a seemingly overpowering evil: "You may even conceive that our intention to be there to stop this nuclear weapon was ineffective, that it was naive, and you'll hear that, and you are going to hear how misinformed we are, but together, this is what we have to do: One by one by one dismantle the weapons of mass destruction, one by one by one, that's the only thing citizens can do." Platte repeatedly described the defendants as citizens, upholding a responsibility that all Americans share: "We also are citizens of the United States. And we consider democracy very important; in other words, we are persons who will seriously study what is going on in this country, what we are doing as a nation." "We felt it was our duty as citizens of the United States to stop the crime." "All of us really must make it happen. God's laws are clear. And in the surrounding body of laws regarding nuclear weapons, they must be dismantled. We, as a nation, have committed to doing so. This is the law." Being a good citizen, in Platte's view, involves critical reflection on the nation's domestic and foreign policy, making oneself aware of those laws that might call the nation's policies and actions into question and acting in response to those policies if conscience (again informed by the confluence of God's law and international law) so dictates.

By the end of the statement Platte was crying, moved by the circumstances that had prompted the defendants' action:

> There are many times when we are tempted to put on sack cloth and sit in ashes as a symbol of our own repentance for not doing enough. We want to bring about a lasting peace. We want to see justice, a banning of war, total disarmament, all over the world. We want the

people in this world to live. Forgive me. This is a passionate plea. And you might think that this is the soap box, but what this is is a heart and spirit and the cry that this world begin to see that we are brothers and sisters. So this is where we come from. If we have to spend the rest of our life in prison, we will. . . . We must do more for peace. We must do more for peace, and if our symbolic disarmament action does any good, thank you, God, and if it doesn't, then we must do more. Thank you. Forgive me for crying.

Platte's opening statement, in keeping with Burns's notion that opening statements present different interpretations of events rather than different facts, made no attempt to deny the charges. Instead, it gave a detailed account of exactly the actions of which she and her co-defendants were accused, told with an emphasis on showing "where we come from." Platte presented the actions not as wanton destruction perpetrated by dangerous criminals eager to avoid punishment, but as the brave and heartfelt response—at any cost, even life in prison—of good, thoughtful, responsible citizens to circumstances that defy more important and obligatory laws than those of the court. Her theory of the case, which the defendants' words and actions throughout the rest of the trial reinforced, rested on this notion of an alternate system of justice that the defendants were upholding, even as they admittedly broke the state's laws: a higher morality that is truer and more binding, on *all* citizens, though only a select few are ultimately compelled to act. Her statement emphasized a vast breach between earthly justice and true justice, suggesting both the necessity and the difficulty of the prophetic task to which she set herself. The significance for the Plowshares of that image—two systems of justice, one true and one false, continually at odds with each other—becomes even more apparent when Platte's statement is placed next to another Plowshares opening statement that in many ways could not be more different. Despite significant variations between the two statements and the two cases that they open, they share a theory of the case anchored by the theme of another, truer, more binding justice—one which shows the justice of the courts to be a sham and its laws unworthy of being upheld.

The Pax Christi–Spirit of Life Opening Statement

The opening statement delivered by the four Pax Christi–Spirit of Life Plowshares activists in 1994 differs from Platte's in several ways, yet it too presents a theory of the case framed by the notion of adherence to a truer justice than that of the courts. The four defendants—Philip Berrigan, John Dear, Lynn Fredriksson, and Bruce Friedrich—had trespassed onto Seymour Johnson Air Force Base in Goldsboro, North Carolina, on a December morning in 1993—Pearl Harbor Day. Despite a throng of air force personnel on the base at the time for special exercises, the four made their way to a nuclear-capable F-15E fighter plane. They hammered on the plane's exterior with household hammers and poured their blood over it. They also poured blood into the air intake valves and placed their statement and a banner reading "Disarm and Live" near the plane. Air force personnel detained them a few minutes later. The four received a felony charge of destruction of government property and were held without bond when they stated that they would not comply with a court order not to return to the base.[12] Their trial began—and quickly ended—two months later on February 15, in North Carolina's district court. Prior to the start of the trial, the judge had denied the defendants advisory counsel. This is uncommon; Plowshares defendants often do avail themselves, without obstacle from the court, of advisory counsel. More typical of Plowshares trials, the judge had also passed a motion in limine, prohibiting the defendants from speaking of their moral and political motivations. Those two pretrial developments were very much on the minds of the four defendants as they co-wrote their opening statement, which Fredriksson began to deliver.

Unlike Platte, Fredriksson did not begin the statement by emphasizing the defendants' religious identity (though Dear was a Jesuit priest—he left the order in 2014—who often wore his Roman collar in the courtroom, Berrigan had been a priest, and Friedrich and Fredriksson both were affiliated with Catholic Worker communities). Nor did she spend any time trying to characterize the defendants as careful or thoughtful, with a detailed description of how they planned for the action and what they did, as Platte would ten years later. As the prosecution and judge had feared, Fredriksson, after briefly acknowledging that the four had in fact perpetrated the action in question, launched almost immediately into a moral and political indictment of U.S. foreign policy.

> On December 7, 1993, the four of us walked onto the Seymour Johnson Air Force in Goldsboro, North Carolina, to nonviolently disarm one F-15E Strike Eagle, a nuclear-capable fighter bomber which has already been used notably in the massacre of Iraqis during the Gulf War. We poured our own blood on one bomber to expose the bloody

warmaking of the entire U.S. military; we hammered on that bomber to begin the process of disassembly and conversion. We acted in the Spirit of Life and the peace of Christ to fulfill the works of the prophet Isaiah: "They shall beat their swords into plowshares, and their spears into pruning hooks; nation shall not lift up sword against nation; neither shall they train for war anymore."[13]

A decade later the judge in the Sacred Earth and Space II trial would overrule the prosecution's objection to Platte's mention of the grace of God, but the judge listening to Fredriksson had other concerns on his mind than the defendants' "talking about God." He heard her description of the United States military—"bloody warmaking," "massacre of Iraqis"—as violations of the motion in limine he had passed, expressly forbidding the defendants from speaking about morals or politics. He ordered her to stop. She did not. A U.S. marshal took Fredriksson's written text of the statement from her, at which point Friedrich continued to read his own copy of the statement. After Friedrich's copy was taken in short order, Dear picked up where Friedrich had left off. "We are not guilty of committing any crime," they read. "The real crimes have been committed by institutions, corporations, and the U.S. government and its military and covert forces that develop, construct, stockpile, and deploy genocidal weapons." That alliance worked together in the service of a nuclearism that "has surpassed even the murderous psychosis of Nazi fascism." To protect the interests of the national security state, said the defendants, the court had denied them access to their advisory counsel, limited their meetings with one another, and placed severe restrictions on their speech. "This court, like all others, protects the interests of the national security state and uses its illegitimate power to suppress the truth and to discourage further acts of resistance." They concluded, "This court has made a fair trial impossible. From this point on, we will not participate in this travesty against justice." The four turned their backs to the judge, recited the Lord's Prayer, and began to sing. Several of their supporters in the courtroom joined them, a handful of whom were eventually charged with contempt of court, as were Fredriksson, Friedrich, and Dear. The judge declared a mistrial that same day, on the grounds that the jury had been, in his words, contaminated. In subsequent individual trials, each of the four received a guilty verdict.

The opening statement delivered by the Pax Christi–Spirit of Life defendants is obviously and significantly dissimilar to the one delivered by Platte ten years later. While Platte was deferential and conciliatory throughout her statement, the Pax Christi–Spirit of Life defendants wrote an intentionally confrontational statement, willfully violating the judge's pretrial motion in order to speak explicitly about foreign policy. (Certainly, the different perspectives of the respective judges made a significant difference as well, with Platte's judge allowing her far more discursive leeway than the Pax Christi–Spirit of Life judge permitted.) As foils for each other, these statements reveal two important characteristics of the Plowshares' trials. First, Plowshares activists have a great deal of autonomy in how they choose to approach their trials. Opening statements are not the only place where defendants exercise that autonomy. Some defendants choose to avail themselves of advisory counsel while others do not; some actively file all manner of pretrial motions while others do not; perhaps most strikingly, some plead guilty while some plead not guilty; some appeal their verdicts while others do not; and, as reflected in these two statements, some defendants follow the conventions of the courtroom more closely than others. In short, there is no one right way for a Plowshares defendant to participate—or not participate—in her or his trial.

Additional factors beyond the defendants' chosen approach (more sympathetic or less sympathetic judges, for example) influence the way the trials play out. I discuss these factors and variations in more detail in the next chapter, but especially because of how different these two opening statements are in many ways, they reveal a second important characteristic of the Plowshares trials: how consistent the Plowshares' theory of the case is. Whether confrontational or deferential, narrative or declaratory, the primary trope around which the theory of the case is structured remains the same: the earthly court is unlawful, its laws unjust and even deadly, its justice a sham, and the defendants' obligation lies elsewhere, to a truer and more binding justice.

Constituting Religious Identity

Although the Plowshares posit a profound schism between earthly justice and true justice, according to which the court system is immoral and not to be held in any regard, they rely on it as a space for making visible, explaining, and authenticating their actions. The trials function in these ways because they are public, because they necessarily involve outsider constituencies, because they are conducive to precisely the kinds of discursive battles that the Plowshares' theory of the case presupposes, and, not least, because they are arenas for the conferral or denial of status, which plays an important role in the notion of success that undergirds the Plowshares' project.

For those outside their milieu, it may seem like quite a stretch to think of the Plowshares' actions as successful. By the activists' own admission, their outcomes are hardly measurable. But as James Gusfield points out in his study of the nineteenth-century American temperance movement, instrumental or observable outcomes are not the only measure, nor always the best measure, of political success. Gusfield argues that even political acts that seem not to achieve instrumental ends can be profoundly effective, in that they enhance or detract from the status of the various groups involved. Political action can be "significant per se" rather than a "means to an end" because it "has a meaning inherent in what it signifies about the structure of the society as well as in what such action actually achieves."[14] In the arena of symbolic politics, where moral crusades often take place, values and prestige are distributed or denied, attitudes and feelings are shaped, and groups are positioned in a social order so that a cause or campaign that may seem illogical or ineffective is transformative precisely because of its demonstrative nature. Gusfield calls his conception of symbolic politics a dramatistic one—that is, it moves an audience as performance, even as it is in some way unreal. And at certain nodes it can become real, actualized, for example, by the legal system. For Gusfield, law is a primary vehicle of symbolic politics, whereby significant noninstrumental effects are achieved that increase or decrease the status of various groups, which is itself an important "real" outcome.

Legislation can both signify and instantiate public approval of a particular behavior, establishing the norms of a socially or politically superior group.[15] Other groups lose status when their behaviors are delegitimated through legislation and when that legislation is enforced by the courts. But for the Plowshares, to lose status in the courtroom—to be deemed a criminal and sent to prison—is to gain religious status. As their theory of the case makes plain, civil disobedience is divine obedience; criminality in the state's view is morality in God's view—and in the eyes of their wider resistance community. I address this point more explicitly later, but the inverse relationship between legal and religious status, crucial to the Plowshares' conception of efficacy, means that the courtroom is a space not merely for the expression of religious identity but for its constitution. What it means for a Plowshares activist to be religious—"truly" religious, as the defendants in this chapter emphasized—comes into being in a profound way in the courtroom as they describe what they did and why they did it, because theirs is a religious ideal based on the value of proclaiming, witnessing, and telling, even (or especially) at great cost to personal freedom.

Going before the courts is useful for the Plowshares because it allows the defendants to convey a message, but, like the actions, going before the courts is also a way to change the world through the public enactment of faith. The role that the activists take on in and through the courtroom is a role that they regard as necessary for the creation of a new world order. Thus, the trials are performative in the same dual sense as the Plowshares' actions: showings that are also doings. They serve as both demonstration and enactment of religious identity, as the negotiation of social roles and boundaries that happens in the courtroom allows for the authentication of the Plowshares' theological claims, even as the activists are often silenced or disparaged in their attempts to speak of conscience and morality and to put the "government Beast" and "Lord Nuke" on trial.

The relationship between religions and the courts is a fraught one in the United States, with the often-contradictory clauses of the First Amendment calling for the courts to determine what does or does not count as legally protectable religion.[16] Religious groups are often depicted as at the mercy of the court, which has the power to acknowledge or limit a claimant's religious rights. The Plowshares' cases, however, are not First Amendment cases. The courts have no interest in quibbling about the legality of the Plowshares' religious practices and generally want very much not to hear about the Plowshares' religion at all. And, as the next chapter shows, the Plowshares often explicitly deny that their religious freedom is the primary issue at hand. Both the courts and the Plowshares, for different reasons, deny that these are cases *about* religion. And yet there is little doubt that the Plowshares' trials serve as arenas *for* religion, unsettling the way scholars have often thought about the relationship between religious groups and the courts as one of control, regulation, and limitation. Unlike in religious freedom cases where religious actors explain their religion and wait for it to be deemed legal or not, Plowshares defendants perform their religion, asserting their own agency in the processes by which religious discourses and identities are constituted in the courtroom.[17] The Plowshares employ religious narratives and language; they cast themselves and their actions, as the two opening statements discussed earlier demonstrate, in explicitly religious terms. And, when they are silenced by objections, Plowshares defendants turn to a repertoire of language and behaviors, through which they not only express but constitute the identity claims that lie at the heart of their religious life. That is, not only do defendants say that they are religious, as Platte did in her statement, but they activate those identity claims by insisting on the "truth," both verbally ("What I tell you is truth") and gesturally (turning their backs to the judge).

In the next chapter I discuss this identity-constituting repertoire more fully, but the Sacred Earth and Space II and Pax Christi–Spirit of Life opening statements present many of its elements in seed form, as do Kabat's, Crane's, and Woodson's emphasis on truth and authenticity, on describing events and motivations so that they are apprehended properly. That truth refers less to facts than to motives, goals, and especially identity.[18]

While Plowshares defendants usually emphasize that true justice is apprehensible by, and binding on, all citizens, they also acknowledge that only a select few feel so bound. There is a tension bound up with the Plowshares' theory of the case, especially apparent in Platte's statement, between a responsibility shared by all citizens to an alternate justice and the special distinction of being open to its dictates and having acted on them. This alternate justice unites people under a common responsibility, but simultaneously it marks as separate those who feel its obligations strongly enough to act on them. In their time before the courts the Plowshares negotiate a tension between unity and distinction. Their trials, as I will show next, feature striking instances of boundary work, both rhetorical and embodied, by which the Plowshares demonstrate their "nonbelonging" before the court.

5

"Your Honor, I Object. . . . She Is Talking About God"

Boundary Negotiations in the Courtroom

Seattle Nuclear rhs

On November 2, 2009, five Catholic activists cut through a series of chain-link and barbed-wire fences surrounding Naval Base Kitsap in Bangor, Washington, where roughly a quarter of the United States' nuclear warheads are reportedly stored and a fleet of eleven submarines equipped to deploy Trident nuclear weapons is stationed. The five unfurled a banner reading "Trident: Illegal + Immoral," poured their blood out of baby bottles over the ground, and beat on the ground and the fences with household hammers before being apprehended and arrested.[1] In a written statement, the five elucidated the biblical motivation behind the Disarm Now Plowshares action, as they called it, beginning the statement with verses from Ezekiel—"I will purify you from the taint of all your idols. I will give you a new heart and put a new spirit within you. I will remove the heart of stone from your body and give you a heart of flesh. I will put my Spirit within you and make you conform to my statutes" (36:25–27)—and ending with their namesake swords-into-Plowshares verse from

Isaiah. In between the Bible verses they explained, "We walk into the heart of darkness. . . . We intend to beat swords into Plowshares as one step up the holy mountain where all nations can unite in peace." They further explained that the sunflower seeds they scatted around the site were meant to "plant the hope of new life."[2] Two of the five were priests, one was a nun, and all were over the age of sixty. Three had participated in several previous Plowshares actions, including Sister Anne Montgomery, who was one of the Plowshares Eight.

In September 2010, not quite a year after completing their action, the Disarm Now Plowshares activists were indicted on counts of conspiracy, trespass, destruction of property on a naval installation, and depredation of government property. One month after their indictment the five defendants submitted a motion to dismiss the charges against them, arguing that they were not valid because the property in question concealed weapons of mass destruction, thereby justifying and even necessitating their action. But the motion to dismiss also offered another option. If the charges were not dropped, the defendants requested that, by court order, they be allowed to speak about nuclear weapons during their trial. Quick on the Plowshares' heels, U.S. attorney Jenny Durkan submitted an opposing request that the court expressly bar any testimony concerning nuclear weapons. She argued that the defendants, in petitioning for the court order, clearly intended to "turn their trial into what they perceive as a referendum on United States defense strategy. They are not entitled, and should not be allowed, to do so."[3] Judge Benjamin Settle agreed with Durkan and denied the defendants' motion in full.[4] A few months later the five stood trial and were found guilty on felony counts of conspiracy, trespass, and damage and injury to federal property. They received prison sentences of six to fifteen months, with an additional year of supervised release, as well as hefty fines.

Motions similar to the one that the Disarm Now Plowshares proposed are submitted routinely by Plowshares defendants or attorneys acting on their behalf. Routinely, they are denied. Even though denial is the likeliest outcome by far, as defendants know from experience, the motions serve an important function as defendants begin, even in pretrial paperwork, to shape courtroom proceedings according to their theory of the case, in which the courtroom is not an arena for proving their innocence but rather for communicating what the activists regard as the truth about the actions and about themselves. Like Susan Crane's reaction to her assault charge, Helen Woodson's satisfaction with her presentencing report, and Ardeth Platte's emphasis in her opening statement on relating only what is sincere and truthful, the Disarm Now defendants' motion to dismiss or to receive certain permissions demonstrates the Plowshares' hope for proper apprehension by the courts, highlighting their communicative aims for the trials.

Platte's opening statement, however, revealed a tension bound up with that communicative aim, which permeates the Plowshares' project. Communication rests, in large part, on the kind of identification with the audience that Platte took pains to achieve. But even as she worked to identify herself with the jury by invoking citizens' common morality and responsibility, she emphasized the activists' particular religious status, as well as the fact that they had embraced responsibility, over and against all those who had not. Platte hinted throughout her statement at the defendants' special role in fulfilling a divinely mandated obligation. That tension between universality and particularity, a common morality versus the Plowshares' distinctive response to it, becomes even more pronounced in the Plowshares' trials once opening statements are completed. Throughout their trials, defendants echo Platte's emphasis on common morality, insisting that they are not unusual or special and have done only what all citizens are called to do. Often they go to great lengths to deny that they are qualitatively different from anyone else in the courtroom. Yet subtle boundary work saturates the Plowshares' trials, in language and behaviors that convey significant distinctions between the defendants and all those who have not done what they have done.

Even more than the secretive actions themselves, the courtroom, a public space regulated by widely known rhetorical and behavioral norms, allows for the performance of boundaries as sites for both the upholding and the elision of difference, as the episodes that I explore in this chapter demonstrate. These episodes come from five trials spanning the Plowshares' thirty years, which reveal with especial clarity—either because they are anomalous or, more often, because they are exemplary—the salient performative tactics that the Plowshares use to convey and enact their identity claims and to negotiate the tension between universality and particularity before the courtroom's audiences.[5] To a greater or lesser extent, all Plowshares trials exhibit the tactics identified here: the use of particular defenses, behaviors and rhetoric that assert nonbelonging, and claims of identification. These representative cases, taken together, provide a complex picture of how the Plowshares' verbal and embodied courtroom performances function within their larger project as potent expressions of symbolic boundaries as well as a means of actualizing social boundaries.

Necessity and International Law Defenses

The courtroom is, foremost, the setting where Plowshares activists hope to explain their actions and motivations, with the intention of changing hearts and minds on the issue of nuclear weapons. In the courtroom they can communicate directly with those outside their immediate circle of supporters, from juries and courtroom personnel to reporters and their readers. Plowshares activists, for whom the trials are freighted with enormous symbolic and tactical significance, do not go to court unprepared. They usually defend themselves, and in doing so they demonstrate an indisputable legal savvy, apparent from the start in their willingness and ability to use legal rather than theological categories to talk about their actions, to communicate effectively with audiences beyond the rather narrow segment of the population that shares their religiopolitical worldview. In a concerted effort to engage the legal system on its own terms, Plowshares activists have turned consistently to two defenses: necessity and international law. When the Disarm Now defendants asked for a court order granting them permission to speak about nuclear weapons in their testimonies, they were asking for permission to use these two defenses, knowing full well that in almost every Plowshares trial to date, the court has barred these defenses (a precedent that was not to be overturned for them). And yet these defenses are a fundamental element of the Plowshares' pedagogical intentions for their trials; asking that they be allowed is a mere formality, since the activists intend to use them, or at least make a determined attempt, whether or not the court grants permission.

Use of a "justification" or "necessity" defense began with the 1981 trial of the Plowshares Eight, who argued that their action had been necessary to avert the danger of nuclear war. According to a necessity defense, conduct is not criminally liable as long as it is a justifiable response to a greater harm—a necessary preventative measure against a demonstrable threat, in a situation where breaking a law does more good, or less harm, than the consequences of following the law. The classic example of a necessity defense comes from an English case, *The Queen v. Dudley and Stephens*, in which the two eponymous sailors were accused of murdering their cabin boy (said to be near death already) after twenty days in a lifeboat following a shipwreck, to eat his remains and thus survive. Their necessity defense did not triumph; Dudley and Stephens were sentenced to death (the sentence was later commuted to six months in prison). Neither did the necessity defense triumph for the Plowshares Eight, whose judge barred its use. After a decade-long appeal process, the Plowshares Eight defendants' original sentences of five to ten years were reduced to time served, when the judge in the 1981 case was determined to have demonstrated bias against the defendants by not allowing them to call on expert witnesses to corroborate the idea that their action was a justified and necessary response to the nuclear threat. But more important to the defendants than a successful appeal was the opportunity to have their case, and their cause, in the news for a decade.

This pedagogical, communicative quality lies at the heart of the necessity defense, and the Plowshares Eight were certainly not the first civil disobedients or antinuclear activists to realize its potential in that regard. Since the 1970s the necessity defense, which has been recognized by the Supreme Court as part of common law, has been used regularly by defendants breaking laws (usually trespass laws) out of moral compulsion. Occasionally it has triumphed in high-profile civil disobedience trials. In 1987, for example, fifteen defendants, on trial for trespassing and disorderly conduct during an anti-CIA protest on the University of Massachusetts–Amherst campus, including well-known political activist Abbie Hoffman and former first daughter Amy Carter, were acquitted based on their necessity defense.[6] But more often it does not meet with that kind of success. In nuclear protest cases, including those of the Plowshares, judges have barred the defense on the grounds that nuclear weapons do not pose an immediate threat and that, moreover, trespassing is not an activity that a protester could reasonably believe would stop the arms race or even disable a weapon to any significant degree. As laid out in chapter 2, however, the Plowshares vehemently deny the characterization of their actions as ineffective, insisting on the instrumentality of symbolic disarmament. Plowshares defendants believe that they have actually disarmed nuclear equipment by hammering on it and pouring their blood over it, and that disarming one weapon, or even one component part or contributing blueprint, is a justifiable response to the threat of global nuclear annihilation. For the Plowshares, a prohibition against the necessity defense is a prohibition against talking about the essential context of their actions. For their judges and prosecutors, however, the necessity defense is an interpretive rather than a factual approach to the matter at hand, as State's Attorney Durkan suggested in her motion to bar its use in the Disarm Now trial.

In employing a necessity defense, the Plowshares Eight were in step with other high-profile civil disobedience cases at the time. But using this type of defense was a striking departure from the Berrigans' earlier legal strategy. In their trials for earlier civil disobedience actions, such as the Catonsville draft board raid, they had relied on defenses based on claims of individual conscience. In contrast, a necessity defense is based on claims about society's shared conscience. It is universalizing rather than particularizing, the significance of which, in the context of the Plowshares' trials, is discussed later. The Plowshares Eight, and Plowshares defendants since, emphasized the universal rather than the particular even more explicitly in their invocations of the Nuremberg principles and international law. The Nuremberg principles, codified as customary international law following World War II (but, as custom, not considered binding in U.S. courts of law), are often invoked in civil disobedience cases in tandem with a necessity defense, where they are intended to corroborate the idea that laws must at times be broken for a greater good, with the idea that personal responsibility rather than following orders or laws is paramount in determining one's moral obligations, especially when those can be shown to be morally suspect.[7] But the judge deemed the Plowshares Eight's invocation of the Nuremberg principles, like the attempted necessity defense, to refer to matters beyond the scope of the charges at hand and to step outside the bounds of the presentation of evidence, to which defendant testimony is limited.

The trial for the 1989 Thames River action, in which seven activists swam and canoed to reach a Trident submarine docked at the Naval Underwater Systems Center in New London, Connecticut, illustrates Plowshares defendants' strenuous refusal to rein in their talk of motivations and justifications, despite objections from their prosecutors and warnings from their judges. The seven defendants left the Connecticut shore at three o'clock on the morning of their action, swimming for over an hour to reach the Trident. They hammered and poured packets of their blood over the submarine and carved the word "death" on its side. Their trial in Hartford Federal Court lasted three days, and the seven were convicted of conspiracy to enter a naval reservation for unlawful purpose.[8] Defendant Kathy Boylan's testimony reveals the discursive battles waged as defendants try to insist on defenses that the court does not allow:

Q. Once you got there [to the submarine], you took the hammer you brought with you and struck the submarine with it?

A. Yes

Q. And the other folks who were with you, the other six all went there with the same plan, is that right?

A. To—to symbolically—

Q. To approach the USS Pennsylvania and strike it with the hammers each one of you had brought?

A. Calling it symbolic disarmament, that's what we had in mind, to disarm the submarine.[9]

Explaining symbolic disarmament as both a motivation and an achievable goal is, for Plowshares defendants, crucial to establishing the necessity of their actions. But by this point in the trial the defendants had been instructed several times not to speak of motives or conscience or necessity. The judge explicitly instructed the jury to disregard the defendants' and witnesses' statements about religion and morality and about nuclear weapons and warned the defendants—repeatedly—not to make such statements at all. In this excerpt, the prosecutor's attempt to keep Boylan from talking about symbolic disarmament is an attempt to keep her from violating the judge's orders, to little avail.

Shortly after the prosecutor attempted to deter her from speaking of symbolic disarmament, Boylan invoked international law:

Q. But you knew as you went under that pier and approached the Trident that you were in an area that the Navy had reserved or restricted access to, did you not?

A. No. I was in God's water.

Q. But you knew that at least in the Navy's belief you weren't supposed to be under their pier or striking their submarine, correct?

A. Well, I'm following the law so—

Q. But you knew as you were doing that that at least the United States Navy believed that you had no business being under their pier or on their submarine, is that right?

A. The United States Navy is subject to international law, then they are required to get rid of the Trident so—

Q. But you knew as you went there that the Navy didn't have the same view that you did?

. . .

A. I don't think they have come to realize the fact that international law applies to them yet.[10]

In this passage the prosecution was indeed asking about intent: in many Plowshares cases, establishing intent is necessary to proving certain charges (in this case, trespass with intent to injure and depredate U.S. property). But even in asking about intent, the prosecution focuses on what it regards as the facts of the case, rather than motives or interpretations—the defendants' intent to enter into forbidden space, not their intent to either symbolically disarm the submarines or remind the navy of its responsibility to uphold what the defendants characterize as a universally binding, international law.

Plowshares defendants' refusal to be bound by the constraints of factual language, evidenced when they choose defenses that rely on interpretive content, challenges the idea that morals are impermissible or irrelevant in court. It also reflects their stance on the impossibility of value-free language, suggesting that a refusal to speak of morality is not a neutral position but an immoral one in the face of nuclear weapons. In this way invocations of necessity and international law, with their refusal to function as value-neutral retellings of events, are appeals to the common underlying moral sensibility that Platte's opening statement emphasized. They are fundamental expressions of the Plowshares' theory of the case. Thus, it may seem odd to suggest that the Plowshares' use of these defenses is strategic, because of their relevance to civil disobedience in general and their particular appropriateness to the Plowshares' project. But given that the use of these defenses is plainly transgressive, as the defendants are reminded at every turn, it is impossible to overlook the intentionality behind their use. Repeated attempts to breach the conventions of testimony are purposeful assertions of the moral distinction posited in Platte's opening statement, setting the defendants apart as those who understand universally binding moral obligations in their proper light and who choose to characterize them as such even when they are told that doing so is not permitted in the courtroom.

Necessity and international law defenses have a pedagogical character especially appropriate for the Plowshares' aims. The utility of these defenses for the Plowshares, however, is not merely pedagogical. Other, more subtle aspects of these defenses come to light upon consideration of the defenses that Plowshares defendants do not use, particularly that of religious freedom. Though Plowshares activists conceive of their actions as deeply religious, meant to respond to divine mandates, to counter what they characterize as nuclear idolatry, to effect metaphysical as well as practical change, and to enact Catholic and Christian identity, they agree with prosecutors and judges who stress that religion is not the issue at hand during their trials. For the court, the Plowshares' religious convictions are not pertinent to the facts of their cases and have no bearing on the illegality of their actions. Plowshares activists disagree, but nonetheless maintain that while their actions are religious, their legal justifications for them need not be and indeed should not be. Even though Plowshares activists are resolute and public practitioners of religion, for whom identity claims are strongly moored to religiosity, defendants characterize defenses based on necessity and international law as more valid than religious freedom defenses, even though the latter has met with far more success than the former in U.S. courts.[11]

One notable exception, from early in the Plowshares' history, is instructive when considering the Plowshares' later rejection of defenses based on religious freedom. In 1983 seven activists entered Griffiss Air Force Base in Rome, New York, and hammered and poured blood over B-52 engines and a bomber. After their trial concluded and they had been charged with conspiracy and destruction of government property, the defendants filed an appeal that emphasized that a violation of their religious rights had occurred when criminal sanctions were levied for actions undertaken out of a sincerely held religious belief, and also that they had acted to counter an establishment of nuclear idolatry. Their appeal documents bear quoting at length:

> Appellants assert that there has been established in this country a national religion of nuclearism. It is a religion in which the bomb is the new source of salvation. It is a religion that compels a quality of loyalty focused on the acceptance of nuclear weapons as sacred objects. . . . The existence of these weapons of mass killing violates the deepest religious beliefs of the Appellants and therefore laws which protect these weapons have as their primary effect, as applied, the inhibition of the Appellants' religious beliefs. . . . Appellants assert that while the statutes under which they were convicted may appear on their face to be neutral, they do in application, violate Appellants' free exercise of religion in so far as . . . they impose criminal sanctions upon those who, in exercise of their sincerely held religious beliefs, act to preserve the existence of the planet in furtherance of their religious obligations. . . . The statutes and practices of the government impose the most severe burdens on the Appellants' most deeply held moral beliefs and practices by requiring their complicity in the unimaginable horror of nuclear war. It should be emphasized here, that central to the Appellants' religious beliefs is the belief that they must act affirmatively to prevent killing and war. It is not enough to simply hold ideas in opposition to the government's conduct. By protecting the government's activities the statutes in question therefore operate against the Appellants' practice of this central tenet of their religion.[12]

Though the judge denied the appeal, he noted that the religious freedom argument, which had been offered already in a pretrial motion, was both clever and compelling, and it is certainly consistent with the logic of symbolic disarmament. But the jury did not have the chance to weigh its merits—neither appeals nor pretrial motions are presented before a jury. During the trial itself, while before the jury, the Griffiss defendants went out of their way to downplay the sentiments that they would later highlight in the appeal, emphasizing their adherence to necessity over and against obedience to a higher religious law. Attorneys for the defendants argued explicitly that the issue at hand was "not obedience to a higher, subjective law, but whether a particular form of opposition to a government's policies or practices is justified and considered so by society." They went on, "For the prosecution to continue to mischaracterize defendants' acts as civil disobedience, or adherence to some 'higher law,' despite defendants' continued reference to the well accepted legal defense of necessity, must be seen as having the purpose of obscuring issues and misleading the court."[13]

The attorneys' grievance is twofold. In addition to pedagogical concerns with the concealment of what is, for the defendants, the issue at hand (nuclear weapons), these statements suggest that for the prosecution to characterize the defendants as adhering to a religiously based higher law is delegitimating, because such a characterization implies that the defendants have been motivated by a particular set of religious beliefs. And as Platte's opening statement made plain, a crucial element of the Plowshares' theory of the case is that they have acted in response to a morality that is universally binding. The conspicuous discrepancy between the Griffiss trial transcript and the appeal documents illuminates one of the primary functions of the necessity defense as a strategic choice for Plowshares defendants. Necessity, when it can go forward, not only enables the defendants to put nuclear policy on trial; it also allows them to appeal to a wider moral sensibility that they argue is not and should not be limited to those of a particular religious background. A religious freedom argument, in which defendants are set apart as a religious minority deserving of special accommodation, does just the opposite, undermining the insistence that the jury is bound by the same morality as the defendants, whether or not they share the defendants' religious convictions.

Thus, though the activists do speak of religious motivations for their actions, they do not typically cite particular religious motivations by way of defense—religious identity is mentioned, as in Platte's opening statement, to establish character and provide context, but it is not proffered as evidence. Rather, defendants invoke an underlying moral sensibility as itself evidence, through necessity and international law defenses. It is, of course, quickly apparent that there is a conflation of more inclusive moral paradigms with the defendants' own religious convictions: Boylan claimed to be enacting international law in "God's water" in the trial excerpt cited earlier, and the actions that the defendants have found necessary to prevent a greater harm were not just any actions, but the specific symbolic disarmaments that they understood and framed in religious terms. Thus, while the image of a common, underlying moral sensibility is meant to take the place of, and be more effective than, claims to a particular religious sensibility, there is a good deal of overlap between the two. But it is a striking aspect of the Plowshares' trials that defendants insist on the latter's subservience to the former, limiting their claims to religious particularity while before the jury and resisting strenuously when such claims are made on their behalf by the prosecution.

While defendants, for the most part, turn to necessity or international law defenses as "well accepted" and more satisfactory than the higher law or religious freedom defenses that the Griffiss appeal invoked, they in fact expect, based on more than three decades of experience, that necessity and international law defenses will be legally unsuccessful. Even when these defenses are stifled, however—perhaps more so when they are stifled—they are extremely useful for communicating the "truth" with which the activists are principally concerned. The judge in the Griffiss case expressed wary admiration for the religious freedom argument laid out in the pretrial and appeal documents, yet Plowshares defendants have not used that defense again. On the other hand, judges in most Plowshares cases since the first have ruled against the use of the necessity defense and defenses invoking the Nuremberg principles or international law, yet defendants still attempt to use these defenses, despite the fact that more often than not they are quickly derailed. They remain, for Plowshares defendants, the only suitable ways to talk about their actions. Using these defenses is also a strategic choice with implications for the courtroom proceedings as part of the Plowshares' larger project, as other central courtroom practices emerge from the apparent failure of those defenses.

Courtroom Behavior, Situational Propriety, and Nonbelonging

Kathy Boylan, insisting that she acted according to international law, exemplifies the Plowshares' refusal to capitulate when judges or prosecutors attempt to steer them away from using barred, interpretive defenses. Defendants continue to employ language that is, to them, the only appropriate language for talking about their actions. When the judge's limits on that language become especially constraining, they turn to behaviors that indicate a rejection of the court's regulations and a refusal to adhere to them. Defendants regularly flout courtroom protocol by refusing to approach the judge, refusing to stand when instructed to do so, and turning their backs on the judge during sentencing. They have boycotted and walked out of their trials and instructed their attorneys to make no closing statements. Two cases, one from 1985 and one from 1999, nicely illustrate the sorts of noncompliant and nonconforming behaviors that Plowshares defendants use as they attempt to disrupt the normativity of the court, to further highlight the failure of justice that their attempted use of necessity and international law defenses is meant to suggest.

In the trial for the 1999 Plowshares Versus Depleted Uranium action (the trial in which an atypical assault charge was brought against defendant Susan Crane), four defendants were tried for an action at the Maryland Air National Guard Base, in which they hammered and poured blood over aircraft intended to deploy missiles tipped with depleted uranium. According to the activists, depleted uranium disintegrates into radioactive dust that poses serious health hazards, especially an increased incidence of profound birth defects. The judge barred the defense's expert witnesses—scientists prepared to speak about the dangers of depleted uranium—from testifying and forbade the mention of depleted uranium during the trial. The defendants, predictably, tried to talk about depleted uranium anyway, but the judge sustained repeated objections from the prosecution, so Crane eventually read a statement to the court, over the judge's orders for her to stop: "We cannot put on a defense about the dangers of depleted uranium. . . . We will not participate in what amounts to a legal gag order." The four defendants then turned their backs on the judge while one of them read aloud from the Book of Jeremiah, which inspired their supporters in the courtroom to burst into spontaneous song.[14]

This was the second instance of unruly crowd participation during the trial. Earlier the judge repeatedly had tried to ascertain who drove the van that dropped off the activists at the action site. The defendants repeatedly refused to answer. After several rounds of futile questioning, supporters in the unusually crowded courtroom began to stand up one by one and say, and then shout, "I drove the van." Perhaps a dozen individuals stood up to proclaim their supposed culpability before order was restored and the trial continued. But in the second audience outburst, following Crane's reading of the group's statement and the recitation from Jeremiah, the judge's gaveling for order was ignored, and the courtroom was cleared. At that point the defendants refused to participate further in the trial and instructed their attorneys to do the same. The defense made no closing arguments or sentencing appeals.[15]

The 1985 trial of the five Trident II defendants, who hammered and poured blood on Trident submarines at the Electric Boat Quonset Point plant in Rhode Island, features similar instances of resistance to the court's behavioral norms. The judge in the case did allow expert witnesses for the defense to testify as to whether nuclear war was imminent, but he instructed the jury to disregard their testimony, and throughout the trial he barred the defendants from speaking about necessity or justification. To convey their displeasure, the defendants turned their backs to the judge during sentencing, a gesture that echoes moments of what the judge, at least, perceived as noncompliance throughout the two-week-long trial. Some of these instances of noncompliance are direct. For example, one defendant had an additional two months added to his sentence for showing contempt of court in refusing to answer the judge's questions (including, again, who drove the van).[16] But some are more subtle, not described in media coverage but evident from an examination of the trial transcript. At one point the judge interrupted questioning, at a moment when the prosecution was objecting to a response from a defendant on the stand because it dealt with necessity, to address the following to one of the defendants not on the stand at the time: "I will tolerate absolutely no misconduct in this courtroom. That includes putting arms on the back of the bench, and slouching like you are in a country club." And later he had occasion to continue in the same vein—apparently the defendant had done it again. "My sheriffs are instructed when I see someone crouched down and look at the court a little wounded like a hippopotamus to go out of this courtroom and advise the individual to take their arms off the back of the bench and to sit like gentlemen and ladies."[17]

The judge's metaphor gives a bit of a pause, but makes quite clear his mounting frustration with the defendants' gestures and postures: they are not proper to the setting; they are fit not for the courtroom but for the country club or the zoo. The judge's insistence on the maintenance of the courtroom's behavioral standards, however undefined (acting like gentlemen and ladies, not hippopotami), reveals his desire for what sociologist Erving Goffman terms "situational propriety." A person who adheres to situational propriety is acting in accordance with the norms, specifically the social and relational norms, of any given situation. Maintaining situational propriety is often largely unconscious—shaking a proffered hand, for example—but even the unconscious maintenance conveys a great deal about a social actor's attunement to the norms of a given social context. Of particular interest to Goffman (and particular importance to the judge in the Trident II trial), what is communicated through adherence to situational propriety is a "kind of respect and regard for that to which attachment and belongingness are owed. At the heart of it is a kind of concern that shows one to be a part of the thing for which one is concerned."[18] The emphasis on respect and attachment helps to explain why the judge became so frustrated with the defendants' poor posture. Flouting situational propriety is not always deliberate. A person visiting a foreign country may not know the norms of that country, for example. But the judge referred to misconduct and threatened punishment. Clearly, he believed the defendants to be flouting situational propriety on purpose—as, indeed, they were. In refusing to answer the judge's questions or continue their testimonies, in slouching and rolling their eyes and turning their backs to the judge, Plowshares activists conveyed, quite intentionally, not only a lack of respect for the earthly justice that in their worldview condemned Jesus to die and protects nuclear weapons, but a lack of attachment to it—a nonbelongingness. Their performance was not lost on the judge.

Considering the Plowshares defendants' actions in the courtroom in comparison to the legal activities of other religious groups highlights the significant difference between the Plowshares, who do not typically make religious freedom arguments, and groups such as the Mormons and Jehovah's Witnesses and Christian Scientists, who have used the courtroom as a space in which to argue their constitutional right to free exercise of religion. Scholars have noted that these latter groups' participation in courtroom proceedings, in which they defended the respective practices of plural marriage or proselytizing or faith healing, was intended to demonstrate their adherence to the American political and legal processes and their status as good citizens. Their time in the courts, variously successful in terms of promoting or changing legislation, had the effect of destigmatizing them in society's eyes, by showing "their willingness to voice a kind of principled defiance to state authority within the accepted political framework of the judicial system," according to one scholar's analysis of religion-based medical neglect cases.[19] While the Plowshares, too, see a great benefit to participating in the judicial system, their participation, laden with gestures of noncompliance and nonbelonging, demonstrates the converse—their refusal to be destigmatized, to be perceived as fitting within the judicial system or being agreeable to its parameters.

Clearly, behaviors that indicate disrespect for the courts are different from, for example, Platte's crying during her opening statement, which revealed not frustration at being silenced but rather heightened emotion brought on by the words that Platte was allowed to speak. It is likely that Platte's tears had a different effect on the judge and jury than the angry gestures of the Depleted Uranium and Trident II defendants. It is even possible that Platte's tears intentionally or unintentionally forged a connection between herself and the jury rather than asserting a disconnect, as the latter defendants' behaviors may well have done. But crying too can be a transgressive behavior, out of keeping with the norms and expectations of the court, which value and insist on objective accounts of events, free of emotional content. Courtney Bender, examining how people find ways to communicate meaning and values in situations where shared meaning cannot be presumed, argues that behaviors that "break the rules" allow for the assertion of meaning by permitting nonofficial meanings to be exposed and foregrounding "what matters" to individuals in spaces where their priorities or values or interpretations are challenged or stifled by "official" rhetoric and rules.[20] For Bender, these moments of rule breaking bring some people together while simultaneously establishing distinctions between rule breakers and representatives of official behavior.

Those who break the rules, for Bender, may still be partly—even largely—invested in the groups or situations that they transgress; they are simply expressing their simultaneous alternate commitments and their overlapping, rather than antithetical, worlds of meaning. The Plowshares' various kinds of rule-breaking behavior, then, while quite different in their potential for either drawing distinctions or making connections, can be located at various points on the spectrum between Goffman's and Bender's interpretations of rule breaking. Crying and smirking at the judge, for example, assert different levels of nonbelonging. Platte's tears, in keeping with her statement, suggested that she was in fact deeply invested in the courtroom proceedings. The anonymous Trident II defendant's hippopotamus-like gestures of displeasure did not. Yet both kinds of behavior perform the same ideology and speak to the same conception of what matters. Additionally, both kinds of behavior reveal the Plowshares' reliance on the courtroom as an arena where the expression of emotions that are kept out of the actions themselves, such as anger and frustration, can take place. Despite the passionate conviction that incites their actions and the fear that many Plowshares participants report feeling in the days and hours before the actions, descriptions of the actions themselves suggest that, typically, they are carried out quite calmly. Activists often attribute the calm to a feeling of absolute peace that comes over them during the actions. But as social movement theorists note, during nonviolent civil disobedience, strong emphasis is placed on the need to temper one's anger and other forceful emotions to convey nonviolent intentions or to replace it with gentle love, in the Gandhian paradigm, as a means consistent with the desired ends.[21]

Paradoxically, then, while the Plowshares see the courtroom as a space that sharply curtails their freedom to express their motivations and ideologies, they also take advantage of a greater license in the courtroom to express emotions, especially through gestures and behaviors that need to be carefully modulated during the actions themselves, from crying to fuming. Employing a variety of behaviors that reside at different points along a spectrum of noncompliance, defendants demonstrate with their bodies, and conscious of an audience, the distinction between the court's law and the moral principles to which they subscribe, on which the necessity defense is based—and, moreover, their passionate adherence to the latter, which entails "nonbelongingness" from the former.

The Performance of Linguistic Incompetence

Many Plowshares defendants are paragons of courtesy and respect in the courtroom, but even the most decorous defendants communicate nonbelonging. Often they do so by claiming to misunderstand legal language and protocol, as Platte did almost immediately in her opening statement, from the previous chapter: "I'm sorry, I don't understand all the laws here." But Platte had already participated in three Plowshares trials by the time of the Sacred Earth and Space II trial, and, as a longtime resident of Jonah House, she had attended several others. She had made it her business to thoroughly understand the laws. Similarly, in the trial for the Trident II action, defendant Frank Panopoulos stated, "Forgive me if I do not say this in the right way, I'm not experienced."[22] Panopoulos was twenty-six years old and being tried for his first Plowshares action, so the claim of inexperience seems credible enough at first. But the trial transcript makes plain that, like Platte, Panopoulos was in fact well versed in the regulations of the courtroom and savvy in negotiating them. The claim of inexperience is revealed as a rhetorical maneuver in the context of his expert discussion of legal matters elsewhere in the opening statement and throughout the trial. Like Platte, Panopoulos used the trope of incomplete or improper understanding to convey that he was an outsider in the courtroom, with a different conception of justice and morality.

With such assertions Plowshares activists perform a lack of the practical competence that Pierre Bourdieu argues is necessary and is revealed in the use of "legitimate language" (here, the language of the courts).[23] It is not for lack of familiarity that Plowshares defendants cannot use the court's legitimate language; rather, in refusing to use it, they are making the claim that it has not been inculcated in them—and further, that they have actively resisted and refused its inculcation in favor of divine obedience. A declaration of misunderstanding, then, is a performance of incompetence not unlike crying or slouching. Such a declaration is a way for defendants to distance themselves from the centers of immoral earthly justice, as is its corollary: their insistence on speaking their own rather than the court's language, as in Boylan's determination to talk about symbolic disarmament when the prosecution wants to talk about hammering on a submarine. Using illegitimate language in a context where they know—or can anticipate, in Bourdieuian terms—that it is illegitimate is another way to assert nonbelonging, whether the behavior it accompanies is noncompliant or unimpeachable.

Legitimate language, for Bourdieu and for the Plowshares, reproduces itself while reproducing social norms, by demonstrating differences in levels of linguistic capital and marking off those who have less of it as inferior in the field where a given language is legitimate. But it is precisely in asserting their position on the outskirts of the juridical field that the Plowshares accrue symbolic capital in their religious field. Illegitimate language works to elevate their status, precisely by denigrating it in the eyes of the court. As Plowshares defendants use language and behavior to perform their position on the outskirts of a field and their disavowal of its norms, their loss of status in the courtroom serves to confirm their role as prophets and martyrs. The courtroom's dual audience—composed of close supporters who share their worldview and vocabulary and sense of "true" justice, as well as those who do not (including the representatives of earthly justice, but also those to whom their actions are simply foreign)—makes possible the inverse relationship between status denigration and status elevation. The courtroom is the necessary arena for rhetorical and behavioral performances of nonbelonging, because in the courtroom these performances can be apprehended by a dual audience more so than during the actions themselves, which are usually apprehended only by their supporters (and, even then, at a remove). The dual audience ensures that the performances are invested with the dual, interlocking meanings of status loss and status conferral that they require to be effective.

Identification with a Jury of Peers

Nonbelonging, performed both rhetorically and behaviorally, is crucial to the Plowshares' aims for their time in the courtroom and their larger resistance. But in attempting to effectively communicate their motives and beliefs to courtroom audiences, Plowshares defendants do occasionally declare likeness between themselves and their judges, as when Platte, during a 2000 trial, repeatedly compared her obligation to a higher or deeper law to the judge's obligation to laws of conscience, at one point noting that by performing the action, she was responding to her religious values in exactly the same way that the judge, every time he hears a case, responds to and enacts his own value system. (The judge did not relish the comparison.) But, more often, Plowshares defendants attempt to convey similarity not with their judges or prosecutors, but with the members of their juries. Much of what the Plowshares say during their trials is meant to communicate with the jury through a mechanism of solidarity or identification, similar to the identificatory rhetoric that appears throughout their writings. This was clear when the Griffiss defendants repeatedly attempted to downplay the religious freedom angle of their defense before the jury. It is even more explicit in the defendants' closing argument in the Thames River trial:

> It is fitting that we can directly address people like yourselves [the jury]: ordinary people, since it is in the tradition of our law that we be judged by our peers, by people who precisely because they are unschooled in the technicalities of legal language and procedure, are more immediately in touch with their own humanity and their common sense of right and wrong. You can judge the facts and also see beneath them to the root of all just law, the sacredness of life and the need to protect and nurture it. There is a strong link between common sense and conscience, between the human instinct for what is right and fair, good and just, and the decision to judge and act accordingly. Indeed, the jury has been called the conscience of the community, and, as such, you are the deciding voice in this courtroom.[24]

The jury members are explicitly labeled "peers," but, more subtly, the description of the jury echoes the activists' descriptions of themselves: we the defendants and you of the jury may be unschooled in the law, but we and you are people of conscience; we and you know what is truly right, in contrast to the warped justice of the courts; we and you are in touch with humanity, not just facts. The same trope of misunderstanding and inexperience that Plowshares defendants use to distance themselves from their judges and prosecutors reappears here, but now with the intention of linking the defendants to members of the jury—people who, like the defendants themselves, are unschooled in the technicalities of legal language and procedure. For defendants and jury members alike, lack of experience with legal language and procedure correlates directly to common sense, humanity, and conscience.

Platte's opening statement relied on a similar notion of defendants and jury members united as American citizens concerned with the well-being of the planet and the upholding of democracy. But while opening statements, are the preeminent constructive moment in the trial, in which the theory of the case is put forth, closing arguments are both reconstructive of the theory of the case that has been employed and deconstructive of the opponent's theory. The party offering a closing argument, then, stays within the theory and themes established throughout the trial—here, themes of conscience, obligation to a more just and binding law than that of the courts, and the duty to make one's voice heard—but also critiques the factual or normative bases of the opponent's case.[25] Because factual information is seldom in dispute during a Plowshares trial, Plowshares' closing arguments critique the normative basis of the prosecution's argument, as is apparent in this example: the prosecution may be schooled in legal protocol, but it values adherence to particular laws above a "common sense of right and wrong," or "the human instinct for what is right and fair, good and just, and the decision to judge and act accordingly." The defendants characterize their actions as responses to this common sense or instinct, and in characterizing the task of the jury in the same terms, they present anew the idea of a common, underlying moral sensibility on which their theory of the case relies and from which their rhetoric and behavior in the courtroom derive.

Claims of Similarity and Assertions of Difference

As is clear in Platte's opening statement, while the theme of a universally binding morality permeates the Plowshares' trials, so does the certainty that others will not respond to its obligations as the Plowshares do. Platte's regret at the us-versus-them distinction she invoked in her statement is palpable. The cases discussed in this chapter, however, illustrate that though the distinction is a strict one in theory, Plowshares activists frequently resist or refigure the notion of distinction when claims of identification and assertions of difference better serve their communicative purposes. Identificatory moves like the ones described here might seem to counter the idea that the Plowshares rely on a characterization of themselves as marginal for the efficacy of their actions, argued throughout this book. Indeed, the tension between the rhetoric and behavior of distance (noncompliant behavior and illegitimate language) and the rhetoric of similarity (inherent in the necessity defense and made explicit in the language of identification) reveals an underlying tension between the Plowshares' theology of solidarity and emphasis on a shared moral sensibility and their self-characterization as fulfilling a special role meant only for a few. The Plowshares do not speak directly of being specially called to occupy the role of prophet or sentry, during their trials or elsewhere. Though they do suggest that notion obliquely in various ways, they explicitly present these roles as available to all and the attendant responsibilities as expected of all. At the same time, they believe themselves to be substantively changed by the actions, as discussed in chapter 2.

This tension emerges even within the Plowshares' claims of identification with the jury. The Thames River closing statement is exemplary. Following the appeal to similarity, the statement reminded the jury that blood has been poured in the action as a "symbol of sisterhood and brotherhood, of the willingness to make a small sacrifice that others may not have to make the ultimate one, and, hopefully, to make any sacrifice rather than to kill." The passage echoed earlier testimony from defendant Arthur Laffin, who explained, "I then proceeded to pour blood—my own blood—to symbolize what the end result of the Trident would be should it ever be used, and to express the belief that I have and that we all have that we are prepared to give our life rather than to ever take life."[26] The juxtaposition of these passages reveals that even claims of solidarity ("sisterhood and brotherhood") provide the context for the assertion of the defendants' greater commitment: you may be people of conscience just as much as we are, but your conscience lies dormant, as evidenced by the fact that we are acting in a way that you are not and would not—and more, that you do not have to, because we are. The distinction that such language suggests, a verbal recapitulation of the boundaries demonstrated during the actions, is facilitated rather than countered by claims of similarity, in that a measure of similarity allows for the recognition of where that similarity ends. Carl Kabat expressed the tension between claims of identification and difference when, leaving the courtroom after a 2009 trial, he called the jury his "brothers and sisters" but lamented that they are "ordinary people" who "don't understand the power they have."[27] As in the Thames River closing statement, asserting similarity with jury members sets the stage for claims of difference. The jury members are like the defendants, but they do not realize or do not embrace that similarity.

But whatever substantive otherness the Plowshares feel they possess because of their actions, they seldom express it in direct verbal terms in the courtroom. There, claims of difference are indeed crucial, but they are embedded in claims to similarity and identification and the idea of shared potentiality that anyone can realize—themes that unite the defendants with the jury. The striking discrepancy between the Griffiss appeal documents, which make a vigorous case for the defendants' religious rights, and the same defendants' insistence while before the jury on a common moral sensibility rather than religious particularity demonstrates the Plowshares' investment in rhetorically uniting themselves with members of their juries. Neither claims of difference nor claims of identification, then, tell the whole story. Plowshares defendants, even while stressing their similarity with jury members, believe in and value their own difference, as was evident during a debate about jury selection for the Trident II trial. The defendants wanted, counter to usual procedure, to question potential jurors individually and in private. In keeping with their belief that they are widely misunderstood and criminalized, the defendants argued that if potential jurors were questioned in view of their fellow citizens, any among them who felt sympathies for the defendants and their actions would be prevented from giving honest answers about those sympathies because of "water-cooler anxiety": worry over fitting in with their peers, in whose eyes the Plowshares were surely seen as heinous criminals. The implication is that it would be a rare juror who would maintain such sympathy, facing what was sure to be a unified mass of disapproval.[28] Public disapproval from a society in thrall to Lord Nuke frames that Plowshares' self-understanding and their conception of the actions as efficacious; their trials are essential components of their larger project in part because they are manifestations of this disapproval.

Plowshares activists use their trials as opportunities to characterize their actions in quite different terms than the courts do, thereby insisting on discursive discrepancies that provide a context in which they are able to assert their claims to difference. Even claims of identification that defendants use to communicate their theological and political messages to the jury are opportunities for defendants to assert the ideals of distinctive self-sacrifice and martyrdom that they perform during the actions. Thus, the trials have not failed as communicative endeavors when defenses are stifled or defendants refuse to participate. Rather, such "failures" are themselves the means for the communication of the Plowshares' ideas about their identity, specifically the claims of marginality and persecution that they use to link themselves with Jesus.

Outsiders and Efficacy

At a first glance the drama seems uneven: the high emotion, risk, and visceral impact of the Plowshares' actions versus the apparent passivity of the courtroom, as defendants await their fate. But to regard their time in court in this way is to misunderstand the Plowshares and their project. Acquittal is not the Plowshares' primary concern, and defendants are far from passive during their trials. Instead they make active use of the courtroom's characteristics, bringing to the fore those most conducive to their project to turn the courtroom into an analogous space to their action sites, where similarly important religious work takes place. Specifically, both the actions and the trials take place in highly regulated spaces, the norms of which activists transgress to highlight humanity's failure to live up to God's demands. At the action sites activists enter illicit space and perform ritual actions meant to resacralize those spaces. To echo that sense of transgression during their trials, defendants go to great lengths to demonstrate that they are not welcome or do not belong in the courtroom.

The trials, like the actions, serve as arenas in which the Plowshares perform moral boundaries. But these performances require authentication from the courts, most handily in the form of guilty verdicts. Sometimes, however, the court varies from its expected role as arbiter of the earthly justice that the Plowshares posit as a foil for true justice, showing sympathy for the defendants and corroborating rather than impeding their performances of identity. In the opening statement analyzed in the previous chapter, Ardeth Platte began by asking God to bless the jury members and be with them in their decision-making process. The prosecuting attorney interrupted almost immediately: "Your Honor, I object. . . . I don't think this is a proper opening statement. She is not talking about the evidence. She is talking about God." But the judge overruled the objection: "Well, I respectfully disagree. She is actually making a rhetorical or poetic transition from that statement to fair comment on the evidence in the form of its description."[29] Though the judge's characterization of religious content as merely rhetorical is not in keeping with the Plowshares' own understanding of their religious talk, this episode shows the court facilitating rather than hindering the defendants' communicative intentions, acknowledging and even supporting the defendants' attempts to talk about the religious and moral aspects of their actions.

In choosing certain defenses and modes of discourse, Plowshares defendants insist on an illegitimate language intended to call into question the authority of the court and to assert nonbelonging as a moral imperative tied directly to the aims of their actions. Other parties, however, play a role in how the Plowshares' assertions are received. Just as personnel at the action sites become unwitting yet crucial participants in the actions, whose presence is necessary for their success, prosecutors, judges, and juries function as more than the Plowshares' audience. They also serve the important role of authenticating the Plowshares' related theological and social claims: inasmuch as Plowshares activists are punished by legal consequences, their rhetoric of marginality becomes an actual social martyrdom, by which they, as sacrificial victims mirroring the redemptive death of Jesus Christ, fulfill their theologically mandated role and thus change the world. The trials are opportunities for the confirmation of the Plowshares' tandem claims to marginality and to efficacy, which together reside in their identification with Jesus as deemed illegal by earthly courts. Constituencies other than the Plowshares and their supporters play a crucial role in the substantiation of these claims, delineating a margin for the Plowshares to occupy and then placing them there.

Given that so much of each trial's process and outcome is determined by circumstances outside the defendants' control, including the temperament of these other constituencies, and so much of the effective presentation of the defendants' theory of the case relies on the court presenting the opposite theory, it bears considering to what degree these other constituencies affect the Plowshares' interpretations of the actions as successful. The metaphysical effects that the activists assign to symbolic disarmament no doubt are considered to remain intact independent of legal outcomes. Whatever the outcome, the combination of symbols means that the actions function as sacramental, redemptive irruptions of the sacred, as well as performances of symbolic boundaries. But because punishment from the courts is necessary for symbolic boundaries to become socially instantiated, are the actions' social effects undermined when a judge acknowledges the validity of the action, for example, rather than stifling the defendants' invocations of necessity? How do defendants continue to assert their claim to nonbelonging in the courts, and their status as martyrs, when there are fewer impediments placed in their way? Though in every case the trials function as pedagogical opportunities and as performances of identity and ideology, and the actions function metaphysically for the activists because of the semiotic work that takes place, what does it mean for the social function of the trials and for the actions themselves when the courtroom proceedings do not bolster the defendants' claims to marginality—when judges and juries demonstrate sympathy and support for the actions?

Because both criminalization and trivialization are coded in the Plowshares' rhetoric as persecution, it is not insurmountably problematic when, for example, charges are dropped before a case goes to trial, as has happened on occasion. Activists interpret dropped charges as the court's attempt to sweep the actions under the rug, as in the case of the Plowshares Eight, because of the threat the activists represent. Dropped charges can easily be made to corroborate the Plowshares' prophet discourse, even as they may undermine the martyr discourse. But the martyr discourse is automatically strengthened by the simple fact that Plowshares activists in the United States have never been wholly acquitted. More than once, however, they have been validated, at least in part, by the court. In the 1984 Sperry Software Pair trial, in which two activists poured blood and hammered on computer equipment intended to provide navigation systems for bomber planes, the judge allowed the necessity defense, noting its validity for civil disobedience cases in general. When the two defendants were convicted nonetheless of destruction of government property, the judge suspended their six-month sentences. And in the 1996 Weep for Children trial, the judge disagreed vehemently with the prosecutor's closing assertion that the four defendants were "just like the Oklahoma city bomber" by replying that they were indeed following a higher law.[30] He sentenced them to one thousand hours of community service—not a particularly difficult charge for nuns who spend much of their time working with the poor.

It should come as no surprise that these cases are not held out as particular successes by Plowshares activists, nor are the actions from which they resulted deemed more efficacious because of the support for the defendants that was demonstrated. The corollary will be equally unsurprising: the Plowshares actions that have received the most attention are those in which punishments were the harshest, such as the Silo Pruning Hooks action and, more recently, the 2002 Sacred Earth and Space II action, in which, perhaps because of its close proximity to the events of 9/11, the three participants were charged with sabotage rather than the more usual criminal trespass (without the appearance of greater threat that had been present in the Silo Pruning Hooks action) and faced thirty-year sentences. Media attention as well as popular support for the participants swelled to unprecedented levels in these cases.

These trials were, in many ways, great successes, allowing for wider dissemination of the Plowshares' ideology, based on an either-or confrontation between earthly justice and its foil of "true" or "common sense" or "good" justice. The emphasis on such a confrontation is essential to the Plowshares' sense of self. Even as they rely in their trials on aligning themselves with larger society, Plowshares defendants rely simultaneously on the notion of a rift that cannot be bridged except by action, between those who choose to act in accordance with the demands of true justice and those who, bound by the laws of earthly justice, do not. The defendants intend their challenges to the courtroom's norms as performances of their distinction from the society that pledges immoral allegiance to nuclear idols and from the courtroom, where those idols are defended and safeguarded against challenges. It is because the courts act as protectors and legitimators of nuclear idolatry that the defendants assert their ultimate nonbelonging. Carl Kabat remarked during a 1984 sentencing, "Whether this [court]room is a part of God's kingdom, [is] a real question mark for me."[31] The Plowshares perform their symbolic disarmaments in the firm belief that by doing so they can sacralize the unholy ground of nuclear manufacture or storage. Performing their nonbelonging in the courts, the Plowshares express their doubt over whether the courts can be similarly reclaimed—whether even the most inclusive boundaries that they draw can incorporate the purveyors of corrupt earthly justice. For the sake of their status as marginal prophets, it is a doubt on which they must insist.

But to regard as failures the trials that proceed and close quietly, in which judges demonstrate a measure of support for the defendants' position, would be an analytic misstep. Such trials may not provide the opportunity for the same kind of strenuous boundary work that the more difficult trials do, but they are still crucial in shaping boundaries—if not the external boundaries between the Plowshares and the sinful world, then the internal boundaries between the Plowshares and their closest activist kin, who share their worldview. It is to this more subtle form of boundary work, performed during even the least difficult trials, to which I turn in the conclusion.

Conclusion

After Jackie Hudson's death in August 2011, the Dominican Sisters of Grand Rapids, Michigan, where she had been a nun for fifty-eight years, published an obituary that included an excerpt from an essay Hudson had written years before, reflecting on her work for peace and justice and specifically on her antinuclear activities—activities that many of her fellow sisters apparently did not quite understand, though "all who knew her loved her and admired her courage and conviction," according to the obituary. "Will my efforts bring about change in my lifetime?" Hudson had asked. "Hard to tell; the important thing is that all of us remain faithful."[1]

Many Plowshares activists have similarly acknowledged that the instrumental outcomes of their actions are uncertain, but that whatever else the actions may or may not do, the most important result is the continued faithfulness of those who undertake them. It is a sentiment at the heart of the Plowshares' project, evident from its beginnings in Philip Berrigan's notion of the one or two faithful who would change the world. For the Plowshares, whose actions strike many as absurdly ineffective, the embodiment of particular personal characteristics (faithfulness, commitment, and truthfulness, for example) is central to their understanding of the actions as deeply efficacious, both symbolically and practically. The actions function as they are meant to function because the activists, in performing them, become who they are mandated to be. The roles to which they are called (prophet, martyr, sentry, shepherd, and more) are oriented around a notion of faithfulness that depends, as the previous chapters have shown, on making, and making again, public declarations of "true" religious commitment.

Those declarations—at the action sites, in the courtroom, and on the page—both express and enact the Plowshares' sense of distinction from all those who do not resist as they do. From trespassing and pouring their own blood, to describing themselves as sentries and shepherds, to pleading ignorance of the courtroom's linguistic norms or flouting its behavioral conventions, the Plowshares conceive of, carry out, and explain their actions and trials as ways to demarcate sociomoral space and situate themselves within it. According to a religious logic that is social, embodied, and emotive as well as cognitive, transgressing spatial and behavioral norms imposed by the state—and upheld, in their view, by the Catholic Church—is a way to instantiate as social boundaries the symbolic boundaries that undergird the Plowshares' religiopolitical worldview. Identity and ideology coalesce in the Plowshares' orientation toward sincerity, responsibility, commitment, and especially self-sacrifice as the vehicles for their actions' efficacy. Paul Kabat expressed that amalgamation of identity and outcome when he answered the question of what he and his fellow activists accomplished: "At least we are a continuing testimony of our concern for humanity and for real disarmament."[2] Their actions, their trials, but especially *the activists themselves* are a testimony, and that testimony is the goal. A resistance project that may at first seem decidedly counterintuitive in terms of both social movement development and political reform possesses, for the activists, a logic of identity that is "deeper than reason."

The Plowshares insist that such deep logic is available to all and, more, that answering the obligations it poses is a responsibility shared by all. But by performing and talking about their actions in the ways that they do, Plowshares activists both demonstrate and enact their belief that real resistance—and, indeed, real Christianity—requires them to occupy the margins of state and church, where few will follow them. That most others do not and would not do the same thing is not a circumstance the Plowshares lament or work against, because it is precisely the point. Plowshares activists set out to do

Plowshares need to be at the margins

something dangerous and extraordinary as a means to fulfill what they understand as their divinely mandated roles. Being criminalized and trivialized and remaining a small group are essential components of those roles. As Anne Montgomery wrote, "To make our prayer and action one, to reach out to the 'other' in a personal way, requires that we emphasize depth and relationship rather than numbers and high-powered organization."[3] Proper motivation and authenticity—proper faithfulness and thereby effectiveness—can be assured only if numbers remain small.

The punishments the activists face play a significant role in keeping their number small. Enduring prison, even welcoming it, is central to Plowshares identity, a mark of extreme commitment—for some, the only commitment worth making. Philip Berrigan, in prison for the Prince of Peace Plowshares action, wrote to McAlister in 1997, "I thank God daily for this dumpster. If one can't do time here (people of our confession), they don't belong in resistance."[4] It should be noted that even Philip acknowledged his uncompromising standards for what constitutes proper Christian witness as perhaps too rigorous; nonetheless, the emphasis on prison is a constant among Plowshares activists, even when more gently formulated.[5] Prison's ability to demarcate the Plowshares even from their close allies is clear is Philip's comment, "Let's begin by saying that jail is the bottom line. Most American peace people never come to grips with that."[6] And its importance to the Plowshares' sense of self was expressed by one activist, weighted down with a sense of failure she experienced upon agreeing to the court's conditions to have her sentence reduced (a compromise that many, though certainly not all, Plowshares activists refuse) and her feeling that she betrayed the other activists who participated in the action with her: "I basically promised not to break the law and not to go on a military installation and to pay the restitution. I had a real hard time when I first got out. Feeling guilty because I'd agreed to all the things. Violated what I thought were absolute principles. I'd think, 'Jean would never do this' or 'Ardeth would never do this.' I had some big adjustments, just coming to terms with what I did."[7]

The harsh consequences are a mixed bag

Others in their wider resistance community express the same sense that harsh consequences are inextricably bound up with what it means to be a Plowshares activist and, like the Catholic Worker quoted earlier who said, "I continue to be challenged by the Plowshares people and feel a call to do more but feel . . . that it's not possible for me," feel regret that those consequences prevent them from following the Plowshares' example of resistance. This Catholic Worker's statement speaks to the questions that have shaped my analysis of the Plowshares' boundary work. First, does "doing more" refer only to harsh punishments, or are the Plowshares' actions themselves, independent of their consequences, regarded by their peers as "more?" If so, how do they come to be regarded that way, as Catholic resistance par excellence, so that those who do not choose to follow in their footsteps feel some measure of regret? By no means am I suggesting that everyone in the wider Catholic peacemaking community shares the feelings of the Catholic Worker quoted here. But there is no doubt that some do, which in turn leaves no doubt that Plowshares actions, and those who perform them, have been deeply influential in shaping the religious worlds of their peers.

I have used the term "performance" in this work in a dual sense, to mean both showing and doing. But considering the Plowshares as shapers of their peers' religious worlds suggests yet another level of meaning, a tripleness to performance rather than a doubleness. As I have argued throughout, the Plowshares' interlocking rhetorical and embodied performances of identity are central to their religiopolitical project and their notion of efficacy. Yet in some measure, sometimes large measure, the success of those performances, which are meant to both convey and constitute identity, depends on outsider constituencies. This is true in the actions, when apprehension by outsiders is essential, and, even more strikingly, during the trials, when the way the trials proceed and the eventual verdicts have as much to do with prosecutors, judges, juries, and observers as with the defendants themselves. Outsiders shape the Plowshares' religious world, variously helping or hindering the fruitful performance of identity. The third aspect of performance that the case of the Plowshares suggests lies in the corollary: as outsiders shape the Plowshares' religious world, the Plowshares, virtuosi within a wider resistance community in which not everyone does what they do, shape the way their peers experience and express and constitute their own religiosity. The performance of religious boundaries, which the Plowshares intend to separate them from the sinful outside world, helps to produce the religious world of their close peacemaking kin by assigning particular content to shared concepts and categories. The "doing" aspect of performance is itself double, referring both to the Plowshares constituting their own identity, as they display and describe it, and to their constituting the religious worlds of their friends and supporters, both near and far.

Even as they stress solidarity and continuity with their larger community, the Plowshares convey a sense of sociomoral distinction not only by the punishments they endure but also through the semiotic, embodied, and discursive repertoires on display in their actions, their trials, and their copious writings. According to those repertoires, the Plowshares are distinct from the sinful world in thrall to Lord Nuke and the lackadaisical church that fails in its duty to call the state to task. The symbols they use in their actions signify their orientation toward extreme self-sacrifice as well as their degree of commitment and preparedness. Anne Montgomery suggested as much when she wrote of the special preparation required for a Plowshares action, more "intense and prolonged" than for other types of civil disobedience. The metaphors that anchor the Plowshares' rhetoric move them to the extreme ends of the discursive domains they share with their wider community, as when they identify their project with Jesus's work, a saving act done on behalf of humanity, and the consequences they face as the "only real credential ... of discipleship." Their performances of nonbelonging in the courts, both subtle ("I don't understand all the laws here," as Platte claimed) and overt (refusing to participate in the trials), testify to their extreme commitment to "true" justice, again on behalf of all those who do not so respond to its mandates.

But those in the best position to apprehend and understand the Plowshares' boundary work are not the parties from which they would hope to distinguish themselves, not the audiences for whom their performances of nonbelonging are, at least immediately, aimed. On the contrary, the semiotic logic of symbolic disarmament and the discursive domains the Plowshares use when talking about their actions and themselves resonate most strongly within the wider Catholic resistance community. These fellow Catholic peace activists share the Plowshares' logic and discourses, and often they share the Plowshares' sense of what constitutes true religious commitment and efficacious symbolic action. It is this wider Catholic peacemaking community that reads and disseminates and reprints the Plowshares' writings, as the Catholic Worker Reprint Series has done with both *The Time's Discipline* and *Swords into Plowshares*, even though, as detailed in chapter 3, many of those writings are ostensibly written for the benefit of people who are baffled by their actions—a category that does not include their supporters and peacemaking allies. Those who circulate these writings do so not for their explanatory power but as a religious activity—an activity, that is, that reinforces sacred norms and holds up the exemplars of those norms. This activity reiterates the motivations and aims of the Plowshares' actions, but it is not the only Plowshares-related religious activity in which members of the broader Catholic peacemaking community engage. Members of this community also travel long distances to attend the Plowshares' trials, write letters to jailed Plowshares activists, and flood their websites with message of support. All these religious activities are engendered by the Plowshares' project, a project that serves as an important component in the religious lives of their peers.

As they perform boundaries between themselves and the sinful world, Plowshares activists distinguish themselves from their close supporters for whom they explicitly express only solidarity and continuity. The case of the Plowshares is a case of a religious group attentive to boundaries—those distinguishing themselves from a corrupt world (full of the protectors of Lord Nuke, whose laws dismiss the sovereignty of God) and also, though less intentionally and explicitly, those distinguishing themselves from their closest Catholic peace activist peers (who, while understanding the logic and motivations of the Plowshares and supporting their efforts in crucial ways, nonetheless do not make quite the same commitment by which the Plowshares define their Christian witness). Their form of resistance is idiosyncratic, but their attention to boundaries is not, though boundary work is often regarded as a mere consequence of the other, more "really" religious things that religious communities do. Consideration of the Plowshares' religious world attunes us to the complex social dynamics at play in religious communities—even those often perceived as one-dimensional, whether foolishly or dangerously so—by which the constitution of religious identity, achieved across a range of social settings, itself crosses boundaries, as religious groups continually break into, make, and remake one another's religious worlds, as well as their own.

NOTES

Introduction

1. Laffin and Montgomery, *Swords into Plowshares* (1996), 9.

2. Jewish Publication Society, *Tanakh*.

3. Plowshares Eight, action statement, box 1, Berrigan-McAlister Collection.

4. My account combines those found in P. Berrigan, *Lamb's War*, 183; and Norman, *Hammer of Justice*, 23–30. Norman's primary informant is the security guard, Robert Cox; and his superior, identified as Captain Drobek.

5. Philip Berrigan to Daniel Berrigan, May 3, 1978, box 1, Berrigan-McAlister Collection.

6. Most sentences are in the one- to two-year range. The action that occasioned the anomalous eighteen-year sentences is discussed in a later chapter. For several years Plowshares activists maintained a website chronicling the Plowshares' actions, including a chronology, descriptions, and background on the activists, archived at http://web.archive.org/web/20130925030826/http://www.craftech.com/~dcpledge/brandywine/plow/. Much of the information on the earlier actions appears also in a book co-edited by Plowshares activists Arthur Laffin and Anne Montgomery, *Swords into Plowshares*, which reports on Plowshares actions first through 1986, then, in a revised edition, through 1996. Jonah House, the intentional community of Philip Berrigan, Elizabeth McAlister, and numerous other Plowshares activists and considered the Plowshares epicenter, maintains a website with information on the past half-dozen actions; see www.jonahhouse.org/archive/.

Plowshares activists in other countries—notably Sweden, the Netherlands, Great Britain, and Ireland—have been acquitted, as discussed in Nepstad, *Religion and War Resistance*. Nepstad's work treats Plowshares activism in the other countries where it has appeared, which is beyond the scope of my project. (The domestic actions constitute almost two-thirds of all Plowshares actions.) Nepstad's book also includes a chronology of U.S. Plowshares actions through 2006 (233–38).

7. Courtney Bender has shown skillfully how the so-called spiritual but not religious identity is produced through and by various institutions and argues that we should attend to those same types of institutional dynamics and processes in the production of religious identity. See *New Metaphysicals*. See also Bender, Cadge, Levitt, and Smilde's introduction to *Religion on the Edge*, in which they make the argument even more pointedly, calling for attention to the complex and diverse ways that religion is expressed and produced outside of congregational settings.

8. Gieryn, "Boundary-Work."

9. For two thorough review articles, see Lamont and Molnar, "Study of Boundaries"; and Pachucki, Pendergrass, and Lamont, "Boundary Processes."

10. For a collection of approaches to boundary work studies, with an emphasis on the various cultural means by which class distinctions are conveyed and carried (musical tastes and food preferences, for example), see the essays in Lamont and Fournier, *Cultivating Differences*.

11. Lamont and Molnar, "Study of Boundaries," 168.

12. See, for example, Yukich, "Boundary Work." Yukich's examination of boundary work in inclusive religious groups—those that, due to an ideology of inclusion, ostensibly refrain from othering—illustrates one type of complexity involved in thinking about religious boundary work.

13. See, for example, Becker, *Outsiders*; Bourdieu, *Distinction*; and Tilly, *Identities*.

14. See, for example, Schmidt, "Church-Going People."

15. Moore, *Religious Outsiders*, esp. chap. 1, "How to Become a People."

16. C. Smith, *American Evangelicalism*, 118.

17. Though my focus in this project is on boundaries that religious groups choose and work to instantiate, it is not my intention to override the fact that not all boundaries on the American religious landscape are chosen by the group being demarcated and not all of them prove easily permeable to the extent that the group on one side or the other would wish.

18. Rowlandson's captivity narrative was published in 1682 in a U.S. edition, closely followed by a British edition that gave the work a very different title. The difference is telling. British readers pored over *A True History of the Captivity and Restoration of Mrs. Mary Rowlandson, a Minister's Wife in New England, Wherein Is Set Forth, the Cruel and Inhumane Usage She Underwent amongst the Heathens, for Eleven Weeks Time, and Her Deliverance from Them* (London: Poole, 1682). The title of the U.S. edition, meanwhile, emphasized not the Indians' cruelty, but God's goodness toward his chosen, covenanted people: *The Sovereignty and Goodness of God, Together, with the Faithfulness of his Promises Displayed, Being a Narrative of the Captivity and Restoration of Mrs. Mary Rowlandson* (Cambridge, Mass.: Green, 1682). The U.S. title especially reflects one of the uses to which Mary's narrative was put in colonial America—to shore up precisely those boundaries, between God's chosen people and the heathenish Indians, that she had noted as permeable during her captivity.

19. Edgell, Gerteis, and Hartmann, "Atheists as 'Other.'"

20. Two recent examples of work in American religious studies that begin with boundary questions are Yukich, "Boundary Work"; and Taysom, *Shakers*. Several of the essays in Bender and Klassen's edited volume, *After Pluralism*, also engage this issue.

21. Schechner, *Essays on Performance Theory*. The work of Schechner and other early performance theorists is often eclipsed by the important contributions of theorists such as Judith Butler, whose notion of unfixed selves constituted by iterative performance is also applicable to religious selves in general and to the Plowshares specifically (see *Gender Trouble*). I focus here on Schechner because his work foregrounds performers' intentionality, which is central to my analysis of the Plowshares.

22. Grimes, "Religion, Ritual, and Performance," in Gharavi, *Religion, Theatre, and Performance*, 35.

23. Several founding figures of social movement studies, as well as more recent thinkers, have moved away from defining a social movement as necessarily involving large numbers of participants and observable political results, toward definitions that emphasize common goals, solidarity, and more subjective outcomes such as cultural transformation. See Epstein, *Political Protest*; Jasper, *Art of Moral Protest*; Tarrow, *Power in Movement*; and Guigno, McAdam, and Tilly, *How Social Movements Matter*. Decades earlier James Gusfield, in his discussion of the temperance movement, suggested that "expressive movements" and "status movements" worked at ends beyond the immediately political. Despite my preference for thinking of the Plowshares as something other than a movement, I have found Gusfield's categories in *Symbolic Crusade* to be useful and return to them later. Dan McKanan, in his review of Sharon Nepstad's book, *Religion and War Resistance*, suggests that Verta Taylor's term "abeyance structure" is more accurate than "movement" in describing the Plowshares. An abeyance structure is a smaller group that continues the vision of an already-subsided movement; see Taylor, "Social Movement Continuity." I agree with McKanan that this seems a closer fit than "movement," but "abeyance structure" implies an attachment to the past that the first Plowshares activists did not emphasize, as I discuss in chapter 1.

Chapter 1

1. Gray, *Divine Disobedience*, 227, x; Gray, "Profiles"; "Berrigans."

2. Clifford, "Berrigans," in van Etten Casey, *Berrigans*, 36.

3. Andrew Greeley famously rails against the Berrigans in "Turning off 'The People,'" *New Republic*, June 27, 1970; and "Berrigans," *Holy Cross Quarterly*, January 1971. In his 1974 book *Building Coalitions*, he castigates Philip for his thoughts on being an American and a Catholic—not "love it or leave it," but, more dangerously, "You can't love it without leaving it" (416).

4. For two recent examples, see Peters, *Catonsville Nine*; and Marsh and Brown, *Faith, Resistance, and the Future*.

5. Jasper, *Art of Moral Protest*.

6. P. Berrigan, *Lamb's War*, 83.

7. D. Berrigan, *To Dwell in Peace*, 94.

8. P. Berrigan, *Lamb's War*, 97.

9. See Dunning, *Aliens and Sojourners*.

10. Roth, "Socio-historical Model"; Roth, "Religion and Revolutionary Beliefs." For Roth, the Berrigans exemplify a host of Weberian categories (virtuosity, charisma, ethical and exemplary prophecy).

11. hooks, "Marginality," in Ferguson et al., *Out There*, 337–340; J. Smith, *Relating Religion*, 237.

12. Polner and O'Grady, *Disarmed and Dangerous*, 143–44.

13. Peters, *Catonsville Nine*, 41.

14. By the time the Berrigans came to prominence, there had been an active Christian nonviolence movement in the United States for decades, which pioneered some of the techniques and tropes on which the Berrigans later would innovate. The Berrigans, however, were among its first Catholic stalwarts (along with Dorothy Day and Thomas Merton), and, as Joseph Kip Kosek notes in his history of Christian nonviolence, they moved the older nonviolent groups to the "cutting edge of radical Christian nonviolence . . . [and] pushed Christian nonviolence another step beyond the innovations of the civil rights movement and the early Vietnam protests" (*Acts of Conscience*, 235).

15. See McGreevey, *Catholicism*; and Dolan, *American Catholic Experience*.

16. Dolan, *In Search*, 146; Marty, *Invitation*, 147–79.

17. O'Brien, "Social Teaching," 202.

18. For more on especially Daniel Berrigan's initially enthusiastic response to the message and potential of Vatican reforms, see McNeal, *Harder Than War*, 188–89.

19. On Vatican reform, see, for example, Maines and McCallion, *Transforming Catholicism*; O'Connell, *Vatican II*; and Wilde, *Vatican II*.

20. O'Brien, "What Happened?," in Weaver, *What's Left?*, 255–82.

21. See Gathje, *Cost of Virtue*, esp. chap. 6.

22. Cogley, *Catholic America*, 290.

23. Appleby, "Daniel and Philip Berrigan," in Lippy, *Twentieth-Century Shapers*, 35.

24. Appleby, "Present to the People," in Dolan, *Transforming Parish Ministry*, 63–64, 91; Cogley, *Catholic America*, 273–74.

25. Byrne, "In the Parish," in Dolan, *Transforming Parish Ministry*, 154–70.

26. Dolan, *In Search*, 198–200.

27. D. Berrigan, *Geography of Faith*, 77.

28. Nelson and Ostrow, *FBI and the Berrigans*; O'Rourke, *Harrisburg Seven*, 7.

29. Nepstad, *Religion and War Resistance*, 53; Polner and O'Grady, *Disarmed and Dangerous*, 298; P. Berrigan, *Widen the Prison Gates*, 258, 261.

30. Gathje, *Cost of Virtue*, esp. chap. 6.

31. P. Berrigan, qtd. in Nangle, "Berrigan Recalled."

32. P. Berrigan and McAlister, *Time's Discipline*, 125; McAlister, "Prison Letter."

33. P. Berrigan and McAlister, *Time's Discipline*, xvii.

34. P. Berrigan, *Lamb's War*, 184.

35. Molly Rush, qtd. in Norman, *Hammer of Justice*, 133–35.

36. Frosch, "Battlefields Shift," A10.

37. Daniel Berrigan, desk calendar, September 1980, box 1, Berrigan-McAlister Collection.

38. Polner and O'Grady, *Disarmed and Dangerous*, 345.

39. Elizabeth McAlister to Carol and Jerome Berrigan, August 1980, box 1, Berrigan-McAlister Collection.

40. The Plowshares Eight trial is still cited as an illustration of the difficulty of using a necessity defense, which will be discussed

at greater length in later chapters. See, for example, Quigley, "Necessity Defense"; and Cohan, "Civil Disobedience."

41. See Toussaint, *Contemporary U.S. Peace Movement*; and Rojecki, "Freeze Frame," in Rochon and Meyer, *Coalitions and Political Movements*, 107–26.

42. The figures in this section are generated from information in Laffin and Montgomery, *Swords into Plowshares* (1987 and 1996), Nepstad, *Religion and War Resistance*, and on the Jonah House website, www .jonahhouse.org.

43. Broad, "Nun Who Broke," A1.

44. Mannheim, "Problem of Generations," in Wolff, *From Karl Mannheim*, 365, 367, 379.

45. Jonah House does go out of its way to make contact with younger generations, hosting college immersion trips during which students experience faith-based intentional community and may be invited to participate in low-risk civil disobedience activities. These immersion trips do function, in a sense, as recruitment for Catholic activism in general and sometimes to the specific cause of nuclear resistance. But Jonah House and the Plowshares, while closely related, are not coextensive, and while the Jonah House community does invite participation in many of the activities it sponsors, it does not recruit for the high-risk Plowshares actions.

46. See Wittner, *Toward Nuclear Abolition*. Or, for a more concise presentation, see Wittner, *Confronting the Bomb*.

47. See Epstein, *Political Protest*.

48. Rochon and Meyer, "Nuclear Freeze," introd. to Rochon and Meyer, *Coalitions and Political Movements*, 1–21.

49. Ibid., 2. According to Rochon and Meyer, the freeze movement "stands out among movements of the 1970s and 1980s . . . because it was conceived from the beginning as a nationally coordinated campaign to enact a specific policy reform" (2).

50. See Arthur Laffin's description of the response of the Nuclear Freeze Campaign and the southeast Connecticut peace community to his 1982 action, in Riegle, *Crossing the Line*, 120.

51. See Nepstad, *Religion and War Resistance*, esp. chap. 3.

52. For more on the Catholic Worker movement, see Zwick and Zwick, *Catholic Worker Movement*; Miller, *Harsh and Dreadful Love*; and Day's own writings, including *House of Hospitality* and *Long Loneliness*.

53. See Troester, *Voices*, esp. chaps. 9–10.

54. Nepstad, *Religion and War Resistance*, 39, 92.

55. McKanan, *Catholic Worker*, 88–89.

56. In Laffin and Montgomery's *Swords into Plowshares*, participants from each action up to the time of publication are listed, and almost everyone is described as active in another movement. Often this is simply the "peace and justice movement," but the civil rights movement, the antiwar movement, and various workers' rights and Latin American solidarity movements appear frequently as well.

57. Troester, *Voices*, 206. The same sentiment is reported in Effler, *Laughing Saints*, 117.

58. Trident Nein/Plowshares #4 Support Committee, meeting notes, 1983, box 2, Maas Collection.

59. P. Berrigan, "Jail Witness," Jonah House, accessed January 25, 2016, www .jonahhouse.org/archive/jail_witness.htm.

Chapter 2

1. The Transform Now Plowshares' account of their action is online; see "Story of the Action," accessed January 25, 2016, http://transformnowplowshares.wordpress .com/about/story-of-the-action/.

2. The group's statement and description of their action can be found at "A Statement for the Y-12 Facility," Transform Now Plowshares, accessed January 25, 2016, http://transformnowplowshares.wordpress .com/about/statement/. Several local and national media outlets also covered the story.

3. P. Berrigan and McAlister, *Time's Discipline*, 174; "Disarm Now Plowshares Statement," Disarm Now Plowshares, December 5, 2009, http://disarmnowplow shares.wordpress.com/2009/12/05 /disarm-now-plowshares-statement/.

4. For more on the roles and responses of Catholic episcopacy and laity to the nuclear issue, see Au, *Cross*.

5. Norman, *Hammer of Justice*, 25.

6. P. Berrigan and McAlister, *Time's Discipline*, 159–60.

7. P. Berrigan, *Lamb's War*, 185.

8. For more on spatial transgression, see Cresswell, *In Place*.

9. Laffin and Montgomery, *Swords into Plowshares* (1996), 76.

10. P. Berrigan, *Lamb's War*, 185.

11. Elizabeth McAlister, notes for testimony, Griffiss Air Force Base Plowshares trial, box 1, Maas Collection.

12. P. Berrigan and McAlister, *Time's Discipline*, 107–8.

13. Peters, *Catonsville Nine*, 33.

14. Philip and McAlister, *Time's Discipline*, 31n4; Peters, *Catonsville Nine*, 76, 92.

15. P. Berrigan and McAlister, *Time's Discipline*, 31n4; Riverside Plowshares, "Riverside Plowshares Statement," Jonah House, May 2003, www.jonahhouse.org/archive/RiversidePS.htm.

16. P. Berrigan, *Lamb's War*, 88.

17. P. Berrigan and McAlister, *Time's Discipline*, 31n4.

18. Ibid., 110; Montgomery, "Divine Obedience," 30.

19. Fink, *New Dictionary*, 45; Lang, *Dictionary of the Liturgy*, 28; McCall, *Do This*, 136.

20. D. Berrigan, qtd. in Baggarly et al., *Disciples and Dissidents*, 21.

21. Laffin and Montgomery, *Swords into Plowshares* (1987), 60, 31.

22. Connell, "Sacrifice of the Mass," in *New Baltimore Catechism*, 209.

23. Paul Kabat, qtd. ibid., 155.

24. Marcia Timmel, personal statement, box 1, Maas Collection.

25. Paul Kabat, qtd. in Laffin and Montgomery, *Swords into Plowshares* (1987), 154.

26. "Four Arrested After Missile Silo Is Damaged," unidentified newspaper clipping, box 2, Maas Collection.

27. Transform Now Plowshares, "Statement for the Y-12."

28. McAlister, notes for testimony.

29. P. Berrigan and McAlister, *Time's Discipline*, 107. Thomas Merton, a Trappist monk who wrote prolifically on issues of spirituality and social justice, was a close friend to the Berrigans.

30. Laffin and Montgomery, *Swords into Plowshares* (1987), 29.

31. Reagan, Address; Jackson, "Heal the World"; Schönberg, "Epilogue."

32. Laffin and Montgomery, *Swords into Plowshares* (1987), 30.

33. Arthur Laffin, qtd. in Riegle, *Crossing the Line*, 118.

34. Mark Colville, qtd. in Baggarly et al., *Disciples and Dissidents*, 22; Plowshares Number Four, action statement, box 1, Maas Collection.

35. Marcia Timmel, qtd. in Laffin and Montgomery, *Swords into Plowshares* (1987), 86.

36. P. Berrigan, "The Time of Dry Wood," Jonah House, accessed January 25, 2016, www.jonahhouse.org/archive/DryWood.htm.

37. Laffin and Montgomery, *Swords into Plowshares* (1996), 49; Nepstad, *Religion and War Resistance*, 57–58.

38. Paul Kabat, qtd. in Laffin and Montgomery, *Swords into Plowshares* (1987), 155.

39. *Kitsap Sun*, qtd. in Friedrich, "Antiwar Demonstrators."

40. Security guard, qtd. in Norman, *Hammer of Justice*, 27.

41. W. P. Houley, qtd. in Thames River Plowshares action, presentencing report, box 3, Maas Collection.

42. Laffin and Montgomery, *Swords into Plowshares* (1996), 54–55.

43. Ibid., 55.

44. Bivins, *Fracture of Good Order*, 14–15; Bell, *Ritual Theory*, 74; Grimes, "Religion, Ritual, and Performance," in Gharavi, *Religion, Theatre, and Performance*, 38–39.

45. Laffin and Montgomery, *Swords into Plowshares* (1987), 30.

46. Lincoln, "On Ritual," 492.

47. Ibid., 492–93.

Chapter 3

1. Susan Crane, "Why We Are Disarming the A-10 Warthogs: A Letter Written to Friends Explaining Our Plowshares Action," Jonah House, December 1999, www.jonahhouse.org/archive/crane_ltrDU.htm.

2. Pershing Plowshares, "Declaration of Conscience: Passover/Easter, 1984," Internet Archive, accessed January 25, 2016, http://web.archive.org/web/20111005012658/http://www.craftech.com/~dcpledge/brandywine

/plow/statements/ppsState.htm. The Pershing Plowshares activists—Per Herngren, Paul Magno, Todd Kaplan, Tim Lietzke, Anne Montgomery, Patrick O'Neill, Jim Perkins, and Christin Schmidt—were convicted of depredation of government property and conspiracy and sentenced to three years in prison and fines.

3. "Statement of Jubilee Plowshares," in Laffin and Montgomery, *Swords into Plowshares* (1996), 104–5.

4. Riverside Plowshares, "Riverside Plowshares Statement," Jonah House, May 2003, www.jonahhouse.org/archive/RiversidePS.htm.

5. Martin Holladay, "Journey to Missouri," in Laffin and Montgomery, *Swords into Plowshares* (1987), 141, 144, 145.

6. Bauerlein, "From Ambler to AVCO," in Laffin and Montgomery, *Swords into Plowshares* (1987), 146; Greg Boertje-Obed, "Reflections from Blount County Jail," Transform Now Plowshares, September 3, 2012, http://transformnowplowshares.wordpress.com/category/reflections/.

7. Laffin and Montgomery, *Swords into Plowshares* (1987), xxi.

8. Fernandez, *Persuasions and Performances*, 8, 7, 10–11.

9. See Jasper, *Art of Moral Protest*, esp. chaps. 12–13.

10. D. Berrigan, *To Dwell in Peace*, 94.

11. The titles alone are illustrative. See, for example, P. Berrigan, *Punishment for Peace*, and D. Berrigan, *They Call Us Dead Men*.

12. Orsi, "Between Memory and Modernity," in Appleby and Sprow-Cummings, *Catholics*, 11–42; Fisher, *Catholic Counterculture*, esp. chaps. 1–3.

13. Fisher, *Catholic Counterculture*, 56–57.

14. D. Berrigan, *Portraits*, 84, 78, 85.

15. D. Berrigan, *To Dwell in Peace*, 69–72.

16. D. Berrigan, *Dark Night*, 94–97.

17. D. Berrigan, "Martyrs' Living Witness," in Gottlieb, *Liberating Faith*, 225.

18. D. Berrigan, *Dark Night*, 24.

19. The brothers had an extremely close and admiring relationship, complementing one another's personalities and proclivities. Throughout their published writings and private correspondence, Daniel praises Philip's leadership qualities while Philip extols Daniel's theological imagination as a framework for his own thinking about resistance.

20. D. Berrigan, *Dark Night*, 144.

21. See, for example, Vree, "Stripped Clean."

22. P. Berrigan and McAlister, *Time's Discipline*, 57–58, 88.

23. Dean Hammer, qtd. in Cappon, "We Have Laid Down."

24. For more on the biblical legitimation of Plowshares actions, see Nepstad, *Religion and War Resistance*, 64–78.

25. Ardeth Platte, Carol Gilbert, and Jackie Hudson, "Sacred Earth and Space Plowshares," Jonah House, accessed February 25, 2016, www.jonahhouse.org/archive/sacred_earth.htm. Platte and Gilbert, Dominican sisters, are two longtime Jonah House residents and Plowshares stalwarts.

26. P. Berrigan, "Jail Witness," Jonah House, accessed January 25, 2016, www.jonahhouse.org/archive/jail_witness.htm.

27. McAlister, "Love of the Children," in Berrigan, *For Swords into Plowshares*, 32.

28. P. Berrigan and McAlister, *Time's Discipline*, 182–83, 185–86. In his autobiography, however, Philip titles a chapter "Letters from the Gulag: Waging Peace in Prison."

29. Ibid., 197; emphasis added.

30. Dishneau, "Kicking the Bomb."

31. See Riegle, *Doing Time for Peace*.

32. Crane, "Why We Are Disarming."

33. Bauerlein, "From Ambler to AVCO," in Laffin and Montgomery, *Swords into Plowshares* (1987), 148; Boylan, "Letter from Newport News," in Laffin and Montgomery, *Swords into Plowshares* (1996), 103; P. Berrigan and McAlister, *Time's Discipline*, 34.

34. "Opening Statement of Sr. Ardeth Platte, OP," Jonah House, April 2003, www.jonahhouse.org/archive/platte_openstm.htm.

35. Woodson, "Inside Line."

36. Carl Kabat, Greg Boertje-Obed, and Michael Walli, "WMD Here Plowshares," Jonah House, June 20, 2006, www.jonahhouse.org/archive/WMD%20Here%20Plowshares/WMD%20Statement.htm.

37. Paul Kabat. qtd. in Laffin and Montgomery, *Swords into Plowshares* (1987), 154.

38. Dean Hammer, Todd S. Kaplan, Vern Rossman, Jim Perkins, letter from prison, December 1984, box 2, Maas Collection.

39. Paul Kabat, qtd. in Laffin and Montgomery, *Swords into Plowshares* (1987), 154–55.

40. Snow and Anderson, "Identity Work," 1348.

Chapter 4

1. "Statement of the Sacred Earth and Space Plowshares II," Internet Archive, accessed January 25, 2016, http://web.ar chive.org/web/20090825072447/http://www .craftech.com/~dcpledge/brandywine/plow /sacred_earth%20statement.htm.

2. McAlister, "Love of the Children," in Berrigan, *For Swords into Plowshares*, 33.

3. Dunn, "Priest Jailed."

4. Dunn, "Protesting Priest."

5. "Protesting Nuns."

6. Helen Woodson, "An Excerpt from a Letter from Helen Woodson in the Bates Co. Jail," Jonah House, August 20, 2004, www .jonahhouse.org/archive/Woodson0804.htm; emphasis added.

7. "Shalom, Salaam, Shanti, Peace: Carol, Jackie, Anne, Ardeth," Internet Archive, accessed January 25, 2016, http:// web.archive.org/web/20090825072457/http:// www.craftech.com/~dcpledge/brandywine /plow/E&S%202%20Bios.htm. "Anne" is Sister Anne Montgomery, a Sister of the Sacred Heart of Jesus and, until her death in August 2012, one of the most active Plowshares participants. (She participated in the first Plowshares action, as well as one of the most recent, and several in between.) She did not go to the Colorado site with Platte, Gilbert, and Hudson—she was serving on a Christian Peacemaker Team in Hebron at the time—but was considered a participant "in spirit" and added her name to their action statement and her biographical statement to theirs. This is not common practice.

8. Burns, *Theory of the Trial*, 37.

9. Ibid., 50.

10. Unless otherwise noted, quotations in this section come from Ardeth Platte's opening statement in the Sacred Earth and Space II Plowshares trial; see "Opening Statement of Sr. Ardeth Platte, OP," Jonah House, April 2003, www.jonahhouse.org/ar chive/platte_openstm.htm. Many quotations

follow the conventions of spoken rather that written English; I have reproduced them as they appear in the transcript.

11. Kainz, *Natural Law*, 17.

12. Laffin and Montgomery, *Swords into Plowshares* (1996), 80–81.

13. The Pax Christi–Spirit of Life defendants' opening statement is reproduced in Laffin and Montgomery, *Swords into Plowshares* (1996), 135–36.

14. Gusfield, *Symbolic Crusade*, 166.

15. Ibid., 166–67.

16. See Sullivan's groundbreaking *Impossibility of Religious Freedom* for a revealing case study that illustrates the inherent difficulty of religious freedom as a legally protectable right. See also the essays collected in Sullivan et al., *Politics of Religious Freedom*.

17. Tobey, "Beyond Religious Freedom."

18. The Plowshares are not alone in using legal settings as contexts for the performance of identity. See, for example, the essays on the construction of indigenous identity in Graham and Penny, *Performing Indigeneity*; see also Johnson, *Sacred Claims*.

Chapter 5

1. The group's press release is at "Disarm Now Plowshares," Jonah House, November 2, 2009, www.jonahhouse.org /archive/Disarm_Now_Plowshares/state ment.htm. See also Friedrich, "Antiwar Demonstrators."

2. "Disarm Now Plowshares Statement," Disarm Now Plowshares, December 5, 2009, http://disarmnowplowshares .wordpress.com/2009/12/05/disarm-now -plowshares-statement/.

3. The court documents referenced in this chapter are a matter of public record. The "Government's Consolidated Response to Defendant's Expanded Motion," submitted by U.S. Attorney Jenny Durkan, case 3:10-cr-05586-BHS, Doc. 64, November 5, 2010, can be accessed at http://disarmnow plowshares.files.wordpress.com/2009/12 /ausa-response.pdf.

4. Judge Benjamin Settle's ruling on the motions, case 3:10-cr-05586-BHS, Doc. 77, November 22, 2010, can be accessed at

http://disarmnowplowshares.files.wordpress.com/2009/12/ruling-re-dismissal.pdf.

5. I focus mainly on the trials of these five actions: Griffiss (1983), Trident II (1984), Thames River (1989), Plowshares Versus Depleted Uranium (1999), and Sacred Earth and Space II (2002).

6. Wald, "Amy Carter."

7. See Cohan, "Civil Disobedience."

8. See Laffin and Montgomery, *Swords into Plowshares* (1996), 69–70. See also Ketcham, "About Long Island."

9. Thames River Plowshares trial, transcript, box 3, Maas Collection.

10. Ibid. The jury in this case did acquit all but one of the defendants of the intent charge; all were convicted of conspiracy to enter a naval base for unlawful purposes.

11. Religious freedom defenses, based on the Free Exercise Clause of the First Amendment, certainly have not always met with success. But they have often protected the interests of minority religious groups, including Jehovah's Witnesses, Seventh Day Adventists, and the Amish, among others.

12. Griffiss Air Force Base Plowshares trial, appeal documents, box 2, Maas Collection.

13. Ibid.

14. D. O'Reilly, "Activists Draw Jail."

15. "Peace Activists Refuse."

16. See "Five Who Damaged" and McLean, "Former Spy."

17. Trident II trial, transcript, box 2, Maas Collection, 19–20.

18. Goffman, *Behavior in Public Places*, 196.

19. Peters, *When Prayer Fails*, 108. See also Gordon, *Mormon Question*. Both texts discuss minority religious groups who have regarded their time before the courts as opportunities to prove themselves as upstanding citizens invested in the American legal and political processes and to counter negative public opinion about their practices and beliefs.

20. See Bender, *Heaven's Kitchen*, esp. chap. 3.

21. See Goodwin, Jasper, and Polletta, "Why Emotions Matter," introd. to Goodwin, Jasper, and Polletta, *Passionate Politics*, 3–4.

22. Trident II trial, opening statement, box 2, Maas Collection.

23. See Bourdieu, "Production and Reproduction," in Thompson, *Language and Social Power*, 43–65.

24. Thames River trial, closing statement, box 3, Maas Collection; emphasis added.

25. Burns, *Theory of the Trial*, 67–70.

26. Thames River trial, closing statement.

27. Carl Kabat, qtd. in Dunn, "Protesting Priest."

28. Trident II trial, transcript. In his explanation of why he chose to be on Saddam Hussein's defense team, Ramsey Clark, who has defended or advised several sets of Plowshares activists, noted that he feels obliged to represent defendants against whom public opinion is already negatively fixed so that these defendants too receive a fair trial: "Both international law and the Constitution of the United States guarantee the right to effective legal representation to any person accused of a crime. This is especially important in a highly politicized situation, where truth and justice can become even harder to achieve." If the same kind of thinking—about a tide of public disapproval standing in the way of truth and justice—informs Clark's decision to be involved with the Plowshares, it is clear that at least one of their more frequent (and prominent) legal advisers is reinforcing their underdog claims. See Clark, "Why I'm Willing."

29. "Opening Statement of Sr. Ardeth Platte, OP," Jonah House, April 2003, www.jonahhouse.org/archive/platte_openstm.htm.

30. Laffin, *Swords into Plowshares*, 61–62; Renner, "Women Who Raided."

31. Carl Kabat, qtd. in Silo Pruning Hooks trial, transcript, box 3, Maas Collection.

Conclusion

1. "In Loving Memory: Sr. Jacqueline Hudson, OP," obituary, Dominican Sisters, 2012, www.grdominicans.org/sister/jacqueline-hudson/.

2. Paul Kabat, qtd. in Laffin and Montgomery, *Swords into Plowshares* (1987), 155.

3. Anne Montgomery, qtd. ibid., 27.

4. Philip Berrigan to Elizabeth McAlister, April 2, 1997, box 36A, Berrigan-McAlister Collection.

5. For example, Ciaron O'Reilly of the 1991 ANZUS Plowshares action writes, "Prison is the setting where we can enter into the deepest solidarity with the poor." "ANZUS Plowshares," in Klejment and Roberts, *American Catholic Pacifism*, 186. For a sample of Philip Berrigan's self-analysis, see *Lamb's War*, 169: "I happen to be quite good at what I do. . . . I have a great capacity for work, initiative, and leadership. These are talents, but they have a dark side: I'm inclined to compare my own commitment to that of others, to my advantage."

6. P. Berrigan, "Jail Witness," Jonah House, accessed January 25, 2016, www .jonahhouse.org/archive/jail_witness.htm.

7. Troester, *Voices*, 214. Jean Gump and Ardeth Platte are two other Plowshares activists.

157

BIBLIOGRAPHY

Appelbaum, Patricia. *Kingdom to Commune: Protestant Pacifist Culture Between World War I and the Vietnam Era*. Chapel Hill: University of North Carolina Press, 2009.

Appleby, R. Scott. "Daniel and Philip Berrigan." In *Twentieth-Century Shapers of American Popular Religion*, edited by Charles H. Lippy, 30–36. New York: Greenwood Press, 1989.

———. "Present to the People of God: The Transformation of the Roman Catholic Parish Priesthood." In Dolan, *Transforming Parish Ministry*, 1–107.

Appleby, R. Scott, and Kathleen Sprow-Cummings, eds. *Catholics in the American Century: Recasting Narratives of U.S. History*. Ithaca: Cornell University Press, 2012.

Au, William A. *The Cross, the Flag, and the Bomb: American Catholics Debate War and Peace, 1960–1983*. Westport, Conn.: Greenwood Press, 1985.

Baggarly, Steven, Philip Berrigan, Mark Colville, Susan Crane, Stephen Kelly, and Tom Lewis-Borbely. *Disciples and Dissidents: Prison Writings of the Prince of Peace Plowshares*. Edited by Fred Wilcox. Athol, Mass.: Haley's, 2001.

Barth, Frederik. *Ethnic Groups and Boundaries: The Social Organization of Culture Difference*. Boston: Little, Brown, 1969.

Bauerlein, Agnes. "From Ambler to AVCO: A Reflection on the AVCO Plowshares Witness." In Laffin and Montgomery, *Swords into Plowshares* (1987), 146–49.

Becker, Howard S. *Outsiders*. New York: Free Press, 1963.

Bell, Catherine. *Ritual Theory, Ritual Practice*. New York: Oxford University Press, 1992.

Bender, Courtney. *Heaven's Kitchen: Living Religion at God's Love We Deliver*. Chicago: University of Chicago Press, 2003.

———. *The New Metaphysicals: Spirituality and the American Religious Imagination*. Chicago: University of Chicago Press, 2010.

Bender, Courtney, Wendy Cadge, Peggy Levitt, and David Smilde, eds. Introduction to *Religion on the Edge: De-centering and Re-centering the Sociology of Religion*, 1–20. New York: Oxford University Press, 2013.

Bender, Courtney, and Pamela Klassen, eds. *After Pluralism: Reimagining Religious Engagement*. New York: Oxford University Press, 2012.

Berrigan, Daniel. *The Dark Night of Resistance*. New York: Doubleday, 1971.

———. *The Geography of Faith*. With Robert Coles. Boston: Beacon Press, 1971.

———. "The Martyrs' Living Witness: A Call to Honor and Challenge." In *Liberating Faith: Religious Voices for Justice, Peace, and Ecological Wisdom*, edited by Roger S. Gottlieb, 222–30. Lanham: Rowman and Littlefield, 2003.

———. *Portraits of Those I Love*. New York: Crossroad Press, 1982.

———. "Swords into Plowshares." *The Catholic Worker*, October–November 1980.

———. *Ten Commandments for the Long Haul*. Nashville: Abingdon Press, 1981.

———. *They Call Us Dead Men: Reflections on Life and Conscience*. New York: Macmillan, 1966.

———. *To Dwell in Peace: An Autobiography*. San Francisco: Harper and Row, 1987.

Berrigan, Philip. *Fighting the Lamb's War: Skirmishes with the American Empire*. With Fred A. Wilcox. Monroe: Common Courage Press, 1996.

———. *A Punishment for Peace*. New York: Macmillan, 1969.

———. *Widen the Prison Gates: Writings from Jails, April 1970–December 1972*. New York: Simon and Schuster, 1973.

Berrigan, Philip, and Elizabeth McAlister. *The Time's Discipline: The Beatitudes and Nuclear Resistance*. Baltimore: Fortkamp, 1989.

Berrigan-McAlister Collection. Special Collections and Archives. DePaul University Libraries, Chicago.

"Berrigans: Conspiracy and Conscience." *Time* 97, no. 4 (1971): 12–17.

Bivins, Jason. *The Fracture of Good Order: Christian Antiliberalism and the Challenge to American Politics*. Chapel Hill: University of North Carolina Press, 2003.

Bourdieu, Pierre. *Distinction: A Social Critique of the Judgment of Taste*. Cambridge. Mass.: Harvard University Press, 1984.

———. "The Production and Reproduction of Legitimate Language." In *Language and Social Power*, edited by John B. Thompson, translated by Gino Raymond and Matthew Adamson, 43–65. Cambridge, Mass.: Harvard University Press, 1991.

Boylan, Kathy. "Letter from Newport News City Jail." In Laffin and Montgomery, *Swords into Plowshares* (1996), 103.

Broad, William. "The Nun Who Broke into the Nuclear Sanctum." *New York Times*, August 11, 2012.

Burns, Robert P. *A Theory of the Trial*. Princeton: Princeton University Press, 1999.

Butler, Judith. *Gender Trouble: Feminism and the Subversion of Identity*. New York: Routledge, 1990.

Byrne, Patricia. "In the Parish but Not of It: Sisters." In Dolan, *Transforming Parish Ministry*, 154–70.

Cada, Chryss. "Three Nuns and a Test for Civil Disobedience: Antiwar Protesters Resigned to Prison in Colorado Case." *Boston Globe*, May 27, 2003.

Cappon, Patricia. "We Have Laid Down Our Lives." *Post-Standard* (Syracuse), November 28, 1983.

Casanova, Jose. *Public Religions in the Modern World*. Chicago: University of Chicago Press, 1994.

Castelli, Jim. *The Bishops and the Bomb: Waging Peace in the Nuclear Age*. Garden City, N.Y.: Doubleday, 1984.

Chernus, Ira. *Dr. Strangegod: On the Symbolic Meaning of Nuclear Weapons*. Columbia: University of South Carolina Press, 1986.

Clark, Ramsey. "Why I'm Willing to Defend Hussein." *Los Angeles Times*, January 24, 2005.

Clifford, Richard J., SJ. "The Berrigans: Prophetic?" In *The Berrigans*, edited by William van Etten Casey, SJ, 31–59. New York: Praeger, 1971.

Cogley, John. *Catholic America*. New York: Dial Press, 1973.

Cohan, John Alan. "Civil Disobedience and the Necessity Defense." *Pierce Law Review* 6, no. 1 (2007): 111.

Connell, Francis J. "The Sacrifice of the Mass." In *Father Connell's New Baltimore Catechism, No. 3*, 207–13. Rev. ed. New York: Benziger Brothers, 1949.

Cresswell, Tim. *In Place/Out of Place: Geography, Ideology, and Transgression*. Minneapolis: University of Minnesota Press, 1996.

Day, Dorothy. *House of Hospitality*. New York: Sheed and Ward, 1939.

———. *The Long Loneliness*. New York: Harper and Row, 1952.

Dear, John, SJ. *The Sacrament of Civil Disobedience*. Baltimore: Fortkamp, 1994.

Dillon, Michele. *Catholic Identity: Balancing Reason, Faith, and Power*. Cambridge: Cambridge University Press, 1999.

Dishneau, Dave. "'Kicking the Bomb' Is the Family Message." *New Haven Register*, February 16, 1986.

Dolan, Jay P. *The American Catholic Experience: A History from Colonial Times to the Present*. Garden City, N.Y.: Doubleday, 1985.

———. *In Search of American Catholicism: A History of Religion and Culture in Tension*. Oxford: Oxford University Press, 2002.

———, ed. *Transforming Parish Ministry: The Changing Roles of Catholic Clergy, Laity, and Women Religious*. New York: Crossroad Press, 1989.

Dunn, Sharon. "Priest Jailed for Missile Silo Stunt." *Greeley Tribune*, August 7, 2009.

———. "Protesting Priest Guilty, Free, Defiant." *Greeley Tribune*, December 23, 2009.

Dunning, Benjamin H. *Aliens and Sojourners: Self as Other in Early Christianity*. Philadelphia: University of Pennsylvania Press, 2009.

Edgell, Penny, Joseph Gerteis, and Douglas Hartmann. "Atheists as 'Other': Moral Boundaries and Cultural Membership in American Society." *American Sociological Review* 71, no. 2 (2006): 211–24.

Effler, Erika Summer. *Laughing Saints and Righteous Heroes: Emotional Rhythms in Social Movement Groups*. Chicago: University of Chicago Press, 2010.

Epstein, Barbara. *Political Protest and Cultural Revolution*. Berkeley: University of California Press, 1991.

Fernandez, James. "The Performance of Ritual Metaphors." In *The Social Use of Metaphor: Essays on the Anthropology of Rhetoric*, edited by J. David Sapir and J. Christopher Crocker, 100–131. Philadelphia: University of Pennsylvania Press, 1977.

———. *Persuasions and Performances: The Play of Tropes in Culture*.

Bloomington: Indiana University Press, 1986.

Fink, Peter E., ed. *The New Dictionary of Sacramental Worship*. Collegeville, Minn.: Liturgical Press, 1990.

Fisher, James Terence. *The Catholic Counterculture in America, 1933–1962*. Chapel Hill: University of North Carolina Press, 1989.

"Five Who Damaged Missile Sub Sentenced to Year in Prison." *Ocala Star-Banner*, October 19, 1985.

Friedrich, Ed. "Antiwar Demonstrators Cut Fence at Bangor Sub Base." *Kitsap Sun*, November 3, 2009, http://tdn .com/news/antiwar-demonstra tors-cut-fence-at-bangor-sub-base /article_95bd9233-a854-555c-8540 -7d571aeddbef.html.

Frosch, Dan. "As Battlefields Shift, Old Warrior for Peace Pursues the Same Enemy." *New York Times*, September 6, 2009.

Gathje, Peter Ronald. "The Cost of Virtue: The Theological Ethics of Daniel and Philip Berrigan." PhD diss., Emory University, 1994.

Gaustad, Edwin Scott. *Dissent in American Religion*. Rev. ed. Chicago: University of Chicago Press, 2006.

Gieryn, Thomas F. "Boundary-Work and the Demarcation of Science from Non-Science: Strains and Interests in Professional Ideologies of Scientists." *American Sociological Review* 48, no. 6 (1983): 781–95.

Goffman, Erving. *Behavior in Public Places: Notes on the Social Organization of Gatherings*. New York: Free Press, 1963.

Goodwin, Jeff, James M. Jasper, and Francesca Polletta. "Why Emotions Matter." Introduction to *Passionate Politics: Emotions and Social Movements*, edited by Jeff Goodwin, James M. Jasper, and Francesca Polletta, 1–26. Chicago: University of Chicago Press, 2001.

Gordon, Sarah Barringer. *The Mormon Question: Polygamy and Constitutional Conflict in Nineteenth-Century America*. Chapel Hill: University of North Carolina Press, 2002.

Graham, Laura R., and H. Glenn Penny. *Performing Indigeneity: Global Histories and Contemporary Experiences.* Lincoln: University of Nebraska Press, 2014.

Gray, Francine du Plessix. *Divine Disobedience.* New York: Knopf, 1970.

———. "Profiles." *New Yorker*, March 14, 1970.

Greeley, Andrew. "L'Affair Berrigan." *New York Times*, February 19, 1971.

———. "The Berrigans: Phrenetic?" *Holy Cross Quarterly*, January 1971.

———. *Building Coalitions: American Politics in the 1970s.* New York: New Viewpoints, 1974.

———. "Turning off 'The People.'" *New Republic*, June 27, 1970.

Grimes, Ronald L. "Religion, Ritual, and Performance." In *Religion, Theatre, and Performance: Acts of Faith*, edited by Lance Gharavi, 27–41. New York: Routledge, 2012.

Guigno, Marco, Doug McAdam, and Charles Tilly, eds. *How Social Movements Matter.* Minneapolis: University of Minnesota Press, 1999.

Gusfield, James. *Symbolic Crusade.* Champaign: University of Illinois Press, 1963.

Holladay, Martin. "Journey to Missouri." In Laffin and Montgomery, *Swords into Plowshares* (1987), 141–45.

hooks, bell. "Marginality as a Site of Resistance." In *Out There: Marginalization and Contemporary Culture*, edited by Russell Ferguson, Martha Gever, Trinh T. Minh-ha, and Cornel West, 337–340. Cambridge, Mass.: MIT Press, 1992.

Jackson, Michael. "Heal the World." *Dangerous.* New York: Epic, 1991.

Jasper, James M. *The Art of Moral Protest: Culture, Biography, and Creativity in Social Movements.* Chicago: University of Chicago Press, 1997.

Jenkins, Richard. *Social Identity.* 3rd ed. New York: Routledge, 2008.

Jewish Publication Society. *Tanakh: A New Translation of the Holy Scriptures According to the Traditional Hebrew Text.* Philadelphia: Jewish Publication Society, 1985.

Johnson, Greg. *Sacred Claims: Repatriation and Living Tradition.* Charlottesville: University of Virginia Press, 2007.

Kainz, Howard P. *Natural Law: An Introduction and Reinterpretation.* Peru, Ill.: Carus, 2004.

Kanter, Rosabeth Moss. "Commitment and Social Organization: A Study of Commitment Mechanisms in Utopian Communities." *American Sociological Review* 33, no. 4 (1968): 499–517.

Ketcham, Diane. "About Long Island: Waging Protest Against the Machines of War." *New York Times*, October 1, 1989.

Klejment, Anne, and Nancy L. Roberts, eds. *American Catholic Pacifism: The Influence of Dorothy Day and the Catholic Worker Movement.* Westport, Conn.: Praeger, 1996.

Kosek, Joseph Kip. *Acts of Conscience: Christian Nonviolence and Modern American Democracy.* New York: Columbia University Press, 2009.

Laffin, Arthur. *Swords into Plowshares: A Chronology of Plowshares Disarmament Actions, 1980–2003.* Marion, S.Dak.: Rose Hill Books, 2003.

Laffin, Arthur J., and Anne Montgomery, eds. *Swords into Plowshares: Nonviolent Direct Action for Disarmament.* San Francisco: Harper and Row, 1987.

———. *Swords into Plowshares: Nonviolent Direct Action for Disarmament, Peace, Social Justice.* Rev. ed. Marion, S.Dak.: Fortkamp, 1996.

Lamont, Michèle, and Marcel Fournier, eds. *Cultivating Differences: Symbolic Boundaries and the Making of Inequality.* Chicago: University of Chicago Press, 1992.

Lamont, Michèle, and Virag Molnar. "The Study of Boundaries in the Social Sciences." *Annual Review of Sociology* 28 (2002): 167–95.

Lang, Jovian P., OFM. *Dictionary of the Liturgy.* New York: Catholic Book, 1986.

Lincoln, Bruce. "On Ritual, Change, and Marked Categories." *Journal of the American Academy of Religion* 68, no. 3 (2000): 487–510.

Lofland, John. *Polite Protesters: The American Peace Movement of the 1980s*. Syracuse: Syracuse University Press, 1993.

Lynd, Staughton, and Alice Lynd. *Nonviolence in America: A Documentary History*. Maryknoll, N.Y.: Orbis Books, 1995.

Maas Collection. Special Collections and Archives. DePaul University Libraries, Chicago.

Maines, David R., and Michael J. McCallion. *Transforming Catholicism: Liturgical Changes in the Vatican II Church*. Lanham: Rowman and Littlefield, 2007.

Mannheim, Karl. "The Problem of Generations." In *From Karl Mannheim*, edited by Kurt H. Wolff, 351–98. 2nd exp. ed. New Brunswick: Transaction, 1993.

Marsh, James L, and Anna J. Brown. *Faith, Resistance, and the Future: Daniel Berrigan's Challenge to Catholic Social Thought*. New York: Fordham University Press, 2012.

Marty, Martin E. *An Invitation to American Catholic History*. Chicago: More Press, 1986.

Marvin, Carolyn, and David W. Ingle. "Blood Sacrifice and the Nation: Revisiting Civil Religion." *Journal of the American Academy of Religion* 64, no. 4 (1996): 767–80.

McAlister, Elizabeth. "For Love of the Children." In *For Swords into Plowshares, the Hammer Has to Fall*, edited by Daniel Berrigan, 32–36. Piscataway: Plowshares Press, 1984.

———. "A Prison Letter." *Radix*, May–June 1977.

McCall, Richard D. *Do This: Liturgy as Performance*. Notre Dame: University of Notre Dame Press, 2007.

McGreevey, John T. *Catholicism and American Freedom: A History*. New York: Norton, 2003.

McKanan, Dan. *The Catholic Worker After Dorothy: Practicing the Works of Mercy in a New Generation*. Collegeville, Minn.: Liturgical Press, 2008.

———. Review of *Religion and War Resistance in the Plowshares Movement*, by Sharon Erickson Nepstad. *Journal of the American Academy of Religion* 79, no. 2 (2011): 544–47.

McLean, Milly. "Former Spy Says Nuclear War 'Imminent.'" United Press International, August 13, 1985.

McLellan, Bill. "Anti-Nuke Priest, Carl Kabat, Readies for Next Plowshares Witness." *St. Louis Post-Dispatch*, August 3, 2009.

McNeal, Patricia. *Harder Than War: Catholic Peacemaking in Twentieth Century America*. New Brunswick: Rutgers University Press.

Miller, William. *A Harsh and Dreadful Love: Dorothy Day and the Catholic Worker*. New York: Liveright, 1973.

Montgomery, Anne. "Divine Obedience." In Laffin and Montgomery, *Swords into Plowshares* (1987), 25–31.

Moore, R. Laurence. *Religious Outsiders and the Making of Americans*. New York: Oxford University Press, 1986.

Morgan, Michael, and Susan Leggett. Introduction to *Mainstream(s) and Margins: Cultural Politics in the Nineties*, vii–xi. Westport, Conn.: Greenwood Press, 1996.

Nangle, Richard. "Berrigan Recalled, Holy Cross Holds Mass." *Sunday Telegram* (Worcester, Mass.), January 26, 2003.

"Necessity." In *West's Encyclopedia of American Law*, edited by Shirelle Phelps and Jeffrey Lehman, 217–20. Vol. 7. 2nd ed. Detroit: Gale, 2005.

Nelson, Jack, and Ronald J. Ostrow. *The FBI and the Berrigans: The Making of a Conspiracy*. New York: Coward, McCann, and Geoghegan, 1972.

Nepstad, Sharon Erickson. "Disciples and Dissenters: Tactical Choice and Consequence in the Plowshares Movement." *Research in Social Movements, Conflict, and Change* 25 (2004): 139–60.

———. "Persistent Resistance: Commitment and Community in the Plowshares Movement." *Social Problems* 51, no. 1 (2004): 43–60.

———. *Religion and War Resistance in the Plowshares Movement*. New York: Cambridge University Press, 2008.

Nieves, Evelyn. "For Three Nuns, a Prairie Protest and a Price to Pay: Sisters Reconciled to Prison for Actions at Missile Site." *Washington Post*, May 21, 2003.

Norman, Liane Ellison. *Hammer of Justice: Molly Rush and the Plowshares Eight*. Pittsburgh: Pittsburgh Peace Institute, 1989.

O'Brien, David J. "Social Teaching, Social Action, Social Gospel." *U.S. Catholic Historian* 5, no. 2 (1986): 195–224.

———. "What Happened to the Catholic Left?" In *What's Left? Liberal American Catholics*, edited by Mary Jo Weaver, 255–82. Bloomington: Indiana University Press, 1999.

O'Connell, Timothy E., ed. *Vatican II and Its Documents: An American Reappraisal*. Wilmington, Del.: Glazer, 1986.

O'Reilly, Ciaron. "ANZUS Plowshares: A Nonviolent Campaign." In Klejment and Roberts, *American Catholic Pacifism*, 171–86.

O'Reilly, David. "Activists Draw Jail in MD Incident." *Philadelphia Inquirer*, March 24, 2000.

O'Rourke, William. *The Harrisburg Seven and the New Catholic Left*. New York: Crowell, 1972.

Orsi, Robert. "Between Memory and Modernity: How Catholics Are American." In Appleby and Sprow-Cummings, *Catholics*, 11–42.

Pachucki, Mark A., Sabrina Pendergrass, and Michèle Lamont. "Boundary Processes: Recent Theoretical Developments and New Contributions." *Poetics* 35, no. 6 (2007): 331–51.

"Peace Activists Refuse to Participate in Military Vandalism Trial." AP State and Local Wire, March 23, 2000.

Perry, Lewis. *Civil Disobedience: An American Tradition*. New Haven: Yale University Press, 2013.

Peters, Shawn Francis. *The Catonsville Nine: A Story of Faith and Resistance in the Vietnam Era*. New York: Oxford University Press, 2012.

———. *When Prayer Fails: Faith Healing, Children, and the Law*. New York: Oxford University Press, 2008.

Polner, Murray, and Jim O'Grady. *Disarmed and Dangerous: The Radical Lives and Times of Daniel and Philip Berrigan*. New York: Basic Books, 1997.

"Protesting Nuns Seek Acquittal, New Trial." AP State and Local Wire, April 15, 2003.

Quigley, William P. "The Necessity Defense in Civil Disobedience Cases: Bring in the Jury." *New England Law Review* 38, no. 3 (2003): 111–75.

Reagan, Ronald. Address to the Forty-Second Session of the United Nations General Assembly. September 21, 1987. www.reagan.utexas.edu/archives /speeches/1987/092187b.htm.

Reger, Jo, Daniel J. Myers, and Rachel L. Einwohner. "Identity Work, Sameness, and Difference in Social Movements." Introduction to *Identity Work in Social Movements*, edited by Jo Reger, Daniel J. Myers, and Rachel L. Einwohner, 1–17. Minneapolis: University of Minneapolis Press, 2008.

Renner, Gerald. "Women Who Raided Navy Base Sentenced." *Hartford Courant*, October 1, 1996.

Riegle, Rosalie G. *Crossing the Line: Nonviolent Resisters Speak Out for Peace*. Eugene, Ore.: Cascade Books, 2013.

———. *Doing Time for Peace: Resistance, Family, and Community*. Nashville: Vanderbilt University Press, 2012.

Rochon, Thomas R., and David S. Meyer, eds. *Coalitions and Political Movements: The Lessons of the Nuclear Freeze*. Boulder: Rienner, 1997.

———. "The Nuclear Freeze in Theory in Action." Introduction to Rochon and Meyer, *Coalitions and Political Movements*, 1–21.

Rojecki, Andrew. "Freeze Frame: News Coverage of the Freeze Movement." In Rochon and Meyer, *Coalitions and Political Movements*, 107–126.

Roth, Guenther. "Religion and Revolutionary Beliefs: Social and Historical Dimensions in Max Weber's Work." *Social Forces* 55, no. 2 (1976): 257–72.

———. "Socio-historical Model and Developmental Theory: Charismatic Community, Charisma of Reason, and the Counterculture." *American Sociological Review* 40 (April 1975): 148–57.

Schechner, Richard. *Between Theater and Anthropology*. Philadelphia: University of Pennsylvania Press, 1985.

———. *Essays on Performance Theory, 1970–1976*. New York: Drama Book Specialists, 1977.

Schmidt, Leigh Eric. "'A Church-Going People Are a Dress-Loving People': Clothes, Communication, and Religious Culture in Early America." *Church History* 58, no. 1 (1989): 36–51.

Schönberg, Claude-Michel. "Epilogue." *Les Miserables*. New York: Universal Republic Records, 2012.

Smith, Christian. *American Evangelicalism: Embattled and Thriving*. Chicago: University of Chicago Press, 1998.

Smith, Jonathan Z. *Relating Religion: Essays in the Study of Religion*. Chicago: University of Chicago Press, 2004.

Snow, David A., and Leon Anderson. "Identity Work Among the Homeless: The Verbal Construction and Avowal of Personal Identities." *American Journal of Sociology* 92, no. 6 (1987): 1336–71.

"Statement of Jubilee Plowshares." In Laffin and Montgomery, *Swords into Plowshares* (1996), 104–5.

Sullivan, Winnifred Fallers. *The Impossibility of Religious Freedom*. Princeton: Princeton University Press, 2005.

Sullivan, Winnifred Fallers, Elizabeth Shakman Hurd, Saba Mahmood, and Peter G. Danchin, eds. *The Politics of Religious Freedom*. Chicago: University of Chicago Press, 2015.

Sullivan, Winnifred Fallers, Robert A. Yelle, and Mateo Taussig-Rubbo, eds. *After Secular Law*. Stanford: Stanford University Press, 2011.

Tarrow, Sidney. *Power in Movement: Social Movements and Contentious Politics*. New York: Cambridge University Press, 1998.

Taylor, Verta. "Social Movement Continuity: The Women's Movement in Abeyance." *American Sociological Review* 54, no. 5 (1989): 761–75.

Taysom, Steven C. *Shakers, Mormons, and Religious Worlds: Conflicting Visions, Contested Boundaries*. Bloomington: Indiana University Press, 2011.

Tilly, Charles. *Identities, Boundaries, and Social Ties*. Boulder: Paradigm Press, 2005.

Tobey, Kristen. "Beyond Religious Freedom: Religious Activity in the Civil Disobedience Trials of Plowshares Anti-Nuclear Activists." *Journal of Religion* 96, no. 2 (2016).

———. "'Have We Made Ourselves Inaccessible?': Plowshares Disarmament Activists' Rhetoric of Marginality." *Journal of Political Theology* 13, no. 1 (2012): 76–92.

Toussaint, Laura L. *The Contemporary U.S. Peace Movement*. New York: Routledge, 2009.

Troester, Rosalie Riegle. *Voices from the Catholic Worker*. Philadelphia: Temple University Press, 1993.

Turner, Victor. *Dramas, Fields, and Metaphor: Symbolic Action in Human Society*. Ithaca: Cornell University Press, 1974.

———. *The Ritual Process: Structure and Anti-Structure*. Ithaca: Cornell University Press, 1969.

Vree, Dale. "'Stripped Clean': The Berrigans and the Politics of Guilt and Martyrdom." *Ethics* 85, no. 2 (1975): 271–87.

Wald, Matthew L. "Amy Carter Is Acquitted over Protest." *New York Times*, April 16, 1987.

Wilde, Melissa J. *Vatican II: A Sociological Analysis of Religious Change*. Princeton: Princeton University Press, 2007.

Williams, Rhys. "Religious Social Movements in the Public Sphere." In *Handbook of the Sociology of Religion*, edited by Michelle Dillon, 315–30. Cambridge: Cambridge University Press, 2003.

Wittner, Lawrence S. *Confronting the Bomb: A Short History of the World Nuclear Disarmament Movement*. Stanford: Stanford University Press, 2009.

———. "A Modest Revival." *Bulletin of the Atomic Scientists*, June 13, 2007.

http://thebulletin.org/rebirth-an
ti-nuclear-weapons-movement
/modest-revival.

———. *Toward Nuclear Abolition: A History of
the World Disarmament Movement*, 3
vols. Stanford: Stanford University
Press, 2003.

Woodson, Helen. "The Inside Line: From
Ft. Worth." *Nuclear Resister* 130
(September 3, 2002), www.nuker
esister.org/static/nr129/130inside
line.html.

Young, Ralph E. *Dissent in America*. 2 vols.
New York: Pearson, 2005.

Yukich, Grace. "Boundary Work in Inclusive
Religious Groups." *Sociology of Religion* 71, no. 2 (2010): 172–96.

Zwick, Mark, and Louise Zwick. *The Catholic
Worker Movement: Intellectual and
Spiritual Origins*. Mahwah, N.J.:
Paulist Press, 2005.

INDEX

173

Lightning Source UK Ltd.
Milton Keynes UK
UKHW04f2334050818
326769UK00001BA/118/P